Kenneth W. Mack is the author of *Representing the Race: The Creation of the Civil Rights Lawyer*. He is a professor at Harvard Law School and lives in Newtown, Massachusetts. **Guy-Uriel Charles** is a law professor and the founding director of the Duke Center on Law, Race, and Politics. He lives in Durham, North Carolina.

BY KENNETH W. MACK

Representing the Race: The Creation of the Civil Rights Lawyer

EDITED BY GUY-URIEL E. CHARLES

Race, Reform, and Regulation of the Electoral Process:
Recurring Puzzles in American Democracy
(with Heather K. Gerken and Michael S. Kang)

THE NEW BLACK

What Has Changed—
and What Has Not—
with Race in America

Edited by
Kenneth W. Mack
and Guy-Uriel E. Charles

THE NEW PRESS

NEW YORK
LONDON

"Immigration and the Civil Rights Agenda" by Cristina M.
Rodríguez originally appeared in the *Stanford Journal of Civil Rights
& Civil Liberties* 6:1 (2010): 123–44. "The Right Kind of Family:
Silences in a Civil Rights Narrative" by Jonathan Scott Holloway is
adapted from chapter 5, "The Silences in a Civil Rights Narrative"
of *Jim Crow Wisdom: Memory and Identity in Black America
Since 1940* by Jonathan Scott Holloway. Copyright © 2013 by the
University of North Carolina Press. Used by permission of the
publisher. www.uncpress.unc.edu.

Requests for permission to reproduce selections from this book
should be mailed to: Permissions Department, The New Press,
38 Greene Street, New York, NY 10013.

Published in the United States by The New Press, New York, 2013
Distributed by Perseus Distribution

ISBN 978-1-59558-677-3 (pbk)
ISBN 978-1-59558-799-2 (e-book)
CIP data available

The New Press publishes books that promote and enrich public
discussion and understanding of the issues vital to our democracy
and to a more equitable world. These books are made possible by
the enthusiasm of our readers; the support of a committed group
of donors, large and small; the collaboration of our many partners
in the independent media and the not-for-profit sector; booksellers,
who often hand-sell New Press books; librarians; and above all by
our authors.

www.thenewpress.com

Composition by dix! Digital Prepress
This book was set in Minion

Printed in the United States of America

10 9 8 7 6 5 4 3 2 1

To the memory and legacy of Dr. John Hope Franklin—
mentor, role model, and friend.
May your work and life's example continue to inspire and awe.

CONTENTS

CONTENTS

PREFACE

Orlando Patterson

In coming to terms with what has changed—and what has not—
with race in America at the beginning of the twenty-first century,
one must first grapple with a deep paradox that lies at the heart
of black-white relations today. The relationship between African
Americans and Euro-Americans is at the heart of the race problem
in the United States, although of course there are many other racial
and ethnic groups now struggling to find their place in an increasingly diverse society. On the one hand, African Americans have been
wholly accepted into the public sphere of American life, which is
the greatest achievement of the civil rights movement. On the other
hand—despite undeniable breakthroughs, most evidently the election of an African American as president of the United States—
they still remain largely excluded from the private lives and private
sphere of Euro-American society.

In less than a generation, the legal and political infrastructure
that defined American race relations for most of the twentieth century has been dismantled. The civil rights and voting rights acts
of the 1960s opened the way not only for black individuals to receive
basic respect from their fellow citizens, but also for their full participation in the nation's public life. Black Americans are an essential
component of the Democratic Party, and they have run for and been
elected to offices at all levels, all over the country, from mayor to
senator to governor. President Obama's election was simply the fit-
ting culmination of this great process of political inclusion.

A striking example of the integration of blacks into the nation's public life is the transformation of the military—the repository of the nation's honor and power. Traditionally, blacks were excluded from all but the lowliest functions in the American armed forces. That exclusion had its roots, in part, in the historic influence of white southerners in all branches of the armed forces. White southerners were traditionally steeped in a code of militant honor that had its basis in the degradation of blacks under slavery and later Jim Crow, as the late historian John Hope Franklin has argued. Hence the need to exclude blacks from military honor as part of the racist system of humiliating them and defining them as permanent outsiders. The integration of the armed forces, beginning with the administration of President Harry Truman, worked a veritable revolution in one of the most conservative institutions in America. The subsequent rise of blacks at all levels in the military, now including over 10 percent of the army's officer corps, and Colin Powell's appointment as the nation's highest-ranking military officer are achievements almost on a par with Obama's election.

The rise of a black middle class is another great advance that any objective observer of American race relations must acknowledge. The opening up of the nation's schools at all levels to African Americans, following the Supreme Court's celebrated decision in *Brown v. Board of Education*, led to enormous new opportunities for blacks. The decision, augmented by the 1960s-era civil rights acts, led to a dramatic lessening of the achievement gap between black and white students. As a consequence, many blacks achieved middle-class and even upper-class status in the nation's civil service, professional occupations, and even its businesses. A number of the nation's largest corporations have been headed by African Americans, including American Express, Time Warner, and Merrill Lynch, while an African American woman has risen to the top of the Xerox Corporation. Finally, although many might view this development with mixed feelings, one can certainly take pride in the embrace of black popular and elite cultural productions, and in the prominence of African Americans in the nation's sporting arenas.

Just as assuredly, however, any honest observer of the present state of race relations and racial inequality must acknowledge the continued exclusion of most blacks from a range of private spheres, including housing, schools, communities, and the more-desired workplaces of Euro-American life.[1]

First and foremost, there are the persisting inequalities that beset black life: the black poor remain at the bottom of the nation's class system with a poverty rate almost as high as it was three decades earlier. Indeed, the rate began to climb again during the years of George W. Bush's presidency. In the year 2000, the median net worth of non-Hispanic whites ($79,400) was 10.5 times that of black householders (estimated at $7,500). This gap widened substantially during the Bush years, the white net worth having climbed to $88,000 in 2002 while that of blacks fell to $6,000.[2] That disparity grew even wider as a result of the housing crisis, which disproportionately devastated black homeowners. Equally important is the fact that inequality within the black population is even greater than that between blacks and whites. One must be quite skeptical about measuring the progress toward racial equality by the emergence of successful blacks. As John Hope Franklin noted, the role of successful blacks in American society may be merely to ensure "that there is sufficient sway in America's still racist structure to provide the "give" necessary to protect that structure against the winds."[3]

While this news is distressing, it is hardly surprising to learn about another widely discussed report that the Pew foundation published in 2007, which showed that the black middle class is not reproducing its status. Middle-class black status is characterized by rampant downward mobility, with more than half its children failing to earn as much as their parents. More than a quarter of them are falling to the very bottom of the income ladder.[4]

Another paradoxical element in the present racial situation is the persistence of racial segregation, in spite of all the progress—a segregation that includes the black middle class. Segregation harms whites as well as blacks, and it does so in spite of the protestations of those African Americans who have romanticized the warmth and harmony—that soulful sense of community—that was presumed to have emerged from the tight-knit ghettos imposed by Jim Crow. As other contributors to this volume have noted, racial segregation and deliberate exclusion still play a significant role in access to jobs, housing, and other resources. But one should be especially distressed by the persistence of segregation in the nation's schools. Several widely discussed studies show that, in 2009, the average black child was more likely to attend a school that was all, or nearly all, black than in 1970.[5]

However, the most disappointing aspect of our present racial predicament is the desperate condition of black youth. Nowhere is the paradoxical condition of African Americans more acutely exhibited than in the condition of young people, especially black male youth. They are trapped in a seemingly intractable socioeconomic crisis. Only between 52 and 61 percent (depending on method of calculation) of those entering high school graduate, compared with between 71 and 79 percent of white males. A third of all black men in their thirties now have a prison record, as do an astonishing two-thirds of all high school dropouts. Violence has become endemic, with a homicide mortality rate of 34.4 per 100,000 among males ages 15–17. Only 20 percent of black youth not in school are employed at any given time. Their lives are often impoverished, unhealthy, and short, leading one group of social scientists to describe them as an "endangered species."

The bias against black men goes deep into the nation's history, and tragically, one of the negative consequences of this history is that some African Americans themselves seemed to have inculcated this bias. Indeed, there has been a recent revival of sociological discourse on the nature and explanatory significance of culture[6] in understanding the problems of black youth. Nonetheless, young African Americans are the creators of the most dazzlingly original popular cultural productions in the nation and the world. All aspects of their cultural creations are avidly consumed by white and other Americans, and nonblacks of all ethnicities idolize African American sports and entertainment heroes.

What, then, is the "new black" that we must confront in the

twenty-first century? If black is a metaphor for America's long struggle with its race problem, the racial problem of our times is a study in contradictions. What about this new world of contradictions is new, and what seems like a simple holdover from the old and familiar regime of racial segregation? Is the election of an African American president the end point of the civil rights movement, or something else? What are the questions that should be asked about race relations, and racial inequality, in a new and undeniably different century? The essays in this volume are a welcome and provocative beginning in defining, and grappling with, a deep divide in the American soul, as the nation continues to confront its oldest social problem in a new century.

THE NEW BLACK

INTRODUCTION

The New Black and the Death of the Civil Rights Idea

Sometime in the past decade or two, a core idea important to several generations of Americans has begun to unravel. We might call this the civil rights idea. That idea—in reality a set of ideas—emerged from the struggle for racial equality that occupied Americans, and many people around the world, in the second half of the twentieth century. The civil rights idea defined America's race problem as the problem of two relatively cohesive racial groups—blacks and whites. It prompted Americans to take action to reduce the persistence of inequality between those two groups—inequality that could be measured in terms of economic progress, educational achievement, political power, and social freedom. That inequality was assumed to be the product of discrimination, past and present; the unfinished struggle for civil rights was the continuing effort to combat that discrimination and its effects.

The civil rights idea affected the way that history was written, the way that social science was done, the way that law was argued about, and the way that politics was organized. For historians, it focused much writing on the nation's long struggle for racial equality, and on the promise of a better future. For social scientists, it forced writers to grapple with and analyze the historical causes of present black-white inequality. For lawyers, policymakers, and the American public at large, it guided them to legal strategies and government policies which might lessen that inequality. It was an idea that focused, most of all, on blacks and whites; but for many thoughtful persons it seemed to apply in full force to other groups such as Asian Americans and Latinos, and to provide a program for assessing and hastening their integration into the mainstream. The civil rights idea also provided a measuring stick by which American race relations could provide a model to nations around the world as they struggled with racial, ethnic, and religious diversity.[1]

In time, political conservatives as well as liberals would embrace the civil rights idea. Conservatives coexisted uneasily with the civil rights initiatives of the 1950s and 60s, but by the 1970s they began to embrace the language as their own. The seeds of the suburban revolt against civil rights initiatives were taking root as early as the 1940s, and gained steam in the ensuing decades.[2] Many Americans have long been skeptical of the idea that government has a "special obligation" to help minorities because of past discrimination.[3] For them, discrimination hardly seems like the special problem of racial minorities, and civil rights programs must be race neutral. By the 1970s, political conservatives were tapping into a long-simmering revolt against the civil rights idea, and were claiming a version of it for themselves. For them, "civil rights" organizations and initiatives should be focused, first and foremost, on the abolition of racial preferences, even if, and perhaps most especially, those preferences seemed like special dispensations to aid minorities.[4] With the proliferation of anti–affirmative action ballot initiatives, and a conservative majority on the Supreme Court that is deeply skeptical of most governmental uses of racial preferences, the idea that the phrase "civil rights" carries with it any particular program for lessening racial inequality seems to have finally lost its potency.

"The new black"—the deliberately provocative phrase that we have chosen for the title of this book—is intended to prompt readers of this volume to question the continued relevance of the civil rights idea as we enter more fully into the twenty-first century. The contributors to this volume do not agree on the exact meaning of the phrase, or even on how much has changed, and how much has not, with race relations over the past generation. What they do agree on, however, is the proposition that the civil rights idea no longer provides an easy way to describe, or address, America's continuing race problem. If "black" is a metaphor for America's long-standing struggle with race discrimination and racial inequality, as Orlando Patterson contends in his preface to this book, then the civil rights idea, with its focus on lessening black-white inequality, seems like an organizing principle whose validity for thinking about and working for racial equality is increasingly under siege. Popular support for the civil rights idea was always tenuous at best, and has declined over the past generation.

At the same time, the idea that America's race problem is the problem of black and white, at least as these two groups were conceived during the civil rights era, no longer seems to describe the social reality of America. Some have pointed to the pronounced class and wealth differences within the black population, and argued that some African Americans have more in common with wealthy whites than they do with other blacks.[5] Poor black youth, on the other hand, seem increasingly segregated, isolated, and swept into the expanding criminal justice system—while good schools and unskilled jobs have often disappeared from their communities.[6] Much of modern inequality seems beyond the reach of traditional civil rights remedies.[7]

Others commentators have pointed to the transformation in the country's racial composition, particularly through immigration. The most oft-cited statistic encapsulating these trends is that within a few decades, a majority of Americans will identify with groups that were once seen as racial minorities. Yet, the situation is even more complicated than this, as younger Americans with no memory of the civil rights movement increasingly self-identify, and marry, across racial lines, pushing back against conventional racial categorization. Perhaps race is becoming merely a marker of voluntary cultural affiliation rather than a measurable economic or social difference.[8] Many scholars, however, resist such conclusions, contending that the old racial hierarchy has simply reappeared in a new guise and has perhaps become even more entrenched.[9] *The New Black* is an attempt to write the beginnings of a story that we are only starting to grasp—the story of a world of race relations that could hardly have been imagined during the civil rights era.

For some, *The New Black* is a clarion call to rethink the role that race does, and should, play in social organization and activism. In their groundbreaking essay, Lani Guinier and Gerald Torres propose a new concept that they call "political race." For racial identity to continue to be an organizing principle for politics and social action in a rapidly changing America, they argue, group identity should be seen as less connected to physical appearance and cultural heritage than it is to one's position in society. "The new black" for them is a place where people of varying backgrounds can organize based on what racial minorities learned long ago—that the American dream of fair play and hard work remains a chimera to many people. Taeku Lee, by contrast, focuses on a hotly debated topic: the role of "political independents" in national politics, and as part of the coalition that elected the first African American president. Countering the popular image of political independents as undecided white voters, he shows that the unaffiliated voters who were key to Obama's first election and who are thought to hold the balance in national elections are disproportionately black and brown. Cristina M. Rodríguez, on the other hand, challenges the idea that the political organizing models that were created during the civil rights era—models developed by both black and Latino activists—apply at all to recent Latino immigrants in their struggle to be recognized as full citizens.

These calls to help define "the new black" seem especially pressing in light of the election of Barack Obama as the first black president of the United States—an event that, as Lee notes, was not foreseen by even careful students of American racial politics. Obama rose to prominence by parsing the two versions of the civil rights idea—liberal and conservative—and questioning whether the United States should be seen as a nation of competing interest groups. Obama's most famous statement on race relations, his "A More Perfect Union" speech delivered in 2008, was an adroit deployment of that familiar theme, applied to the black-white divide. It was an effective stratagem, but it also highlighted the deeply conflicted role that racial division still plays in American life. For instance,

4

while Obama was more successful than previous Democratic presidential nominees in attracting the support of white voters in certain states, in much of the Deep South white voters were actually less likely to support him than his predecessors.[10] Other researchers have shown that during the 2008 election cycle and Obama's first term in office, the American electorate was driven by race-based attitudes and assumptions—both hopeful and resentful—more than in any comparable period in recent memory.[11] Subsequent election cycles brought even more confusion. Black Republican candidates, such as Tim Scott (elected to Congress from South Carolina and now a U.S. senator) and Herman Cain (temporary front-runner for the 2012 Republican presidential nomination), made inroads among voters who were hardly predisposed to support Obama. At the same time, the inauguration of the nation's first African American president prompted an outpouring of resentment, causing many Americans to deny even empirically verifiable facts—such as his birth within the United States.

The Age of Obama seems to be the age of both hope and resentment, and many of the essays in this volume use the racial politics that have surrounded him to offer some provocative thoughts on what has changed—and what has not—with race in America. In a deliberately controversial essay, Paul Butler compares "the two most powerful black men in the United States," President Obama and Supreme Court Justice Clarence Thomas, arguing that both men embrace a "postblack" identity. Neither man denies that he is African American but, Butler argues, both of them downplay the continued existence of race discrimination, question the usefulness of affirmative action and race-based public policies, and mount cultural critiques of their fellow African Americans. In sum, each man has risen to prominence by distancing himself from core components of the civil rights idea. Glenn C. Loury argues that, of necessity, the nation's first African American president remains disconnected from what he calls the historical "prophetic tradition" in black political thought and action, which emphasizes "an outsider's and underdog's critical view on the national narrative of the United States of America." Mobilizing an array of social science data on racial inequality, Loury argues that we have hardly put the struggles of the civil rights era behind us, and that the election of an African American president, paradoxically, makes America less likely than it otherwise would be to make significant progress in addressing that inequality.

Poet and cultural critic Elizabeth Alexander, by contrast, connects Obama to a long-standing tradition of what she calls "free black men," those who "teach us how to think outside the proverbial box," those "who can imagine . . . black selves beyond the reach of the pernicious roadblocks to our full and flourishing personhood." Reading the imagery and language that surrounded Obama during the 2008 election cycle and his first term in office, she suggests that in the surprising juxtaposition of a black man as president, we may see the emergence of a picture of black manhood that simply does not fit within our racial expectations—whether those expectations be conformist, rebellious, or other. But for Alexander, the question of whether a black president can be a free black man remains just that—a question whose answer we will debate for years to come.

Yet, the most difficult questions that emerge from the unraveling of the civil rights idea are those that ask how it should be modified, or perhaps replaced with something else. How should we think about the future of racial identity and race relations, while not forgetting America's troubled racial past? How should we write history, argue about law, do social science, or create public policy in a world where something undoubtedly new is at work in our world of race? What exactly is this "new black"—the new organizing principle that will influence thinking about race in a variety of fields? Patterson offers some brief thoughts on this subject in his preface to this volume, where he describes the long-running debate over the role of "culture" in explaining present racial inequality.[12] Other essays in this volume delve deeper.

Luis Fuentes-Rohwer takes up this project in his analysis of the future of civil rights law, as viewed from the vantage point of the Supreme Court, where a conservative majority of justices is deeply skeptical about the constitutionality of portions of the iconic civil rights acts of the 1960s. Fuentes-Rohwer argues that we have arrived at a point where the validity of the "Second Reconstruction" is being questioned because of the idiosyncratic opinions of one justice, Anthony Kennedy, who has wielded disproportionate influence within the Court on this subject. Kennedy's conflicting impulses in this area, however, merely reflect "a general ambivalence in the culture at large" on this issue. Americans never reached consensus on the "meaning of freedom as codified in our civil rights laws and Reconstruction Amendments." As the conservative version of the civil rights idea comes to displace the liberal one in the Supreme Court, the tragedy lies not only in the result, Fuentes-Rohwer argues, but also in the fact that Justice Kennedy and his colleagues are unlikely to offer any organizing principle that would point toward some new consensus on the core ideas that should undergird civil rights law.

For some, those core ideas may emerge from recent studies which conclude that implicit biases—unconscious attitudes and stereotypes—are widespread in contemporary culture. It has been well documented that conscious racial attitudes—for instance, opposition to interracial marriage or unwillingness to vote for an African American presidential candidate—have changed markedly over the past generation.[13] Researchers who study implicit bias, however, argue that unconscious attitudes—for example, an association of "African American" with negative characteristics—remain entrenched. An even larger set of researchers have contended that individual attitudes and actions often have no direct relationship to conscious purpose and cognition—results with profound implications for the continuing validity of the civil rights idea.[14] What if people don't "choose" to discriminate based on any conscious motive? What if judges, policymakers, and other public officials who are supposed to be unbiased are, in fact, guided by unacknowledged unconscious impulses? What if members of minority groups themselves are likely to respond in unforeseen ways to policies engineered on their behalf? What if color-blind law and decision making—the core of the conservative version of the civil rights idea—cannot be achieved? Both Jeannine Bell and Angela Onwuachi-Willig ask questions such as these and reach some counterintuitive conclusions.

Bell examines the seemingly surprising persistence of what some call "move-in violence" but she calls "anti-integrationist violence"—arsons, cross burnings, physical assaults, verbal abuse, vandalism, and the like—that sometimes happens when a member of a racial or ethnic minority group moves into a predominantly white neighborhood. Assembling a database of such incidents occurring since 1990, Bell argues that anti-integrationist violence happens in many neighborhoods where white residents believe themselves to be tolerant, and is sometimes even perpetrated by people who regard their own motives as race neutral. For a partial explanation, Bell turns to the Implicit Association Test and concludes that many whites choose to live in—and defend—largely whites-only neighborhoods unconsciously while still genuinely professing their tolerance.

Onwuachi-Willig, by contrast, zeros in on one famous incident—the 2009 arrest of Harvard professor Henry Louis Gates Jr. at his home by Cambridge Police sergeant James Crowley, "a man with considerable antiracist credentials." The arrest, following a report of a possible break-in at Gates's home and a confrontation between Gates and Crowley, prompted widely diverging descriptions of both the incident and its causes. Those who condemned Crowley as an old-fashioned bigot and those who claimed that he was motivated by solely nonracial impulses are both wide of the mark, contends Onwuachi-Willig: "There is no reason to think that Crowley is anything other than what he suggests—a good man who does not harbor [conscious] prejudice against black people." Mobilizing data from studies of unconscious bias, she contends that Crowley may have internalized racial assumptions that led him to interpret the facts leading to his confrontation with Gates, and the confrontation itself, in a manner that led him to place the Harvard professor under arrest. Taken together, Bell's and Onwuachi-Willig's essays suggest that much has changed—and much has not—about the nature of race prejudice in the twenty-first century, and that what needs to change most of all is our model of discrimination and perhaps the laws designed to combat it.

Yet, probably the most profound change in twenty-first-century race relations may involve the way politics is organized. The oft-cited figure capturing this trend is the coming of a majority-minority America. The conventional way to talk about this change is a hold-over from the civil rights idea—that a nascent majority coalition of "people of color" is forming, united by their opposition to the legacy of white racial prejudice. But as Lee reminds readers of this volume, the situation is far more complicated than that. "People of color" often have a looser affiliation to a particular party—or a particular set of issues—than is often realized, he contends, particularly among "panethnic groups like Latinos and Asian Americans." The future of American politics may lie in the hands of the party or the candidates who are most successful in creating flexible organizing strategies that cast aside many traditional associations of political loyalty.

Cristina Rodríguez likewise pushes back against the conventional assumptions about group identity in arguing that the "civil rights paradigm"—which focuses on the integration of outsider groups as full members of our society—may be of limited use in forming a political coalition to address the problem of undocumented immigration. A striking fact of our own times, she contends, is that we can now usefully distinguish between organizing strategies that focus on Latino citizens, and those that focus on undocumented Latino immigrants. While the civil rights idea might still be politically useful for the former subgroup of Latinos, newer pragmatic ideas seem more appropriate for the latter. Taken together with Guinier and Torres's idea that "political race" should replace conventional racial affiliation, both Lee's and Rodríguez's essays suggest that "the new black," in the context of political organizing, forces us to discard the idea that there is any easy link between group identity and specific politics.

History is yet another battleground site in the struggle to define race and racial inequality in a rapidly changing world, for we inevitably remember the past filtered through the needs and imperatives of the present. The past is the repository of foundational stories and of cultural heritages, and several contributors to this volume remind us that those stories themselves are in need of revision. Orlando Patterson does this explicitly in his reinterpretation of the life and works of the eminent historian John Hope Franklin. Born into Jim Crow in early-twentieth-century Oklahoma, Franklin lived long enough to participate in the civil rights movement and become one of the most lauded scholars of his generation. While many claim Franklin's life as an integrationist story that fits comfortably into the mainstream civil rights narrative, Patterson offers a dissenting perspective. For him, Franklin stands for a series of often uncomfortable truths: that the effects of past racism and social division continue to make themselves felt in the present lives of both blacks and whites, and that the election and re-election of an African American president is by no means the end point of the race relations history that Franklin so famously chronicled.

In perhaps the most challenging essay in this volume, Jonathan Scott Holloway takes apart many of the comforting stories that we might tell about the civil rights movement. Both the comfortable image of "the entire nation . . . linked arm in arm with Martin Luther King Jr. when he marched for freedom (and jobs)" and the less comforting image of freedom continually denied for outsider groups seem inadequate as descriptions of a now-hallowed period of American history. Indeed, for Holloway, history will not even remain in the past, as a chance encounter while preparing for a history lecture suddenly thrusts Holloway himself into the story that he was preparing to tell his students as an observer of history rather than as a participant. He suggests that history is often about the stories we choose *not* to tell—uncomfortable stories that are perhaps too painful, or simply forgotten due to the fallibility of memory. Indeed, he begins and ends his essay with the poignant question: "What do we tell our children?" Which stories do we choose to remember, and thus enshrine as history, and which might we even purposefully choose to forget, now that the civil rights movement lies more than a generation behind us?

Read alongside Elizabeth Alexander's unsettling interpretation of President Obama's image on the cover of the latest edition of John Hope Franklin's *From Slavery to Freedom*, both Patterson's and Holloway's essays suggest that the foundational stories that we tell to better understand our own rapidly changing world of race relations are anything but foundational. We continue to struggle over what to tell, and not to tell, about our racial past. Indeed that struggle to define and redefine history is just another version of the question that pervades this volume: what has changed, and what has not, with race in America?

We conclude this introduction by noting that the authors of the essays gathered here are less confident in their ability to describe the causes, and cures, for widespread racial inequality than they would be if this book had appeared ten or twenty years ago. They are equally less confident in their ability to describe and analyze the past, and future, of racial identification. That is as it should be. If "the new black" stands for anything, it is the proposition that the less-complicated world of blacks, whites, and their long history, that was encapsulated in the civil rights idea, is falling apart. The world is no longer black and white, if it ever was. *The New Black* is less a manifesto describing a full-blown program or framework for thinking about race than it is a roadmap marking the decline of something that is old and perhaps has outlived its usefulness. That is to be expected at a time when a familiar idea that once allowed us to talk comfortably about the past, present, and future of race in America may be in its death throes.

Kenneth W. Mack
Cambridge, Massachusetts

Guy-Uriel E. Charles
Durham, North Carolina

1

POLITICAL RACE AND THE NEW BLACK

Lani Guinier and Gerald Torres

WHO IS THE NEW BLACK?

When a racial hierarchy is in plain view, people of color typically know where on the hierarchy they will be. And when that knowledge comes from their own experience, it can generate a political as well as an emotional response.

Witness the contrasting reaction of blacks, whites, and Mexicans to the racially coded job assignments that dominated the Smithfield Packing Company in Robeson County approximately ten years ago. Robeson County, near the Cape Fear River, was one of the poorest counties in North Carolina. Smithfield was the biggest employer in the region and the largest pork production plant in the world. At the time, large numbers of Mexicans had been recruited to Robeson County, and the number of Mexicans at the hog plant had increased exponentially in three years.

Whites, blacks, American Indians, and Mexicans were assigned to different jobs—the pecking order was described in stark detail in a *New York Times* article from that time period. The reporter, Charles LeDuff, got a job at the hog plant, and his report was based on inside experience: "The few whites on the payroll tend to be mechanics or supervisors. As for the Indians, a handful are supervisors; others tend to get clean menial jobs like warehouse work. With few exceptions, that leaves the blacks and Mexicans with the dirty jobs at the factory."[1]

The jobs on the cut line were especially cold and brutal. They required work at a furious pace with no letup in a room with no windows, no clock, and no connection to the outside world. These were the jobs held by the Mexicans. Blacks worked on the cut lines too, although a few blacks were a pay grade higher, especially those who were long-term employees.

Criminals were also made to fit within the racial hierarchy in the plant. Like many poor people, white men in prison greens shared something important with Mexicans and blacks. They, too, were on the bottom rung.

But the whites and the blacks had differing interpretations of what it meant to be at the bottom of a racialized hierarchy. For example, Billy Harwood, a white man, had a job at the plant while on work release from the nearby Robeson County Correctional Facility. Despite the word *felon* that was linked with his name, Harwood exuded confidence in the wages of his whiteness. Harwood complained about the work, while simultaneously broadcasting his inherent superiority: "but at least I ain't a nigger."[2] In his mind, being white was his key to upward mobility. "I'll find other work soon," Harwood proclaimed. After all, "I'm a white man."[3] To which a black co-worker responded mockingly, "You might be white, but you came in wearing prison greens and that makes you as good as a nigger."[4]

Harwood was assigned to work the cut lines with the Mexicans. Harwood's place by the conveyor belt put him next to Mercedes Fernandez. Fernandez helped show Harwood the ropes; he was the first white person she had seen on the cut line. Like Harwood, she had little sympathy for the black workers. "Blacks have a problem," Fernandez declared. "They live in the past. They are angry about slavery, so instead of working, they steal from us."[5]

Both Harwood and Fernandez distanced themselves from the black workers at the plant; at the same time they shared a similar emotional response to the sordid working conditions at a plant that, they both agreed, treated its workers like animals. But neither Harwood (the white man) nor Fernandez (the immigrant woman) was ready to assume a political stance.

Wade Baker, by contrast, had a more complex understanding of the role that slavery and Jim Crow played in determining his low status at the hog plant. Baker was a fifty-one-year-old black man who had grown up in the Jim Crow South. His mother was the granddaughter of slaves. Baker had no doubt that "socially, things are much better." But while things had improved socially, Baker told LeDuff, "We're going backwards as black people economically. For every one of us doing better, there's two of us doing worse." In Baker's mind, there was a political and economic explanation: "The system is antiblack and antipoor."[6]

In the break room at the plant, Baker acted on his political consciousness as he whispered to the black workers sitting near him, "We need a union." Unlike Harwood and Fernandez, Baker reacted politically, not just emotionally. But while Baker saw the systemic and not just the interpersonal dimension of the problem, he was reluctant to speak up. He had to whisper because everyone at the plant assumed that talk of a union gets you fired.

An NAACP Chapter of a Different Hue

A thousand miles away and almost ten years later, a very different version of the same racial dynamic was at play. Ben Jealous, the national president of the NAACP, visited the Maine State Prison chapter of the NAACP as part of his effort to revitalize "his aging organization in a racially changing America."[7] At the Maine State Prison chapter of the NAACP, a vast majority of the members were white. Jealous's goal was to recruit new members, whatever their color, and to include those who were presently incarcerated.

After Jealous entered the prison, he passed through a courtyard enclosed by a chain-link fence topped with barbed wire and then walked through a heavy door, one that locks with a definitive metallic snap, into a large room where ninety-two inmates were waiting: "A grizzly bear of a white man with a shock of gray hair on his chin stares from the front row. Near him, a young white guy, arms thick with muscles, leans back in his chair. Three rows behind, a balding white man with blue letters tattooed across his forehead sits quietly. White face after white face, inmate after inmate—a sea of white men with few exceptions."[8]

The NAACP chapter was the largest outside organization in the Maine prison. The president of the chapter was William "Billy" Flynn, a self-described Irish white guy.[9] The vice president was Joseph "JJ" Jackson, a black man. Jackson explained to the reporter covering the story that despite its largely white membership, "this is a black organization." The fact that the vast majority of the prison chapter members were white didn't matter. In Jackson's mind, a white man wearing "prison greens" might as well think of himself as black. Once "you have that felon beside your name [you become a minority]." What does becoming a minority mean? It means, in Jackson's words, "You're treated like you're black. Frankly, everybody needs civil rights here."[10]

William "Billy" Flynn (right) and Joseph "JJ" Jackson are president and vice president, respectively, of the Maine State Prison chapter of the NAACP.
Michael C. York

Jackson's comment that "everybody needs civil rights here" suggests the potential political, not just emotional, power of self-knowledge. Under the right circumstances, knowing where you stand with regard to a racial hierarchy can, in fact, elicit a political, not just an emotional, response.

When it was Ben Jealous's time to speak to the NAACP prison chapter members, he looked closely at the sea of white faces in his audience: "A Native American with long black hair [was] sitting four rows from the front; and two black men, one bald and another with cornrows, [were] sitting in the back row. A Latino man [was] near the front, and a South Asian man [was] in the center of the crowd." Everyone else was white. Jealous explained that the letters NAACP stand for the National Association for the Advancement of Colored People. "That confuses folks sometimes," Jealous said, standing behind the wooden lectern. "As they say, colored people come in all colors." The inmates laughed.[11]

One of the reasons chapter president Billy Flynn (the self-described "Irish white guy") and the other mostly white inmates chose to help start a chapter of the NAACP was because the prison chapter received financial and emotional support from the local NAACP chapter in Portland, Maine. The prison did not allow many organizations, but the one that was permitted and had external resources was the NAACP. By forming a chapter, all of those inmates inside the prison who became members essentially linked their fate to a group outside the prison that was opposed to the dehumanizing impact of the criminal justice system and was "an extra powerful support group on the street" able to command the attention of the prison officials.

Aiming to expand his membership, the national president explains, "Colored people come in all colors."[12] Ten years earlier, at the Smithfield hog processing plant, Billy Harwood had claimed that whiteness trumped prison green, though his black co-worker at the Smithfield plant and later JJ Jackson in the Maine prison both challenged Harwood's self-aggrandizing view. Jackson, for example, understood there was a long-standing, though often masked, connection between race and class. Joined by chapter president Billy Flynn, Jackson's acknowledgment was a political, not just an emotional, act. You didn't need to be black to be a felon, but if you were a felon, you were likely to be socially stigmatized as if you were black.[13]

At a critical race theory (CRT) conference in Iowa a few months before Ben Jealous trekked north to the Maine prison, Frank Valdes, a gay Cuban American law professor, asked the assembled audience of scholars a question that echoed some of the ongoing ambivalence toward black-white alliances. It was a question that we would ultimately understand in conjunction with Jealous's important conclusion that colored people come in all colors. At the time of the CRT conference, however, Valdes's question stumped the audience. None of the attendees at the conference had a ready answer for his question: "What is the *work* we want race to do in the twenty-first century *other than to serve as a site of grievance*?" In part because no one in the critical race theory conference in Iowa had been prepared to answer Valdes's question, we have been pondering it ever since: "What is the work race currently does? And what is the work we ultimately *want* race to do?"

This essay is an effort to answer Professor Valdes's question: what is the work we want race to do other than to serve as a site of grievance? In other work we have called race "the miner's canary," a metaphor that emphasizes the vulnerability of people of color not merely as a site of grievance but as an early warning signal of systemic dysfunction. When the canary gasps for breath, it is not a call to fix the canary. When the canary gasps for breath, it is time for *everyone* to evacuate the mines. Because the canary's respiratory system is more vulnerable, when the canary has difficulty breathing, it alerts others to the growing toxicity of the atmosphere in the coal mines. Race as the miner's canary becomes a metaphor for a vulnerability that affects the miners, not just the canary. Thus, the goal is to fix the *atmosphere in the mines* to benefit the miners as well as the canary.

THE CASE FOR POLITICAL RACE

We propose an analytic shift that we call "political race." Political race starts by identifying the potential political coalitions of people who are white, who are black, who are Latino, who are poor, all of whom are disadvantaged by current structural dynamics. Race becomes a political act, a metaphor for the mobilization of people around issues of race, class, gender, and geography.

But a political race coalition does not arise naturally; it may depend on hard political work that builds an emotional connection among people who are otherwise estranged. Moreover, shared hardships don't necessarily make allies. "As linked fate rises, so does competition," said Michael Jones-Correa, a professor of government at Cornell who specializes in immigration and interethnic relations. "It's like a sibling rivalry," he said. "This is not a painless relationship."

Compare the Maine prison chapter of the NAACP to the workplace in North Carolina. In the case of the prison, the inmates saw themselves and each other as outcasts in need of "civil rights." They all became "colored people," a connection that became foundational for the political work to be done. By contrast, the racialized hierarchy at the Smithfield factory exacerbated the racialized differences that still characterized life in the South and legitimated the cultural attitudes that some of the immigrants brought with them as they came to North Carolina looking for better jobs.[14]

Of course, Latino immigrants don't just enter a preexisting racial hierarchy; they bring with them their own assumptions based on the hierarchies in their home countries.[15] "When we come to the U.S.," said sociology professor Eduardo Bonilla-Silva, who is Puerto Rican, "we immediately recognize whites on top and blacks on the bottom and say, 'My job is to be anything but black.' "[16]

In the prison, race became a political act. The idea of "colored people" in need of "civil rights" not only resonated, it became the basis for connecting the inmates to issues of race, class, gender, and geography. By contrast, in the factory, the old racial animosities informed the assignment of job duties, which formed a hierarchy that undermined the potential for coalition building across racial lines.

By "political race" we mean a group of people who ultimately are defined by their politics rather than by their physiognomy. Race, however, is neither lost nor hidden. Political race uses race and politics to forge an identity that ultimately resists conventional categories and supports democratic renewal. Political race acknowledges racial unfairness but does not rely on an individual's phenotypic identity as the reason to capture social goods or fixed political resources. Instead race becomes a political space for organized resistance around a more transformative vision of the good society. Simply stated, political race is a metaphor that captures the idea of race as a site of emotional connection *and* political engagement.

If blacks are going to make a meaningful difference in the socioeconomic hierarchy that so far defines the twenty-first century, it will not be due solely to a mobilization that only includes other phenotypically black people. Meaningful change is dependent on a "new black," i.e., a cross-racial coalition of disenfranchised groups that mobilize under the umbrella of "political race."

Political race is not a status that depends on phenotype or biology. The idea of political race, for example, would reject Billy Harwood's conviction that he remained white even when dressed in the green uniform of a North Carolina prisoner on work release. Instead, the idea of political race is rooted in the epiphany that accompanied NAACP leader Ben Jealous's visit to the Maine prison chapter a decade later. As Jealous acknowledged, "Colored people come in all colors," taking account of the fact that almost all of the Maine prison chapter's members—including the president—were white men. If blacks are going to make a difference in the twenty-first century, it will not be through their own movement, but through their involvement in a cross-racial coalition with other disenfranchised groups mobilized under the umbrella of what we have come to call "political race." Political race necessarily includes consideration of class as an important determinant of social position.

Race becomes a portal into a space in which to organize, to identify, and to challenge the corrosive structure of material disadvantage and inequality across racial lines. It may show up first in the black community, but it's like the rust decaying the infrastructure of America that endangers everyone. If the bridge collapses from deferred maintenance, it scarcely matters whether those plunging into the river are white or black, Latino or Asian.

Political race means that race in the twenty-first century should become a political space for articulating a multiracial response to the individualism of the American dream. The American dream tells us that if we work hard and play by the rules, we can succeed. The dream has universal appeal; its promise is that opportunity can be shared broadly. Everybody presumably has the chance to succeed as measured by income, a good job, and economic security. Opportunity is presumably earned, if not exclusively, then mostly, through grit and individual effort.

But what happens when individuals work hard, play by the rules, and yet still do not succeed? Those who fail to climb up the ladder of success have no explanation for their failure. The American dream offers an individual explanation for success; simultaneously the American dream fails as an individual explanation for failure. No one wants to accept the explanation that one's lack of success by the conventional measures suggested above was because of one's own lack of talent or drive.

Not surprisingly, for many, race becomes the explanatory variable. After all, race provides a pragmatic explanation of what would otherwise have to be called individual failure: "While it is easy to see success as a sign of merit rather than luck, few people willingly accept an equally self-referential explanation of failure. Race arguably fills the gap, providing a believable account of all that went wrong."[17] In the words of W.E.B. DuBois, the psychological wage of whiteness put "an indelible black face to failure."[18]

Traditionally, race has done a lot of the heavy lifting to justify this dark side of the American dream. Yet, racial group consciousness need not merely be a way to assess blame. Those who see the necessity and efficacy of collective political struggle—i.e., those who are "politically raced black"—are more likely to experience a sense of the structural impediments to individual success and thus to experience that structural analysis as part of a collective consciousness. In Jane Mansbridge and Aldon Morris's words, people of color who identify with their community benefit from a sense of collective injustice that can be an "empowering mental state." Rather than finding fault with themselves or other individuals, they are more likely to experience "an oppositional consciousness" based on righteous anger. That group consciousness then enables them to see their group as having a shared interest in ending or diminishing injustice.[19]

By contrast, those who enjoy the privilege of thinking of themselves only as individuals are left with no explanation when the American dream fails them. They work hard and play by the rules, but if they don't succeed the only reason "must" be that someone is keeping them from achieving what should have been theirs; someone must have "stolen" the American dream. When searching for a likely suspect, conventional racial categories are triggered: the thief is likely a person of color.

We suggest that political race is an important concept because it provides an alternative answer to the dark side of the American dream. Political race suggests that individual effort alone is not a sufficient explanatory variable for either success or failure. Instead, political race sees the experience of those who have been left out, the experience of those who have been denied opportunity as a window on a larger system of structural deficiencies. Political race suggests that blacks and whites, Latinos and Asians all face built-in headwinds that make upward individual mobility difficult for individuals to succeed on their own. The idea of political race not only draws on the kinds of forces that produced the multiracial NAACP chapter at the virtually all-white Maine prison. It also reflects efforts to respond to the racialized economic hierarchy at the pork plant in North Carolina.

Whereas whites like Billy Harwood, the man in green prison garb on work release at the Smithfield packing plant in North Carolina, found themselves on the same bottom rung as blacks and Latinos, it was blacks who wanted a union. The black workers understood that "the system" was "antiblack and antipoor." In places like the hog plant, political race-based mobilization could draw attention to large inequalities in the distribution of job types as well as to the huge disparities in rewards associated with particular job categories.

We want to be clear. In proposing the concept of political race, we are not endorsing transracial universalism, where race is closeted. In transracial universalism race recedes into the background, thus losing the positive contributions that consciousness of race can bring. A sense of community is important as is an oppositional consciousness that can be tapped to mobilize a group to challenge shared injustice. By contrast, transracial universalism focuses on the individual acting alone as the agent of change; it fails to acknowledge the importance of empowering groups of people working together to take action against systematic injustice.

Moreover, we do not suggest that Americans are "postracial." Race still matters. Instead we propose the idea of political race, where race is a tool to diagnose deeper structural problems that affect everyone, not just people of color. Thus, in answer to Professor Valdes's question, race is not just a site of individual grievance. Instead racial disparities are both a problem and a mirror. Political race functions as an invitation to join with others to work together to fix the deeper structural problems, not just to minimize individual experiences with racial inequality.

In sum, political race maps surprising racial dynamics like those in the Maine prison chapter of the NAACP as well as the more commonplace racial hierarchy such as the one at the Smithfield packing plant. Both stories yield an important insight. Race consciousness does not necessarily lead to coalition building. But it can make political consciousness more likely.

Yet, race consciousness alone does not fulfill the promise of political consciousness. At the hog plant in North Carolina, for example, the black workers' desire for a union was not universally shared.

Some of the workers did not blame management; instead, they saw one another as the problem. As we discussed earlier, one of the Mexican workers disparaged her black co-workers, saying "Blacks have a problem. They live in the past. They are angry about slavery, so instead of working, they steal from us."[20]

In what follows, we shall continue this exploration of the potential as well as the limitations of the concept of political race with a paraphrase of a lively conversation that occurred at a Duke University conference in honor of John Hope Franklin, one of America's great historians. We shall describe in some detail an exchange that highlights the challenging aspects of political race.

Too many people already assume that there is an easy coalition possible among people of color without confronting the ways in which historic racial divisions are recapitulated in the discourses of ordinary life.[21] The opposite side of this optimistic vision is composed of those who are confident that cross-racial political alliances are almost always insincere and unreliable. Thus the conversation at Duke reveals some of the difficulties that will have to be overcome for the concept of political race to gain traction, especially because the American dream, with all of its promise, remains elusive. Some are even accused of stealing it from others.[22]

WHAT ABOUT ILLEGAL DON'T YOU UNDERSTAND?

The question political race asks is: With whom do you link your fate? This is a much bigger question than "who is" and "who is no longer" black in any simple sense. Trying to decide who occupies the category of the "new black" was for us at the heart of an exchange at the Duke conference during a session on Latinos and immigration. There were four Latino panelists, each of whom was either an academic or a professional broadcaster.

After the distinguished panelists finished their remarks, a middle-aged working-class black woman dressed in a white sweater and turquoise blouse heatedly took them to task. She punctuated her remarks with vivid gestures, swinging her arms and using her hands for emphasis, speaking almost as loudly with her hands as with her voice. It was as if she were a conductor trying to get a truculent orchestra to play in tune. When she completed her questions, she folded her arms across her bosom and leaned back as if to say: Answer that!

The demographic makeup of the panelists put them at some disadvantage because they were not speaking the same language as their formidable interlocutor.[23] Their scholarly language and examples seemed utterly unpersuasive as a response to a direct challenge by this black woman. She was not buying their sophisticated arguments. For this woman, the question of immigration, especially undocumented immigrants, was easy. Why were these smart alecks making it so difficult?[24]

The black woman had raised her hand to speak in response to a panelist who had just finished describing his view of what elements would have to be part of a just immigration policy. Such a policy would include some path to citizenship. It would require that you earn this privilege by having been here a certain number of years, at least beginning to learn English, and producing evidence that you paid your taxes. The panelist asserted that the IRS already allows undocumented workers to pay income tax through their I-10 form.[25] This enables people to show exactly how long they have been here and what they have been doing. The panelist described a conversation with one of the movers hired by a company to take his household goods from California to Seattle, where he was moving. The moving company employee was undocumented but proudly declared that he paid taxes every year and had been doing so for ten years. When the panelist asked him why, he replied, "I want a record. If I am ever eligible for citizenship I want a very clear record that this is what we can do."

The inquisitor raised her hand and began:

I wonder what happened to enforcement of law. For God's sake, we prosecute people for running a red light. The law is the law. And this applied even back when they had the Jim

Crow laws, but we had to go through the proper process as black people to get our so-called civil rights, which are not quite there yet.

But what ever happened to not breaking the law?

[It seems ludicrous] that somebody wants to document how long they have been breaking the law. It makes no sense to me. Why would you document that you have been in the U.S. illegally for 10–15 years? . . .

Let's do a scenario that everybody understands. When we left home [to come to this conference], we all locked our doors if no one was in the house. If I went home this afternoon and I found one or two or three people in my house that were not supposed to be there, the first thing I would do—and the first thing you would do—would be to call law enforcement. And have them removed. Is that correct?

PANELIST 1: Depends on whether they were cleaning my home or taking care of my children. [panel laughter]

QUESTIONER: These are unauthorized people. I said you locked your door, and you wouldn't lock the door if the maid or the babysitter were there. But what would happen if you came home and someone you don't know anything about is in your house? You would come and that person is in your house, would you not call law enforcement? And what would happen if that person said, "I'm here; you've got to feed me; you've got to provide medical services for me; you've got to provide educational services for me; and there is not a thing you can do about it"?

MODERATOR: I was with you until you described them as strangers, because these are not strangers that we don't know anything about. . . . They are invited to pick our strawberries; pick our tomatoes; pick our lettuce. Raise our children; clean our houses; clean our office buildings. . . . They are invited to be here; recruited to be here; transported to be here; and operate in response to a very efficient transportation network that knows when and whether and where there are jobs all the time. . . . And if they were truly strangers, I think we would have something more to talk about.

QUESTIONER: If they are invited to be here, then why don't they have legal status?

MODERATOR: They are invited to be here and the people who invite them are not prosecuted . . . the out-of-status illegal immigrant *is* prosecuted. The owner of the office, the owner of the janitorial service, the meatpacking plant is not prosecuted . . .

QUESTIONER: Do we not have laws in place that should prevent this?

PANELIST 2: The functional answer is right. If you were to run a red light, what would be the penalty? Would it be the equivalent of deportation? Part of what we are talking about here is whether there is a sense of proportionality between the behavior and the penalty, which is a fundamental principle of the criminal justice system.

QUESTIONER RESUMES: Do we not have laws in place . . .

PANELIST 2: There is also in law enforcement the concept of prosecutorial discretion. . . . Prosecutors don't go after everyone who violates law. Otherwise we'd all be in some form of prison or have to pay some fine. . . . It is the culmination of a moral judgment and a judgment about the appropriate uses of government power that go into that decision, and those are the kinds of values that we're saying need to be brought into this debate that don't seem to be getting an airing because people think that "what part of illegal don't you understand?" is the beginning and ending of the conversation. But that's not true for any aspect of law or any aspect of life, so I don't think this should be true for this context either.

PANELIST 3: I want to go back to a question that was asked earlier about narrative. One narrative proposed by skeptics of undocumented immigrants is to ask, "Why don't people just go back and stand in line and wait their turn?" The answer is simple: there is no line for the people that we are talking about . . .

The Challenges Facing Political Race

In many ways this brief exchange at Duke is a conversation in miniature of a much larger and more complex conversation about how race, class, and ethnicity reveal the challenges facing the idea of political race. For example, it stands in opposition to the individualized understanding of the promise of the American dream. The American dream attempts to explain success: if you as an individual work hard and play by the rules, you as an individual will succeed. Most Americans who are successful think they earned their success. In their minds, virtue leads to success; success is evidence of virtue.

While it is easy to see achievement as a marker of individual merit and hard work, few are inclined to accept a comparable self-referential explanation of failure. As noted previously, race arguably fills that gap. Thus, poor and working-class whites often accept the terms of racial solidarity rather than confront the fundamental need to organize collectively and across racial lines to obtain the benefits already accorded to white elites.

For the poor southern whites in the post–civil rights era, black people got the things that those white people thought they should have rightly had. A similar dynamic is now seen in the tension between blacks and Latinos. What the exchange above captures is that for the black woman questioner the "illegal" immigrants are now "stealing" the American dream.[26] For whites, black people are presumably stealing the American dream because of affirmative action and other programs of racial preference. For blacks, undocumented Latino immigrants are stealing the American dream because they are taking their jobs and violating the rules. The dark side of the American dream is the necessity to produce scapegoats.

Our thesis suggests that the American dream—that honest effort and hard work will be rewarded—is still achievable, but only if the structural impediments that adversely affect all Americans—not just people of color—are exposed and transformed. These impediments are often spoken of in the language of race, but truth be told, they adversely affect everyone. Thus, any safety net we conceive of has to function as a ladder whose rungs are within everyone's reach. Class jumping (otherwise known as upward mobility) is actually quite rare in this country. Those who do move from rags to riches are celebrated; but they do not represent the lived experience of most Americans. The exceptions, most assuredly, do not prove the rule. Indeed, they may function to accomplish just the opposite.[27]

So, who exactly *is* the new black? Blackness has been the marker for those at the bottom of the social, political, and economic pyramid. Is that the insight that should guide our social analysis within the racial and class history of the United States? Is the new black shorthand for those wealthy black professionals and business executives who have exited the "hood" for the mansion with a view? Or is it conceivable that the Latina maid who cleans your hotel room is one of the new black? Or the Latinos on the cutting floor of the North Carolina hog processing plant? What about the Latino men serving time in prison? Or Latino families being deported? Are they members of the new black?

For us, the answer to the question of who is a part of the new black is yes to the Latina maid and probably no to the millionaire. In other words, the new black, like the old black, is a marginalized status reflecting economic class. However, unlike the old black, the new black is less tethered to biologically determined notions of who is black, despite the continued existence of laws like the one-drop rule.[28] Instead, the new black is explicitly linked to one's economic position.

Our answer might cause those who are heavily invested in conventional racial categories to recoil, but we have a view on race that is different than the one in common circulation, one which does not undervalue the ways in which the historic racialization of American culture produced positive, rather than just negative, effects. For us, the new black raises issues not just of biological or phenotypic race but of the complex intersection between race and class. The new black, like the old black, is a marker for where you belong in the hierarchy that defines American life, but it is also a hierarchy that despite its obdurate nature remains officially invisible. At the same time it continues to operate as the dark side of the American dream, meaning blackness becomes the explanation for failure and structural deficiencies can be safely ignored.

The new black, as an expression of political race, is really about the interaction between race and class. This is the lesson from the cutting floor in the Smithfield hog processing plant and the prison in Maine. It doesn't mean race as conventionally understood. These two examples suggest that race is a fluid term, one that defines a class position more than just a biological determinant. You were placed at the bottom of the employment hierarchy if you were black, brown, or a felon. In the prison, everyone was "blackened" by virtue of their imprisonment. One was an employment hierarchy that mapped conditions outside the plant and the other was a flattened hierarchy by virtue of their common fate: incarceration. Both examples illustrated the possibilities of political race.

Indeed, in the Maine prison, all of the inmates knew they would be better off if they linked their fates not only with each other but with the "colored people" outside the prison who made up the Portland NAACP chapter. By contrast, in the hog processing plant, linking fate would have required a direct challenge to the racialized hierarchy that placed undocumented workers at the bottom of the heap along with convicted felons. The workers at the plant were the living answers to the questions posed by the black woman interlocutor at the Duke conference.

In the past, the relationship between race and class was overlooked because of the disadvantage associated with blackness as a racial condition—with all of its burdens and obstacles—needed to be overcome before class could be exposed. Overt concern for economic injustice, for example, took a backseat during the heyday of the civil rights revolution.[29] As Andrew Young, one of Martin Luther King's chief lieutenants, admits, "The civil rights movement was not aimed at ending poverty. It did not focus on economic issues. Not because we didn't think economic issues were important, but because we didn't think we could win on economic issues. . . . We set out to break down the color barriers for those who were exceptionally well qualified and we succeeded."[30]

Exploring the space opened up by the category of the new black also enables us to investigate questions of deserts. What does it take to be treated with equal dignity and respect? After all, aren't these the bedrock principles on which equality and liberty rest? Unlike the French, we did not resolve the tension between equality and liberty by resorting to "fraternity." We resolved it by guaranteeing the right to pursue happiness as each of us individuals shall find it. We are, of course, insisting that possessing an inalienable claim to equal dignity and respect is the source of the binding energy that makes a polyglot and racially complex society like ours possible.

Unfortunately, the new black is a characterization rooted in a meaning that everyone thinks they know. Yet for us, the category has to encompass all of those Americans who are suffering through the current social and political milieu that changes in our technologically driven—but physically outsourced—economy have produced. In our view, the structurally poor may be part of the new black whether they are white people, Latinos, or Asians. Those of us who could afford to move out and move on, by contrast, have often distanced ourselves not just physically but also psychologically from our communities of origin. It is these linkages, and a new understanding of American social life, that lead us to conceive of the concept of political race.

By juxtaposing the words "new" and "black" the title of this volume forced us to contemplate more carefully the relationship between race and class as well as the multifaceted nature of race itself. For us then, the idea of a new black requires a redefinition of race that takes account of the broader historical moment we occupy.

Political race is, for us, the answer because it depends on a new kind of politics in order to support a new kind of economy that recognizes that success comes from cooperation and community, not just raw individual competition.[31]

Race can no longer be answered by the simple question, Who is your daddy? The real question of this century is not who is and is not phenotypically black or Asian or Latino (or how those categories gain priority). In the twenty-first century, a clear understanding of the color line requires us to see beyond the dynamics that regulate the relationships between white and black people. Instead, it is time to explore race as a legal, political, and sociological phenomenon, not for purposes of counting, but for purposes of political mobilization.

Political race is the tool we should use, not because it is the only tool, but because it allows us both to understand emergent phenomena and to suggest the basis upon which transformative mobilizations might occur. Political race is integral to the diagnostic process by which the ills of America's social, cultural, and economic life can be identified. Political race reminds us that the hardships experienced by people of color (the canaries in the coal mines) evidence society-wide vulnerabilities that can only be addressed when poor and working-class people of all colors link their collective fates.

Political race is a self-conscious choice. It "is not something you are; it's something you do. It's a decision you make."[32] Or as Ben Jealous said at the Maine prison when he addressed the predominantly white chapter meeting of the NAACP: "colored people come in all colors."

What this means is that the political and social agenda that defines the new black is an essential part of a transformative political and economic agenda for Americans—all of us. Rather than using race to search for scapegoats, political race continues in the tradition of Martin Luther King Jr., who began this unfinished process.[33] Just before he was killed in Memphis, Tennessee, King marched to defend the rights of Memphis garbagemen and was planning a poor people's march on Washington. As King knew then, it is only by seeing opportunity as an interdependent proposition that the American dream can be brought into the twenty-first century. The vehicle for this, in King's mind, would be new multiracial alliances organized to restructure the architecture of American society. Or as we suggest, the meaning of the new black will be found in the idea of political race.

2

DÉJÀ VU ALL OVER AGAIN?

Racial Contestation in the Obama Era

Taeku Lee

*Herein lie buried many things which if read with patience may show
the strange meaning of being black here in the dawning of the Twentieth Century. This meaning is not without interest to you, Gentle
Reader; for the problem of the Twentieth Century is the problem of
the color-line.*

—W.E.B. DuBois (1903)[1]

W.E.B. DuBois's opening lines in *The Souls of Black Folk* were repeatedly evoked at the dawn of the twenty-first century to intimate
that the color line remained a defining problem of this new millennium. Yet, less than a decade into this new century, a historical moment that would have been inconceivable to almost any American
in DuBois's time was fully inscribed into our daily consciousness.
Many Americans basked in the celebratory afterglow of having an
African American family in the White House, even as they absorbed
as a daily fact of life comic moments like media persona Chris Matthews's infamous remark, "I forgot he was black tonight for an
hour," following President Obama's first State of the Union address.

In perhaps more barbed terms, the election of Barack Obama
invited public speculation over the continued significance of race.
Thus Shelby Steele asked, "Does victory mean that America is now
officially beyond racism?"; Matt Bai asked, "Is Obama the End of
Black Politics?"; Touré asked, "Who's Afraid of Post-Blackness?"; and

the list and litany went on.[2] This essay reflects on Barack Obama's ascendancy as an illuminating lens on racial politics and racial discourse in this new millennium. Rather than tackling head-on the significance of the 2008 and now also 2012 elections and whether they augur a "postracial" future for America, I dig around the edges into some of the unexamined assumptions and hidden transcripts underlying this question.[3] Specifically, the essay reminds readers that 2008 in particular was an *extraordinary* and rare political moment, and not the inevitable culmination of a steadfast march of racial progress. It then revisits the election, paying special mind to the prevailing view that independent voters were the decisive factor in Obama's success. The essay then concludes with some thoughts on what may in fact be changing about America's political landscape and how we might reckon that change.

NORMALIZING OBAMA'S ELECTION?

Contemporary claims to a postracial America in the context of what happened in 2008 are perhaps paradoxical and pernicious. Postracialism—if what is meant by "post" is coda, transcendence, abnegation, or invisibility—is clearly more of an aspiration (for those who espouse it) than a materially achieved reality. There is, alas, no shortage of proof points on the persistence of racial inequality in America. Picking indicia is akin to picking up confetti in Times Square on New Year's morning. So my aim here is not to belabor the point, but simply to note the seeming paradox and irony underlying the persistent discourse on postracialism. The gap between discourse and lived reality is not lost on President Obama himself, who remarked in an address on Martin Luther King Day in 2010, "You know, on the heels of my victory over a year ago, there were some who suggested that somehow we had entered into a postracial America, [and] all those problems would be solved. . . . That didn't work out so well."[4]

Yet if racial schism and inequality persist, from whence does the longing for a postracial America come? The temptation to see the election of a self-identified African American seems, *res ipso loqui-tur*, a beacon signal of the end of what Gunnar Myrdal termed the "American dilemma."[5] Perhaps America's liberal creed of equality no longer stands so strikingly at odds with reality. The symbolism in telling school-aged children that anyone can be president of the United States after 2008 simply carries a prima facie credibility that it did not before 2008. In this aspect, there is clearly a collective investment among many in what David Hollinger refers to as "a possible future" where choice supersedes ascription and strategy displaces destiny.[6]

At the same time, much energy—especially from the academic left—has been focused on demonstrating how plainly and doggedly racism and racial inequality exist and, therefore, how untenable claims to such a possible future are. Some of the most incisive of such demonstrations show that aspirations to a postracial society are intimately linked to an ideology of colorblindness and a willful neglect of racial realities.[7] My aim in this essay is not to rehash these arguments in other contexts. Rather, I take these interventions as a given and take as my point of entry the question of whether there is any paradox at all between the fact of Obama's election, and re-election, and the stubborn persistence of racial inequalities.

The paradox only exists, in effect, if both realities are equal in epistemic status. That is, there is only a tension here if Obama's successful campaigns are an expected electoral outcome in the same way that differential risk rates—unemployment, poverty, educational attainment, incarceration, infant mortality, stress-related chronic health conditions, home default, and the like—are expected outcomes for African Americans (and, to different extents, other racialized minorities). Only if the election of a black man to the White House is seen as an ordinary feature of our electoral system, within a reasonable range of expected outcomes, is Obama's success at odds with other indicia of structural disadvantage, where successes (especially of such a high order) are decidedly extraordinary outcomes.

The point here is simple, but worth pondering nonetheless. It is beguilingly easy to think of the outcome of the 2008 presidential election as unsurprising and perhaps even inevitable. The nation was on the brink of the Great Recession; our military campaigns in Iraq and Afghanistan had driven us even deeper in debt and exacted a ruinous toll on American lives and livelihoods; the incumbent president George W. Bush's approval ratings were hovering around a near-historic low of 30 percent; and so on. Furthermore, there is a clear and well-documented trend over some fifty years in support of the idea that the nation was ready and willing to elect an African American to the White House. Since 1958, the Gallup Poll has asked Americans, "If your party nominated a generally well-qualified person for president who happened to be black, would you vote for that person?" In the first poll in which this question was asked, roughly three out of every five whites were unwilling to vote for someone like Obama, even if "well qualified" and from the political party of their affiliation. By the 1980s, when the Reverend Jesse Jackson twice ran unsuccessfully to be the Democratic Party's nominee, that figure had fallen to less than one in every five whites; in 2008, it dropped even further to fewer than one in every ten whites.[8]

Yet prior to the 2008 election, the state of our researched understanding also painted a clear picture that "the terms *prejudice* and *racism* [remain] important and deeply meaningful facets of the American social, cultural, and political landscape."[9] In the political arena, studies consistently showed that the color of a candidate's skin would predictably handicap African Americans running in a majority white jurisdiction, even controlling for the content of their character and the quality of their political bona fides.[10] At an aggregate, historical level, David Canon's study of 6,667 congressional elections between 1966 and 1996, for instance, found that African Americans won in only 0.52 percent of the cases (no typo there!).[11] At the more microlevel of individual voters, studies showed that whites were not only more likely to favor white candidates over their African American counterparts, but also that they were more likely to favor lighter-skinned African American candidates over their darker-skinned counterparts.[12] Other studies showed a stubborn gap among white Americans between (nearly uniform) endorsement of racial equality and (a much more divided) attitude toward the practices and policies that might achieve that equality. In the breach between principles and practices, moreover, stood divergent attributions of racial inequality, overtly negative stereotyping, and renewed strains of racism, rooted in both socialized symbolic resentments and realistic group competition.[13] Finally, beyond the reach of consciousness and introspection, studies showed a strong unconscious operation of stereotypes, prejudice, and discrimination. By one measure, as high as 88 percent of whites held an implicit bias for whites and against African Americans.[14]

The marrow in these various studies of bias is that Obama's election caught most people—including (and perhaps even *especially*) scholars of race and racial politics—quite by surprise. As an anecdote, I organized a roundtable of six nationally preeminent scholars of racial politics and voting behavior at a political science conference in the spring of 2008. The stellar cast keyed their wits and wisdom on the still-fresh wounds of the ongoing primary contests between Barack Obama and Hillary Clinton, and what they meant for various dilemmas of race and gender politics. Yet none on the panel declared their confidence (or even aspiration) that Obama would win in the general election. The fact that Obama's success ran against the expectations of many experts in the field, of course, may be more of an indictment against the academy than anything else.

The question of whether social science research on race warrants arraignment on its deficits in light of Obama's success deserves a fuller consideration than this essay permits.[15] For the present, I share two vantages that reinforce my point that there is no paradox between Obama's election and the persistence of racism. The first is an observation about the dominant mode of analysis in much of the social science research on race relations and racial politics. This mode relies on quantitative reasoning and explains or predicts outcomes that are most likely to happen under "ordinary," equilibrium conditions of politics. The analysis is commonly couched in the statistical language of central tendencies, expected values, maximum likelihoods, propensity scores, and the like. This practice is often poorly equipped to explain or predict extraordinary events, or does so only by stripping phenomena of their defining contexts or by rendering race as a category of analysis into a reified ghost.[16] Whatever else the 2008 election may have been, it was extraordinary on several dimensions. A looming economic meltdown, a hugely unpopular war (and with it, sitting president), and an unusually strong ground game and record-breaking fund-raising campaign all made for uncommon circumstances. But there was also Barack Obama, an exceptionally fresh and prepossessing candidate, possessed of prodigious powers as a public speaker and an uncommon credibility among a diverse cross-section of Americans. In racial terms, Obama was singularly polysemous and multivocal, enabling voters of multiple stripes—black, multiracial, postracial, immigrant, Pacific Islander, and so on—to see him as a candidate who dignified their experiences and advocated for their interests. Political scientists are adept at deriving statistical models that specify the marginal effects of incumbency, a poor economy, wars, scandals, and even hurricanes and snowstorms on Election Day—but we are not so accustomed to reckoning a candidate like Barack Obama.

In short, the paradox here emerges from the peculiar refracting lens that much of social science research deploys. If the first point is that a single, anomalous, extraordinary moment should not falsify "normal science," a second key point is that the best social science evidence nonetheless suggests that race did in fact play a role in 2008 (as it also would in 2012). While Obama clearly fared significantly better than his Democratic counterpart John Kerry did in 2004, there is some telling local variation in that result. For instance, in some states and counties in the Deep South, Obama actually fared significantly worse among white voters than did Kerry in 2004. These racial gaps, moreover, were especially pronounced in jurisdictions covered under Section 5 of the 1965 Voting Rights Act.[17] An even more robust body of research uses psychometric measures of "racial resentment," "implicit association," and "affect misattribution" and concludes rather clearly that antiblack sentiments were predictive of greater opposition to Obama.[18]

Ultimately, perhaps the best way to decide whether race factored into voters' electoral calculus is through counterfactual reasoning: would the outcome of the 2008 election change if the Democratic nominee were Barack Obama's white doppelgänger—a candidate equal in every respect to Obama but for his race? While Obama's rare traits as a candidate make such counterfactuals a generally limiting exercise in abstraction, the best electoral forecasting models would have predicted a more decisive landslide for the Democratic nominee than Obama enjoyed. This electoral cost of racial prejudice is quantified by several studies as ranging between 3 and 5 percent.[19] The nub here remains that the best research on race before 2008 would not have foreseen a majority-white national electorate ready for a black president. And in fact, far from signifying a shift to a transcendent, postracial "Age of Obama," racial conflicts and competition in 2008 held a renewed ferocity in American political life.

INDEPENDENTS AND THE PANRACIAL VOTE IN 2008

If racial bias is such a regnant force, skeptics might ask: how then did Obama win the presidency and what does that foretell for the future of race relations and racial politics in America? No matter how extraordinary the circumstances or how exceptional the candidate, an election is won or lost by the aggregation of votes. Where then did Obama's margin of victory come from?

On this question, it is useful to revisit and reframe a common narrative about the 2008 election by setting it in bold relief against some election results. Specifically, one of the predominant framing messages in the mass media's coverage of the 2008 election was that independent voters were a critical segment of Obama's electoral coalition. As I have argued elsewhere, this idea depends on several accompanying suppositions: that independent voters are predominantly white; perhaps even that most whites who voted for Obama transcended their own racial group interests and favored the postracial promise of Obama's candidacy. From these priors, it would seem that the longer-term viability of a racially progressive politics in America might hinge on appealing to white independents and espousing a postracial discourse.[20]

Examples of this predominant framing were visible as early as January 2008, when an article in the *International Herald Tribune* carried the headline "In This Race, Independents Are the Prize" (Zeleny, January 6, 2008). The narrative continued into April, with a Real Clear Politics article titled "Obama's Independent Edge" (Avlon, April 29, 2008), and continued into Obama's first year in the White House, with an in-depth report from the Pew Research Center titled, "Independents Take Center Stage in Obama Era" (Pew Research Center 2009). Then, as discontent with Obama began to mobilize, the framing shifted, with articles such as the *Wall Street Journal*'s November 2009 piece, "Obama Is Losing Independent Voters" (Rasmussen and Schoen, November 14, 2009). And following Scott Brown's dark horse Senate victory and the passage of health care reform in April 2010, the *Washington Times* ran a story, "Independent Voters Turn Angry" (Haberkorn, April 2, 2010).

What is illuminating in these headlines (and their corresponding stories) is the nearly total absence of any consideration of race. Such absences—especially when set against a backdrop in which race is clearly a salient consideration, such as Obama's candidacy in 2008—are often accompanied by a presumption of whiteness, and the media coverage of independents is no exception. The dynamic is commonplace, where whiteness is simultaneously nowhere and everywhere; it is simultaneously being defined in direct opposition to the experience of African Americans, and being accepted without interrogation as the "null" hypothesis or "normal" state of affairs.[21]

Absences and assumptions notwithstanding, what are the background facts about race, nonpartisanship, and voting behavior?[22] First, the dynamics of partisanship have been rapidly shifting, and whites are no longer the disproportionate number of nonpartisans in America. In the earliest academic and media polls, independents were a relatively minor and (for the most part) ignored segment of the American electorate. The first Gallup polls in the 1940s showed a range of 15–20 percent of Americans identifying as independents, and the initial American National Election Studies (ANES) surveys in the early 1950s found a range of about 20–25 percent self-identified independents. In these earlier surveys, it raised few eyebrows to presume that independents were whites. From the 1952 ANES through the 1972 ANES, more than 90 percent of all self-identified independents were self-identified whites.

Since the 1960s, however, there have been two important and interrelated trends. One is a growing percentage of Americans who identify as independents or nonpartisans. As early as the 1970s, upward of a third of Americans identified as independents. In more recent years, that figure has crept up above 40 percent. It is now no longer uncommon for independents to constitute a plurality of the electorate. This trend of rising nonpartisanship—and its relationship to corresponding trends of rising distrust and disaffection among voters and rising polarization among party elites—is a significant source of the growing attentiveness to independent voters.[23]

The other trend is the rising number of Latinos and Asian Americans in America—and with that growth, a preference not to associate with either political party. The demographic landscape of America in a post–civil rights era is profoundly transformed and transforming. Changes in U.S. immigration law and global migration trends since the mid-1960s have spurred an influx of immigrants to the United States on a scale unseen since the early twentieth century. One in four Americans today is either an immigrant or a child of an immigrant. Moreover, contemporary immigrants come from Asian, African, Caribbean, and Latin American shores, rather than from across the Atlantic. Up until the first decade of the twentieth century, about 90 percent of new migrants to the United States set sail from European shores. Today, roughly 80 percent of new migrants are Latino or Asian.[24]

Coupled with this demographic change is the fact that Latinos and Asian Americans are especially likely to be nonpartisan. Specifically, the approach that political scientists continue to use to measure affiliation with political parties appears largely irrelevant to many Americans. In two recent surveys—the 2006 Latino National

Survey and the 2008 National Asian American Survey—well over half of the respondents chose not to identify as either Democrat or Republican. The effect here has been a dramatic shift in the racial composition of independents. According to the 2008 ANES survey, less than 60 percent of all self-identified independents were whites. If the trend toward diversity continues, we are likely only a few election cycles away from independents being a majority-minority group. Thus, as a general feature of nonpartisanship, it is simply not the case that independents can or should be thought of as a "white" electorate.

A second implication from 2008 is that the electoral debt Obama owes is more credibly to voters of color, be they independents or partisans. That election was highly vaunted for the investiture of large numbers of Americans into the ranks of first-time voters. Who were these rookie citizens? According to the 2008 Current Population Survey Voting and Registration Supplement (CPS), roughly 5 million new voters were mobilized in 2008. Of these, the CPS estimates that about 2 million were African American, 2 million were Latino, and 600,000 were Asian American. The CPS estimates no statistically significant new mobilization of whites in 2008. If one simply carries through the National Election Pool (NEP) exit poll estimates of vote share by race—that 95 percent of African Americans, 67 percent of Latinos, 62 percent of Asians, and 43 percent of whites voted for Obama—a reasonable estimate would be that Obama enjoyed the support of almost 80 percent of these new nonwhite voters.

Further support for this view comes from keying in on the independent vote itself. Here, the NEP exit poll data show that while the two-way split favoring the Democratic candidate remained unchanged between 2004 and 2008, a slightly higher proportion of independents reported voting for Obama (52 percent) than for Kerry (49 percent). Yet to put this in some perspective, Obama also saw an equivalent percentage increase in support among self-identified Republicans, garnering 9 percent to Kerry's 6 percent of this crossover vote in 2004. Perhaps more crucially, the 3 percent uptick in independents' support for Obama in 2008 was slender compared to the mobilization of the African American, Latino, and Asian American support, where 2008 saw a corresponding increase in turnout of 7 percent, 9 percent, and 6 percent, respectively (vis-à-vis the 2004 figures). The icing on top is the breakdown of the independent vote itself: while Obama enjoyed the support of a majority of independents in 2008, a far greater proportion of this support came from nonwhite independents. Among white independents, only 47 percent reported voting for Obama, compared to roughly 70 percent of nonwhite independents.[25]

DIVERSIFYING THE NEW BLACK?

The first sections of this essay focused on the *plus c'est la même chose* elements of race as a motive force in American politics. That discussion mainly focused on the extent to which prejudice persists in the calculus of American voters, notwithstanding aspirations to the contrary or the successful election of an African American president. Given the broad charge of this volume—to consider whether there is a "new black" that defines race relations in the twenty-first century—it is important to note that Barack Obama is not just a symbol of the continuing negative role of racial bias and conflict.

The extent of Barack Obama's support among African Americans, Latinos, and Asian Americans should force us to consider another symbol for Obama: the positive role of racial solidarity, group mobilization, and collective self-empowerment. Can the same group boundaries that demarcate unequal opportunities and outcomes for communities of color also define a basis for collective action and racial solidarity? While much attention has been paid to the question of whether and how racial bias and conflict have changed post-2008, less attention has been paid to whether and how racial group-ness serves as a basis for shared experiences, common purpose, and collective action. The electoral results portray a mass mobilization across communities of color that have often been pit against one another. This, in my view, is the real surprise and the potentially transformative seedling of change to emerge from this historic event.[26]

It is also a germ of change that reflects the decidedly multiracial and multiethnic future of this country. The racial remix that we have seen over the last half century is expected to continue. If Census Bureau projections hold, the United States will become a majority-minority nation sometime in the next three to four decades, as the self-identified white population falls below 50 percent of the U.S. adult population. Majority-minority status already describes the demographics of New Mexico, Hawaii, and California, as well as many cities throughout the nation. These far-reaching changes in number, moreover, are occurring amid equally sweeping changes in kind and in categorization. Our ethnoracial classification system alone has seen the introduction of a separate *Hispanic* ethnic identifier in 1970; a proliferation of Asian, Pacific Islander, American Indian, Native Hawaiian, and Alaska Native categories in 1980 and 1990; and, in the most recent decennial census, the option of choosing more than one among these categories.

What is unclear from the remaking of the American racial landscape—and with it, a multiplicity and hybridity of identities— is whether the sort of multiracial moment seen in 2008 (and again in 2012) is a harbinger of things to come or a brief pause in an otherwise long history of defeat and disaffection. To many, the 2008 election represents a potential watershed moment of success on a grand national political stage engendered by a *panracial* coalition of African Americans, Latinos, Asian Americans, and racially sympathetic whites. Yet to others, it is the 2010 election that is more representative and reprises the kind of racial backlash that has historically accompanied moments of legislative and electoral triumph. Did the panracial mobilization seen in 2008 give us a peek into our future, or will such an ideal fracture and flounder under the weight of economic crises, partisan polarization, political distrust, and the countermobilization of moral and racial panics?

At risk of excessive navel gazing, political scientists grappling with such questions often seek guidance from an archetypical view of "black politics," in which a shared racial group label is demonstrably bound to a collective group politics. If such a discernible linkage is found among any group in the United States, it is found among African Americans.[27] Thus, the fact that two million African Americans were mobilized as first-time voters in 2008 and that 4.3 million more African Americans voted for Barack Obama in 2008 than voted for John Kerry in 2004 is impressive, but maybe not preternatural.

Does such an archetype help us understand the equally impressive and perhaps more startling mobilization of Latino and Asian Americans in 2008 and 2012? Will it help us to anticipate whether nascent identities like "Latino" and "Asian American" will be a similarly generative force in the years to come? More pointedly, can a common thread of marginalization serve as the basis for an inclusive panracial politics? Does political organizing around "wounded identities" enable or inhibit the pursuit of robust solidarity, democratic politics, and collective engagement? While political theorists have applied themselves to these questions in earnest, they are urgent empirical concerns as well, to which firm answers have been more elusive.[28]

In practice, the search for a "new black" politics archetype in Latinos, Asian Americans, and other groups is more often than not reduced to a search for evidence of the political consequences of "linked fate" (or some other measure of group consciousness) in opinion surveys.[29] As a framework, there are several problems with this mode of inquiring about Latinos and Asian Americans and their capacity to shape the future. First, in stripping a rich concept like Michael Dawson's "linked fate" down to discrete questions on a survey, the origins of group solidarity in the textured history of the African American freedom struggle and its deep linkages to the organizing role of socioeconomic class are lost. Second, in conceiving of black politics as an archetype vis-à-vis a black-white binary, there is a tacit view that the processes that link group labels and a collective politics for these other groups is functionally *isomorphic* either to those for African Americans or those of whites. For that matter, there is often a further tacit belief that Latinos and Asian Americans are also functionally isomorphic to one another.

If anything, panethnic groups like Latinos and Asian Americans are so internally diverse and spiced with crosscutting identitarian claims (around class, gender, national belonging, language, religion, sexuality, and so on) that the strong presumption ought to be that any collective basis for politics for either group is decidedly *not* functionally equivalent to what scholars have found for African Americans or equivalent to one another. A third pitfall, Cathy Cohen and others remind us, is that the African American community itself is characterized by heterogeneity, hybridity, and a multiplicity of crosscutting claims.[30]

Fundamentally, the frameworks we bring to any inquiry and the questions we ask of them have a way of defining the answers we find. Simplified, convenient inquiries on our present day—ones fueled by aspiration and angst rather than tempered with sobering realities—will invite blithe proclamations of postracialism and the pivotal role of (white) independents, and maybe even the rush to judgments on the inevitability of multiracial electoral coalitions and the evolution of a "new black." Put otherwise, if we are in fact living through another reconstruction of America's race relations, we will likely miss this change by clinging to well-worn concepts and frameworks.

As a parting thought, it is useful to keep in mind one constant from the turn of the century that W.E.B. DuBois passed down to our time: the central role of institutions, ideologies, and identities that create a capacity for struggle and resistance. Thus while DuBois bore witness to the lynching of Sam Hose—and in any given year, between fifty to more than one hundred additional Americans of African descent—he also worked with others to spawn intellectual ferment and grow indigenous organizational strength within the African American community. His was an era of the Niagara movement and the Brownsville raid; of the rise of the NAACP, the United Negro Improvement Association, the Brotherhood of Sleeping Car Porters, and the National Urban League; of the Harlem Renaissance and the further maturation of black-nationalist thought and racial uplift ideologies. By contrast, Organizing for America—for all its undeniable strengths and successes in building a twice-winning panracial electoral coalition—cannot be mistaken for a sustainable movement-based organization.

Transformative social change requires the presence of an institutionalized, indigenous countervailing force, wrought from the wellsprings of a robust civil society. Perhaps such wellsprings can be seen in the energy that produced the Occupy movement, or are ready to reemerge in the long wake from the spring 2006 immigration protest marches, or reincarnate from Organizing for America, or appear in some other embodiment of an autonomous demos yet to come. Ultimately, whether "the Obama era" heralds a rupture with our racial past or the unfolding of a panracial or postracial future depends on the meaning and action we give to our present day and on what Max Weber termed the "strong and slow boring of hard boards." In short, it depends on us, collectively.

3

IMMIGRATION AND THE CIVIL RIGHTS AGENDA

Cristina M. Rodríguez

During Congress's efforts to pass comprehensive immigration reform in 2006 and 2007, media and academic commentators characterized the activism that animated the immigrant community as the beginnings of a civil rights struggle[1]—one that would dovetail with the growing political power of the country's Latino population to produce a major new social movement. These predictions were stirring, and the large-scale immigration marches that helped prevent the passage of a House bill that would have made unlawful status a felony rather than adopt a legalization program illuminated the agency and power of immigrant communities. But the intensity of organization reflected in those marches has been difficult to sustain. In addition, the interests of the Latino electorate and immigrants diverge and sometimes directly conflict, thus making a pan-Latino movement focused squarely on immigrants' rights a fraught proposition.[2]

In this essay, I reflect on whether the civil rights paradigm should be invoked in the movement for immigration reform. Do alternatives exist that more accurately capture the stakes involved? Even if the civil rights paradigm does not provide the best framework for debating immigration reform, in what ways do civil rights concerns nonetheless arise in immigration regulation, and what can be done by political and administrative actors to address those concerns?

Civil rights rhetoric and values historically have informed movements for immigrants' rights and remain relevant in immigration reform debates, but the overarching conceptual frame for the immigration debate should use two other paradigms: a more pragmatic concept of mutual benefit and an appreciation for the rule of law that includes valuation of proportionality, accountability, and fairness. First, I discuss the viability of the civil rights paradigm as a general matter. Though the broad question I pose has relevance to many aspects of immigration reform, I focus on unauthorized immigration—the most urgent issue on the reform agenda. I then address the intersection of civil rights principles with the two alternative paradigms—mutual benefit and rule of law. In particular, I focus on how early shifts in the Obama administration's enforcement agenda embody the rule of law properly conceived. But whether we think about the immigrant community within the national civil rights narrative—as heir to the struggles against Jim Crow and race discrimination of the 1950s and 60s—or as a community best served by more ordinary antiexploitation and fairness concerns, the main challenge is to create a regime that serves the national interest and advances the rule of law while also respecting human dignity.

THE CIVIL RIGHTS PARADIGM

Immigration law and policy evolved over the course of the twentieth century alongside the civil rights movement. In a 1948 civil rights message to Congress, for example, President Truman called on the legislature to end the race-based restrictions on naturalization.[3] He vetoed the 1952 Immigration and Nationality Act, despite his belief that it made necessary improvements to the immigration regime as a whole, because Congress elected to maintain the racially discriminatory national origins quotas adopted in the 1920s to limit the admission of immigrants from southern and eastern Europe.[4] The 1965 Immigration Act that finally abolished these racial quotas emerged from the political and cultural milieu that produced the Civil Rights Act of 1964 and the Voting Rights Act of 1965, and members of Congress defended the new immigration regime as the realization of the antidiscrimination aspirations of that era.[5]

Consistent with this linkage between civil rights and immigration, courts in the late twentieth century grappled with whether and how to extend equal protection guarantees to noncitizens. Among other things, they addressed whether immigrants could be denied access to the social goods extended to citizens, such as public schooling, welfare benefits, and other entitlements.[6] The body of cases that emerged represented a meaningful, albeit incomplete, extension of the judicially crafted constitutional protections developed in the wake of *Brown v. Board of Education* to secure the rights of African Americans and other racial minorities. In *Plyler v. Doe*,[7] in particular, the Supreme Court advanced a strong antisubordination, anticaste justification for immigrants' rights by striking down a Texas law that would have denied unauthorized immigrant children access to public schools.

For advocates and social reformers, the appeal of the civil rights paradigm is obvious. It places immigration reform squarely within a central and perpetual national struggle for racial justice and equality. But despite the fact that immigration reform and the civil rights narrative have intersected throughout U.S. history, with the latter helping to shape the former, it remains unclear what it would mean for an immigrants' rights agenda to form a modern-day civil rights movement. I leave to the side the crucial question of what the movement would look like organizationally—how it would be structured, what coalitions it would entail, what tactics it should use, and how it might learn from the successes and failures of the civil rights movement itself. I focus instead on the substantive question: what would the civil rights claim be?

Civil Rights as Incorporation

Defining the core civil rights claim is complicated by the fact that the central question in today's debate is how to make sense of the unauthorized immigrant—a figure to whose presence there has been no formal, legal consent. Do unauthorized immigrants' claims to justice and recognition constitute legitimate civil rights demands?

Does today's population of unauthorized immigrants have a claim to social and political incorporation that is similar to the claims made during the civil rights era by black and Latino citizens excluded from full membership by segregation and discrimination?

A civil rights agenda could ignore this status problem by focusing on immigrant workers' dignity and respect for their rights under labor and employment laws—through a straightforward call for the enforcement of existing laws (which emerged from the New Deal and the civil rights movement) to prevent exploitation in the workplace and protect basic economic interests. In this sense, even for the unauthorized worker, a civil rights claim would be easy to make, not only because unauthorized status can never justify conditions of servitude, but also because the integrity of the labor law regime depends on its enforcement regardless of the status of the workers in question.

But to be properly called a new civil rights movement, these claims would have to be more demanding than a call for basic humane treatment. Recognition of immigrants' interests would have to be justified by something more than the argument that our society depends on enforcement of labor and civil rights laws. The civil rights demand is ultimately one for justice, equality, and incorporation—at the very least in social life, and ultimately in the political process. On a philosophical level, a civil rights paradigm therefore requires arguing that unauthorized immigrants, rather than being treated as lawbreakers, ought to be regarded as persons entitled to respect and membership.

Justifications for this sort of incorporationist agenda certainly exist. The claim that unauthorized immigrants deserve to be incorporated into our society would stem from the fact that they are already members of that society, as a sociological matter. They are taxpayers, workers, and homeowners whose lives are intertwined with legal immigrants and U.S. citizens. They are persons on whose labor society depends.[8]

Legal reality does not, however, match this sociological reality. Unauthorized status means subordination and marginalization.

Unauthorized immigrants lack the capacity to be effective social actors because their status erases them from the political conversation and makes it difficult for them to advocate their interests to others; the broader society feels justified in ignoring immigrants' interests because of illegal status. Unauthorized immigrants are subject to almost unrestrained state power because there are few limits on the government's authority to remove them from the country. That power also facilitates exploitation by employers, and means that unauthorized immigrants risk arrest and deportation when they interact with legal and social institutions. Legal marginalization thus becomes social marginalization. The fact that unauthorized immigrants are overwhelmingly poor and nonwhite deepens the civil rights parallel. Given the sociological characteristics of unauthorized status, then, the desire to situate the debate on the civil rights trajectory makes sense.

Incorporation as Out of Reach

Despite the strong resemblance of the unauthorized phenomenon to the conditions that fueled the civil rights movement, the fit between the civil rights paradigm and the case of the unauthorized immigrant remains an uneasy one. The difficulty stems first from the fact that unauthorized immigrants have broken the law. It would be disingenuous to point to the fact that immigrants organize to defend their interests through protest, and transform themselves through their work into de facto members of society, but to deny immigrants' complicity (at least adult immigrants) in their own status. To be sure, the fact that unauthorized status may be the product of choice does not change the undemocratic nature of the social condition described above. The immigrants' illegal status is not morally irrelevant in the same way that race, or gender, or other characteristics that have defined successful civil rights movements are.[9] This fact alone will make it difficult to transform the movement for immigrants' rights into a broad social movement that appeals to the larger public's sense of moral obligation.[10] In fact, the expectation that immigrants' rights become the next great social movement may be overburdening advocates and immigrants themselves with a heavy historical narrative they may not be able to sustain.

Similarly, the claim for immigrant incorporation cannot be justified along the same lines as the civil rights claims made by blacks and Latinos—as a demand for realization of the principle of equal citizenship enshrined in the Constitution. At the core of the civil rights movement was the existence of a constitutional commitment to equal citizenship regardless of race forged through the Civil War and Reconstruction. As constitutional citizens whose entire lives and histories had been lived as part of American society, civil rights movement activists demanded an equal treatment and respect that they already had been promised by the Constitution, whose breach throughout the Jim Crow era amounted to a repeated failure to honor commitments already made.

This is why even the Supreme Court is uncertain about the propriety of extending equal protection principles that protect racial minorities to noncitizens. The Court recognizes that some forms of discrimination on the basis of citizenship status can be justified because noncitizens have not yet been incorporated fully into the polity. This is because we live in a world of nation-states where citizenship is both a formal status and a participatory practice, and it is only more glaring when illegal immigration is at issue.

Given these tensions—that civil rights concerns are inescapably present in the immigration context but that key features of the civil rights framework are not—the question becomes whether the civil rights paradigm should be abandoned or downplayed. Efforts to protect immigrants' rights and secure immigration reform ultimately can be understood and described through civil rights principles without giving in to the demand that unauthorized immigrants become the next great social movement. To that end, alternative framings of the immigration issue are desperately needed to capture the full range of the interests at stake.

THE MUTUAL BENEFIT AND
RULE OF LAW ALTERNATIVES

I suggest two alternatives to the civil rights paradigm: mutual benefit and the rule of law. Like the civil rights framework, each of these has been present historically in debates concerning how best to design a regime of immigrant admissions and immigrants' rights. At the moment, the mutual benefit framework operates primarily as a rhetorical framing device in public discourse. But a conception of the rule of law that incorporates principles of proportionality, accountability, and due process has shaped the Obama administration's policy in this arena since the president took office. I consider the promise of each framework in turn.

Mutual Benefit and Pragmatism

The mutual benefit framework is fundamentally pragmatic and highlights the social gains that would come from the adoption of particular immigration policies. The concept of mutual benefit involves the recognition that immigration in general and legalization in particular can enhance the welfare of immigrants and Americans alike. The gain to immigrants is evident—job opportunities, acquisition of a stable legal status and the opportunity for long-term incorporation, all of which translate into the opportunity to live a better life. The social gains also include family reunification, as well as the general economic gains and growth in productivity that attend an orderly regime of labor migration, increased tax revenues, and the augmentation of a future tax base to support an aging population.[11]

The case for legalization using a mutual benefit paradigm begins with an acknowledgment of the negative externalities created by illegal immigration. Above I have noted the corrosive effects the present immigration regime has on the labor laws. The vulnerable position of the unauthorized worker, who has strong disincentives to report violations of the law for fear of deportation, makes employer abrogation of labor, health, and safety laws easier. The threat of enforcement places families and communities of mixed status under great economic and social stress, which strains social institutions, such as public schools. The presence of a large unauthorized population also undermines confidence in the government's law enforcement capacities, which contributes to a general distrust of government.

Mutual benefit relies on the premise that it is not in society's interests to allow the persistence of an unauthorized population, and the argument for legalization could be made on the ground that it represents the only solution to the problems outlined above.[12] A legalization program represents a logical policy response to the mutual benefit claim, just as it would to a civil rights claim, but that does not make the two frameworks interchangeable. The social salience of the mutual benefit paradigm comes from its linking of reform to broader social welfare. In addition, the mutual benefit paradigm might be politically appealing, because it does not necessarily coincide with political inclusion, or paths to citizenship. The procedural details of a legalization regime justified by mutual benefit might differ substantially from the regime created through a civil rights approach. Legalization, instead of being a matter of right or obligation that stems from U.S. complicity in the creation of the problem, would be a benefit, which in turn would provide justification for more demanding eligibility criteria. A mutual benefit paradigm is not inconsistent with a legalization program, but mutual benefit does allow for a broader range of political trade-offs.

The Rule of Law and Proportionality

Holistically conceived, a rule-of-law paradigm would emphasize not just law and order, but also protection of individuals from arbitrary government action and abusive state power. A rule-of-law framing does not promise a civil rights movement for our time but rather a balancing of different values. Importantly, these values include not just enforcement and policing, but also norms of proportionality, government accountability, and fairness. A rule-of-law agenda in relation to illegal immigration, in particular, would require more procedural protections in the enforcement process, and the channeling of prosecutorial discretion through the lens of proportionality to focus on high-value targets. The principles of due process and proportionality would encourage, for example, skepticism of intrusive enforcement techniques, such as workplace surveillance, and the development of highly effective but expensive identification-tracking technology whose costs must be born by all people, not just unauthorized immigrants.

Understood in this way, a rule-of-law agenda would advance core interests of the two paradigms already discussed, simultaneously furthering the social (and immigrant) interest in reducing the costs of illegal immigration and promoting the civil rights and liberties interests of noncitizens and citizens alike. But because it dovetails with law enforcement concerns, it has two potential advantages over the other frameworks as a device for framing immigration debates in a way that advances civil rights principles. First, an agenda prioritizing enforcement of the law has potentially significant political appeal. In this sense, the rule-of-law framework need not be seen as a substitute for the civil rights or mutual benefit frameworks, but rather as a complement to be mobilized in the face of political obstacles to more ambitious agendas designed to promote immigrant incorporation.

Second, whereas the paradigms discussed above would focus on legislation, a rule-of-law strategy could help guide not only reform efforts in Congress, but also (and primarily) the work of the executive branch, whose primary responsibility is to enforce the law. The challenge of infusing immigration law with civil rights principles is thus not for the legislature alone. Congress enacts major immigration laws only infrequently,[13] but the various arms of the executive branch that administer the immigration laws manage the system on a day-to-day basis. Alterations in enforcement policy that emphasize proportionality and due process can thus help shape the normative framework that governs the immigration regime as a whole.

Critics of immigration enforcement policy would contend that, over the last decade and a half, Congress and the president have both moved very far from the sort of rule-of-law agenda I describe, with the rule of law becoming synonymous with state coercion. Indeed, members of both political branches have devoted considerable financial and personnel resources to law enforcement operations, both at the border and in the interior, across several administrations. Secretary of Homeland Security Janet Napolitano has made clear that the Department of Homeland Security (DHS) will build on and expand the enforcement regime maintained by the Bush administration, pursuing an aggressive strategy targeting illegal immigration. The rate of deportation indeed went up in fiscal year 2009,[14] and the very fact that the administration's approach to illegal immigration has been to redouble enforcement efforts underscores that the civil rights paradigm may not be a priority for the government.

That said, the first term initiatives of the Obama administration reflect a willingness to incorporate proportionality, accountability, and due process into the enforcement regime and provide a template for a genuine rule-of-law agenda, making it worthwhile to consider some of what has been actually accomplished. As often happens with new administrations and in most regulatory arenas, the Obama administration reviewed the immigration policies of its predecessors and very publicly revised certain positions within the enforcement regime to advance the president's own substantive agenda. As early as 2009, Secretary Napolitano announced various new policies that suggested significant shifts in the underlying priorities of U.S. immigration policy, even as those policies reinforced the emphasis on law enforcement.

The emphasis on proportionality has, for example, guided the administration's approach to the controversial 287(g) program, which allows state and local police to enter into agreements with

Immigration and Customs Enforcement (ICE) to participate in the enforcement of federal immigration law, after receiving training and under ICE supervision. In July 2009, ICE announced that all 287(g) agreements would be governed by a new standard-form memorandum of agreement. The new template departs from the agreements signed by the Bush administration in various ways, the most significant of which is that the template articulates a set of clear enforcement priorities. The template agreement identifies three levels of offenders and encourages participants to target level-one "criminal aliens," or persons convicted of dangerous or violent crimes, as opposed to level-three offenders, who are mere immigration-status violators. This move, in fact, reflects ICE's stated policy of shifting federal enforcement efforts generally toward the apprehension and removal of so-called criminal aliens through the expansion of programs that target serious offenders.[15] By articulating enforcement priorities that reflect principles of proportionality, the DHS appears to be shifting its resources to acknowledge that not all unauthorized immigrants should be regarded as equally in violation of the trust or sovereignty of the United States, thus combining a rule-of-law agenda with an implicit form of humanitarian relief.

Several of the early Obama administration initiatives also advance the accountability component of the rule of law, according to which the use of force, to be justified, must be done by agents accountable for their actions, or subject to supervision to ensure respect for limits on the use of government power, including individual civil liberties. This accountability is also essential to ensuring that enforcement actions produce their intended results—that officers hit the intended targets rather than indiscriminately use force. Changes in the 287(g) program again reflect an intent to promote these values, with ICE promising greater oversight of state and local officials in the program and engaging in more rigorous screening of entrants into the program by requiring that they follow the parameters of the new program template.

In addition to issuing new formal guidelines for reporting and monitoring, the administration also appears to be willing to mete out consequences for failure to conform. In October 2009, several months after the Department of Justice launched an investigation of the use of 287(g) authority by Sheriff Joseph Arpaio in Maricopa County, Arizona, based on accusations that he and his officers engaged in racial profiling, ICE terminated the authority of the sheriff and his deputies to arrest suspected unauthorized immigrants during the ordinary course of policing. This decision, coupled with the more formal references to supervision, may well ensure that Sheriff Arpaio remains an aberrational abuser of the authority granted under the program, rather than a representative example of the consequences of 287(g) programming. The extent to which accountability in form turns into accountability in practice depends on the administration's implementation of its stated objectives. At the very least, however, the creation of accountability mechanisms represents an effort to advance an enforcement agenda that is consistent with a view of limited government designed to protect basic civil liberties.

Some later efforts to keep government officials in check have also been infused with concerns for due process, fairness, and even the protection of human dignity. The most important advance along these lines could turn out to be the renewed attention to the system of civil immigration detention.[16] The head of ICE, John Morton, announced a major overhaul of the detention system in early 2009, with the goal of improving detention center management to "prioritize health, safety and uniformity among our facilities while ensuring security, efficiency and fiscal responsibility."[17] Perhaps the most important long-term commitment made by ICE to this agenda has been the creation of an Office of Detention Policy and Planning, whose responsibilities include to "design and plan a civil detention system tailored to address" ICE's needs. The administration thus has committed resources to developing a detention regime that better promotes the humanitarian interests of detainees[18] and brings the system as a whole into line with the ostensibly civil character of immigration enforcement by eliminating the trappings of criminal confinement.

All of these reforms not only reflect a concern for proportionality, but also reflect a concern for recognition of the greater freedom to which civil immigration detainees ought to be entitled. Moreover, this rule-of-law approach, guided by principles of proportionality, accountability, and fairness, laid the groundwork for the Obama administration's most visible immigration reform so far—the decision to halt deportations of many undocumented immigrants who arrived in the United States as children.

Taken together, these alterations of enforcement policy reflect a paradigm that places respect for law at the center of immigration policy. Importantly, it is a respect for law informed by principles designed to prevent government overreaching and protect the civil liberties of immigrants and the public alike. Though this rule-of-law agenda cannot by its own force eliminate or even substantially curb illegal immigration, this rule-of-law framing can perform a crucial political function that will help make such transformation possible. If the rule-of-law framework succeeds in restoring public confidence in the government's willingness to enforce the law, but in a manner that is humane and advances the interests of society as a whole, this enforcement policy may clear the ground for future reform.

Despite promising to tackle immigration reform during his campaign, President Obama did not make the issue a serious priority during his first term, nor did it rise to the top of his legislative agenda. The shape that immigration reform takes and whether and *how* that reform becomes law, will depend in part on how lawmakers and other interested parties frame the issue. In this essay, I have described three approaches to understanding and addressing the phenomenon of illegal immigration: a civil rights paradigm, a mutual benefit framework, and a rule-of-law agenda. These approaches are not mutually exclusive, nor would a legalization program be wholly incompatible with any of them. But they each appeal to distinct audiences and have been useful at different political moments in time.

The civil rights paradigm, invoked during the dramatic marches organized by immigrants and their allies in the spring of 2006, seeks to frame legalization as a means of fulfilling the promise of the civil rights movement by providing a path out of second-class status for millions of immigrant workers and families. The paradigm demands incorporation in order to bring the legal reality of status in line with the sociological reality of membership. But the limitations of the civil rights paradigm will make it difficult to advance a reform agenda using only the momentum that the paradigm affords—a momentum based on demands that we live up to our ideals as a nation. The general public will demand a justification for immigration reform that links it to their own interests and the "good" of the country—a factor that makes the development of a mutual benefit framework vital. That framework would emphasize that the gains from legalization to immigrants and the broader public would outweigh the costs. All of that said, even if the momentum behind immigration reform and immigrants' rights cannot be built into a morally tinged social movement, important civil rights goals can still be advanced through a rule-of-law agenda focused on enforcement guided by principles of proportionality, accountability, and fairness.

In reality, a complete answer to the civil rights dilemmas that illegal immigration presents will come only by figuring out how to prevent illegal immigration from arising in the first place, or how to reduce it from a large-scale social phenomenon to a nuisance. The focus on legalization, though urgent, is therefore incomplete. In thinking about the future, each of the paradigms I have described may have a role to play, but the usefulness of each paradigm is different when talking about the future versus the current debate over legalization. The civil rights strategy, for example, fits even less well when the concern is no longer noncitizens who are present and integrated, but rather a future class of people whose identities and characteristics are unknown and who cannot be said to have the serious claims on the United States and its citizens described above.

But as with legalization, no matter the moral arguments made or the framework mobilized, political compromises will be necessary to address the problem. Each of these paradigms can be used to broker that compromise. The concepts of civil rights, mutual benefit, and rule of law have always and should continue to shape public deliberation over the nature of our immigrant future.

4

THE PRESIDENT AND THE JUSTICE

Two Ways of Looking at a Postblack Man

Paul Butler

The two most powerful black men in the United States seem to be opposites. One is progressive, and the other is the most conservative person to sit on the Supreme Court in fifty years. One is adored by African Americans and the other is largely reviled. One describes himself as a "feminist" and the other attained his high office despite compelling evidence that he sexually harassed a woman.

What both President Barack Obama and Justice Clarence Thomas have in common, however, are certain aspects of their performance of blackness. They are postblack. Their racial ideology discounts the significance of discrimination, is skeptical about race-based remedies, and contains strong critiques of black culture.

In addition to rejecting racial orthodoxy, Obama and Thomas both use race instrumentally. When being black works for them, they embrace it, and when it does not, they abandon it. You could say they are free of race, or you could say they are so hung up on race—that is, so hung up on not being hung up on it—that it obsesses them. They would deny this, especially the president, but the evidence suggests that they think about race all the time, about how it does not matter to them, or should not, or how they wish it would not. The conundrum of postblackness is that you are still black.

That black people are still black, after all these years, is also a sign of the slow pace of racial progress for African Americans. The California Supreme Court ruled that Chinese people are black, because "black" meant anyone who was not white; but that was in

1854, and now anyone would have to acknowledge that the Chinese have moved on up.[1] They are still not white, but they are no longer black. Irish Americans actually attained whiteness, roughly in the early years of the last century, followed, a few years later, by Jewish Americans.[2] Italians too, even the Polish Americans.[3] African Americans have been black for damn near 500 years.

You can hardly blame a black person, especially a president or a Supreme Court justice, but really any black person, for embracing postblackness when blackness means being at the bottom of virtually every indicia of social and economic well-being. If blackness includes those loud girls on the subway, one screaming about how she is going to "kick that fat bitch's ass," who wouldn't long for postblackness? The "we got to do better" movement in black popular culture occasioned by Obama's election signals a critical moment in race in the United States. Postblackness has a new prestige, and blackness seems hopelessly old school and self-destructive.

This essay is about President Obama's and Justice Thomas's surprisingly similar projects to rush postblackness along, and why those projects will not actually benefit black people.

BLACKNESS, EXISTENT AND POST

The concept of postblackness was first described in the catalog of an art show at the Studio Museum of Harlem. One art critic called the 2001 exhibition "one of the most important shows of the decade not only because of the articulation of this generational transformation where the work of Black artists is no longer absolutely bound by the image or the idea of race, but also its anticipation of that possibility that made Barack Obama the president of the United States."[4] The cultural critic Touré described the participating artists as wanting "to be defined as artists with the freedom that entails, rather than as Black artists, which boxes them in, but they also wanted to retain the liberty to talk about Black subject matter when and where they pleased. They wanted to have it both ways."[5]

Blackness has always been a social construct, not a genetic one.

That is how a person like Barack Obama, whose mother was white, can call himself black. The artist Glenn Ligon, who, along with the curator Thelma Golden, first used the term *postblackness*, said, "Blackness was about group definitions so there could be Black leaders who spoke for Black people in total."[6] James Baldwin discussed an obligation of representation.[7] Blackness included, for many blacks (and not only blacks defined the constructs, whites did, and the law did as well), a set of commitments and practices, including feelings of kinship with other blacks and a recognition that African Americans are victims of racial injustice.

Some African Americans have described the acknowledgment of racial inequality as an important constitutive element of their blackness. "I feel most colored," Zora Neale Hurston wrote, "when I am thrown against a sharp white background."[8] This recognition does not require any particular response; in the same essay Hurston noted that she was not "tragically colored" and did not "belong to the sobbing school of Negrohood that holds that nature had somehow given them a lowdown dirty deal."[9] But part of the social meaning of blackness is an awareness of difference; it is, as Hurston put it, "to know that for any act of mine I shall get twice as much praise or twice as much blame."[10]

Here are some of the ways that Barack Obama is black.[11] He says that he is. He went home to Africa. He is married to a black woman. He plays basketball and walks with a swag, especially in front of other black people. He has benefited from affirmative action. He is very cool.

Here are some of the ways that Barack Obama is postblack. He does not like talking about race. Race discrimination does not appear to have limited his opportunities. He went home to Ireland. His mother was white and his sister is Indonesian. He is not angry. White folks sometimes temporarily forget about race around him.[12] None of his ancestors were slaves.

Here are some of the ways that Clarence Thomas is black. He says that he is. He has phenotypically African features, including dark skin. He is always talking about race. He is angry. He professes kinship with other blacks. He started a black student union when he was in college and left seminary because he thought some of the other novices were racist. He has benefited from affirmative action.

Here are some of the ways that Clarence Thomas is postblack. He is married to a white woman. He is very conservative. He vacations in a recreational van. He performed the third marriage ceremony of Rush Limbaugh and was a guest at the fourth one.[13] He rejects affirmative action.

Both Obama and Thomas embrace the idea of postblackness, even if they haven't used that term to describe their ideology about race. In *The Audacity of Hope* President Obama noted, "As the child of a black man and a white woman . . . I've never had the option of restricting my loyalties on the basis of race, or measuring my worth on the basis of tribe."[14] Justice Thomas said, "Having had to accept my blackness in a cauldron as a youth . . . I had few racial identity problems. I knew who I was and needed no gimmicks to affirm my identity. Nor, might I add, do I need anyone telling me who I am today."[15]

Of course, some African Americans have always resisted racial orthodoxy. What is different about postblackness now is its new prestige, especially now that the most successful black man in the history of the United States is its standard bearer. When Barack Obama bumrushed the ultimate glass ceiling, he changed many African Americans' ideas about blackness, even if not the reality of their "black experience."

When W.E.B. DuBois wrote, in 1903, "one ever feels his twoness," he meant as an American and a Negro.[16] Postblacks have a similar issue, but they have worked out the American thing; the tension they experience is as an African American and what Oprah Winfrey might call their "authentic selves."

Clarence Thomas claims, "I don't fit in with whites and I don't fit in with blacks."[17] Obama checks the box for "black" or "African American" (except, as I will discuss later, perhaps not on his application to Harvard Law School), but his self-image seems to be more complicated. He has described himself as a "man of mixed race without firm anchor in any particular community." [18]

There are two important differences between Obama's and Thomas's performances of blackness. Obama's is more ostentatious and includes his familiarity with and enjoyment of African American cultural tropes like basketball, the black church, and hip-hop music.

Justice Thomas does not perform the same kinds of cultural demonstrations, at least not in public. He reportedly used to play basketball with his law clerks, but, unlike Obama, there are no photographs of the justice's game. The cultural critic Touré asked a number of prominent black people if they would eat watermelon in a room full of white people; many said no because they did not want to support a stereotype. Maybe that is the explanation of why there is no photograph of the justice shooting hoops. More likely, Thomas believes that he has nothing, with regard to race, to prove.

He has, however, made it clear that he cares about what other black people think of him. He told the National Bar Association, the nation's largest association of African American lawyers, that "it pains me deeply, more deeply than any of you can imagine, to be perceived by so many members of my race as doing them harm." [19]

The other difference is their comfort level with talking about race. Justice Thomas does it all the time; the president, since going into politics, does so rarely and reluctantly. When Obama did it most famously, in his race speech, he started by noting that he had not focused on race in his campaign, but it had still "bubbled to the surface." [20] Obama's clearest statement about why he does not talk much about race occurred in a *New York Times* interview in which he gently scolded his attorney general for stating that the United States is a "nation of cowards." In response, Obama said, "I'm not somebody who believes that constantly talking about race somehow solves racial tensions." [21]

As several legal scholars have pointed out, Justice Thomas, in his Supreme Court opinions, has talked about race quite a bit.[22] He has been described as a black nationalist by both Professor Angela Onwuachi-Willig and Professor Stephen Smith (his former law clerk).[23] Famous for not asking questions on the Court (as of the beginning of the 2012–13 term, he had not asked a question in six years), his best-known participation in an oral argument was in *Virginia v. Black*, a first amendment case.[24] He told the lawyers that "a burning cross is unlike any other symbol in our society" and that "there's no purpose to the cross, no communication, no particular message. It was intended to cause fear and to terrorize a population."[25] The *New York Times* noted that "during the brief minute or two that Justice Thomas spoke . . . the other justices gave him rapt attention."[26] At a conference in which the justices were discussing how to vote in a school desegregation case, Thomas said, "I am the only one at this table who attended a segregated school. And the problem with segregation was not that we didn't have white people in our class."[27]

Even more revealing is how Justice Thomas brings up race in cases in which it is not apparently an issue, including in gun control and campaign financing cases. He was part of the majority in *Citizens United v. Federal Election Commission*, which held that corporations had free-speech rights.[28] He recently explained to students that his decision was based on his reading of the 1907 Tillman Act. He said, "Go back and read why Tillman introduced that legislation. Tillman was from South Carolina, and as I hear the story he was concerned that the corporations, Republican corporations, were favorable towards blacks and he felt that there was no need to regulate them."[29] In *McDonald v. Chicago*, in which he wrote an opinion expanding the rights of gun owners, he said, "The use of firearms for self-defense was often the only way black citizens could protect themselves from mob violence."[30]

RACE SAYING AND RACE DOING

I want to highlight three areas in which there is surprising similarity between the racial ideology of the president and the justice. First, they both discount the significance of discrimination. Second, they are skeptical of race-based remedies. Third, they employ cultural critiques of African Americans.

Discounting the Significance of Race Discrimination

My aunt Rosalee, whenever anyone asked her about her arthritis, would reply, "Arthur who?" This kind of willful blindness is the way both Obama and Thomas approach discrimination against African Americans. They don't deny that it exists, but they also do not pay much attention to it.[31]

In the president's case, the reason seems to be that he does not think focusing on race is useful. In his view, such a focus can sometimes cause people to wrongly attribute racial motives, as in the inadequacy of the government's response to Hurricane Katrina. In *The Audacity of Hope*, he wrote that the government's "incompetence was color-blind."[32] Obama responded to criticism from the Congressional Black Caucus by stating, "I think it is a mistake to start thinking in terms of particular ethnic segments of the United States rather than to think that we are all in this together and that we are all going to get out of this together."[33]

Justice Thomas has a more defeatist view; he simply does not trust white people. He has stated that "there is nothing you can do to get past black skin."[34] He commented about "young brothers dying in the street" from inner-city violence and said that "if dogs were being struck down at the same rate and in the same way, there would be a society of blue-haired women to save our canine friends. But these are young black men bleeding in the gutter, and no one seems to give a damn."[35] His views, then, are akin to what the critical race scholar Derrick Bell has described as "racial realism."[36]

Both Thomas and Obama are quick to respond to descriptions of discrimination against blacks by pointing out that other groups have also experienced hardships. On *60 Minutes*, Justice Thomas said, "Do I help, love helping black people? Absolutely. And I do. But do I like helping all people? Yes. In particular I like helping people who are disadvantaged, people who don't come from the best circumstances. Do white people live in homeless shelters? Do Hispanics live in homeless shelters? Is disadvantaged the exclusive province of blacks? No." [37]

Likewise, in his famous race speech, Obama said, "Blacks should bind their particular grievances . . . to the larger aspirations of all Americans—the white woman struggling to break the glass ceiling, the white man who has been laid off, the immigrant trying to feed his family." [38] The president even discounted the significance of racism with regard to his own candidacy. He told the *Los Angeles Times*, "Race is still a powerful force in this country. Any African American candidate, or any Latino candidate, or Asian candidate or woman candidate confronts a higher threshold in establishing himself to the voters. . . . Are some voters not going to vote for me because I'm African American? Those are the same voters who probably wouldn't vote for me because of my politics." [39]

Skepticism of Race-Based Remedies

Both the justice and the president are dubious about the efficacy of race-based remedies. Thomas's critique of affirmative action is well known. He thinks that the Constitution requires that the government be "color-blind." In *Adarand Constructors v. Peña*, for example, he wrote, "There is a 'moral [and] constitutional equivalence' between laws designed to subjugate a race and those that distribute benefits on the basis of race in order to foster some current notion of equality." [40] In a concurring opinion in *Parents Involved in Community Schools v. Seattle School District No. 1*, Thomas stated, "If our history has taught us anything, it has taught us to beware of elites bearing racial theories." [41]

Thomas's distaste for affirmative action is personal as well as jurisprudential. In his autobiography, he wrote that his law degree from Yale was worth "[fifteen cents] when it bore the taint of racial preference." Because of affirmative action, he complained, "Yale meant one thing for white graduates and another for blacks, no matter how much anyone denied it."[42]

Obama's reticence about race-based remedies has not received nearly as much attention. It is more muted and ambiguous than Thomas's. In response to Attorney General Eric Holder's observation that Americans are cowardly when it comes to talking about race, Obama said, "I think what solves racial tensions is fixing the economy, putting people to work, making sure that people have health care, ensuring that every kid is learning out there."[43] During his first presidential campaign he condemned anti–affirmative action ballot measures. He has said that he "undoubtedly" benefited from affirmative action.[44] But in *The Audacity of Hope*, he wrote that the best ways to help black workers "may have little to do with race."[45] He also noted, "An emphasis on universal, as opposed to race-specific programs isn't just good policy: it's also good politics."[46]

Like Thomas, Obama's response to affirmative action has been personal. Reportedly, he didn't list his race on his law school application.[47] He has said that his children should not be eligible for affirmative action.[48] His preference is for a program "where some of our children who are advantaged aren't getting more favorable treatment than a poor white kid who has struggled more."[49]

In his speech about race, Obama supported affirmative action but said the country should "move beyond our old racial wounds. Most working and middle class white Americans don't feel like they have been particularly privileged by their race. . . . As far as they're concerned, no one handed them anything. . . . [Resentment builds] when they hear that an African American is getting an advantage in landing a good job or a spot in a good college because of an injustice they never committed." This feeling is not "misguided or even racist" but "grounded in legitimate concerns."[50]

Cultural Critiques of Blacks

My mother retired after twenty-five years of teaching public school in Chicago and moved, with my stepfather, to Las Vegas. There she sometimes works as a substitute teacher to earn some extra cash. She is an excellent teacher, sought after even, and she can pretty much choose which schools she wants to work at. Principals call early each morning, and she sits listening to their pleas on her answering machine—she still has an answering machine!—and casting judgment. The poor black schools—and in Las Vegas, as in most cities, all the black schools are poor—she will only do around Martin Luther King Day, as her community service. You can just imagine how the kids at some poor black schools treat substitute teachers. If you can't, you don't want to know.

Many of my friends are middle-class African Americans who have made the same kinds of choices that my mother has made about poor black people. Basically, they don't want to be around them, except for charitable purposes. They don't want to live with them, for sure, and they don't want their impressionable young children to go to school with them either. They love them, but from a safe distance, and readily acknowledge that "them" includes some of their close relatives; but still, "them" does not include them. And they have lots of ideas, suggestions really, about why this is. They talk about it all the time.

So do President Obama and Justice Thomas. OK, maybe not all the time in President Obama's case, because it's race, which he does not like to talk about, but does sometimes, as a duty of office. Here is what they say.

Thomas's critiques of black people are actually more populist than the president's. The justice's critiques are focused on black elites. He complained about black leaders watching the "destruction of our race" as they "bitch, bitch, bitch" about President Reagan rather than working with the administration.[51]

Obama has also complained about black elites. He told the Congressional Black Caucus, "I expect all of you to march with me and press on. Take off your bedroom slippers, put on your marching shoes. Shake it off. Stop complaining, stop grumbling, stop crying. We are going to press on." [52]

But Obama's cultural critiques have actually been targeted toward low-income African Americans. Speaking to the NAACP, he said, "We need a new mind set, a new set of attitudes—because one of the most durable and destructive legacies of discrimination is the way we've internalized a sense of limitation; how so many in our community have come to expect so little from the world and from themselves. We've got to say to our children, yes, if you're African American, the odds of growing up amid crime and gangs are higher. Yes, if you live in a poor neighborhood, you will face challenges that somebody in a wealthy suburb does not have to face. But that's not a reason to get bad grades . . . that's not a reason to cut class—that's not a reason to give up on your education and drop out of school. . . . That's what we have to teach all of our children. No excuses. No excuses." [53]

In the same speech, Obama also told black parents, "You can't just contract out parenting. For our kids to excel, we have to accept our responsibility to help them learn. That means putting away the Xbox—putting our kids to bed at a reasonable hour. It means attending those parent-teacher conferences and reading to our children and helping them with their homework." [54]

In a speech at an African American church, President Obama said, "Too many fathers . . . have abandoned their responsibilities, acting like boys instead of men. . . . You and I know how true this is in the African-American community." [55]

During his first campaign Obama joked about the work ethic of "gang bangers," mocking them as saying, "Why I gotta do it? Why you didn't ask Pookie to do it?" [56]

BACK TO BLACK:
POSTBLACK BLACK OPPORTUNISM

Both Obama and Thomas have used blackness instrumentally. They strategically deploy it when it will help them achieve some objective.

Thomas's most demonstrative invocation of racial victimization is famous. It occurred during his confirmation hearings for the Supreme Court. In response to accusations of sexual harassment by Anita Hill, who it bears noting is African American, Thomas said, "From my standpoint, as a black American, it is a high-tech lynching for uppity blacks who in any way deign to think for themselves, to do for themselves, to have different ideas, and it is a message that unless you kowtow to an old order, this is what will happen to you. You will be lynched, destroyed, caricatured by a committee of the U.S. Senate rather than hung from a tree." [57]

In a sense, it is unsurprising to know that the president uses aspects of his identity in a strategic way. That's what politicians do. It is interesting, though, that Obama's usual avoidance of explicitly engaging race sometimes defers to other considerations. This makes the performative aspect of postblackness more evident: being postblack until being black is useful. Then coming, as it were, home.

For example, in the run-up to the 2012 presidential election, concerns were expressed about voter turnout in the African American community, based on the perception that there was less enthusiasm for Obama among blacks during his second campaign compared to the first. In response the White House convened the "African American Policy Agenda Conference" and released a forty-five page report called "The President's Agenda and the African American Community." [58] As the Associated Press put it, "Until now the nation's first black president has carefully avoided putting any emphasis on race." [59] Now, however, in "a shift in White House tactics on the cusp of an election year," Obama "isn't shying away from saying that many of his policies were designed with African-Americans in mind." [60]

THE UNBEARABLE LIGHTNESS
OF POSTBLACKNESS

The two biggest obstacles to postblackness are criminal justice and wealth. Those are the areas with the largest racial disparities. It will be impossible to remedy those inequalities without employing race.

The median wealth of white families is twenty times that of black families.[61] The average black family has $5,677 in wealth, compared with $113,149 for the average white family.[62] This disparity is the highest it has ever been. It is twice as high now as when the government first began compiling these statistics twenty-five years ago.[63]

African Americans are incarcerated at almost six times the rate of white people.[64] One in fifteen black children has a parent in prison, compared with one in 111 white children.[65] For every 100,000 white males, 773 are incarcerated. The comparable number for black males is 4,618.[66]

Justice Thomas began his opinion in *Grutter v. Bollinger*, the infamous affirmative action case, with a quote from an address by Frederick Douglass to abolitionists: "The American people have always been anxious to know what they should do with us. . . . Do nothing with us! If the apples will not remain on the tree on their own strength, if they are worm eaten at the core, if they are early ripe and disposed to fall, let them fall! And if the Negro cannot stand on his own two legs, let him fall also. All I ask is give him a chance to stand on his own two legs. Let him alone! Your interference is doing him positive injury."[67]

President Obama's indifference is gentler than Justice Thomas's, but benign indifference is still indifference. Does the fact that Obama's seems strategic, while Thomas's seems moral, make Obama's worse or better? Obama has not articulated a theory of racial difference, but rather a practice, one premised on his belief that black-focused interventions would doom him politically. As Harvard professor Randall Kennedy has noted, Obama "has consistently attempted to evade racial issues. If he cannot avoid them, he reframes them, minimizing the racial element. If forced to confront a racial issue squarely, he does so in a fashion calculated to assuage the anxieties of whites. This is the Obama way."[68]

President Obama's strategy of helping blacks is often described as "a rising tide lifts all boats." The president's articulation has occurred in statements like this: "Because African Americans and Latinos are often the last hired, it also means that they are the first fired . . . that's why getting the economy moving for everybody is so important because they're disproportionately impacted going up and going down. . . . I do think we've got to focus on economic development in our urban areas. That's not a race-based program, that's a recognition that cities and suburbs, we're all in this together. And we just can't deal with one without dealing with the other."[69]

One instance of the president's own invocation of the phrase "rising tide lifts all boats" demonstrates the inadequacy of the paradigm, especially for delivering racial justice. At a town meeting in Iowa, a man complained about not being able to vote because he had a felony conviction, and that it was difficult to advance beyond low-paying jobs because of his record. Obama responded by saying that he was going to be monitoring voting rights across the country, and that "this is a situation where a rising tide does lift all boats. If the economy is going strong and the unemployment rate is going down generally then that is going to help you as well. All right?"[70]

Well, actually, Mr. President, no. There is nothing about improving the economy per se that would make it easier for the man at the town meeting. The best way—indeed the only way—to end the disabling effect of prior convictions on employment is to eradicate felony disenfranchisement laws. Likewise, as Justice Harry Blackmun noted in an opinion supporting affirmative action programs, "In order to get beyond racism, we must first take account of race. There is no other way."[71] The rising tide lifts all boats strategy only works if you have a boat. And many blacks don't have a boat.

POSTSCRIPT:
THE WAY WE DO POSTBLACKNESS NOW

One of the most sympathetic audiences you could ever imagine Barack Obama having, even though he wasn't there, occurred in the fall of 2011. There was a reunion, a "celebration," the school called it, of the black alumni of Harvard Law School. During the reunion, there was a private gathering in support of Barack Obama. I was one of fourteen co-hosts, and that number did not include the six sponsors. When I arrived at the Cambridge bar where the event was held, I couldn't get in; it was literally overflowing, as though every black person who had ever attended Harvard Law School, except the president and First Lady, were there. I stood outside and listened.

Wonderful stories were told about the president, the audience was advised of ways that they could become involved with his re-election campaign, and then, at the end, Hill Harper, the television actor and author who is also an alumnus, spoke and whipped the crowd into as much of a frenzy as the living black alumni of Harvard Law School are likely to be whipped into.

Harper started with a story about meeting the president when they were both students and the only two people, early one morning, on the law school's basketball court. Point taken. And he ended with a story of attending the president's fiftieth birthday party, and watching him do the "Dougie" on the east lawn of the White House. Everybody smiled, at least everybody who knew what the Dougie is.

The Dougie is a dance that involves a coordinated head, neck, and shoulder movement. It became popular in the summer of 2010 because it looks great and is easy for people to do—by that, I mean easy for black people to do, except this one. I cannot do it, although I wish I could. A few months before the Harvard reunion a friend and I were walking on Ocean Drive in Miami Beach when a car drove down the street blaring the song "Teach Me How to Dougie" by the rap group Cali Swag District. This is the song that inspired the dance, and these two black women who had been sitting at a sidewalk café jumped up and started doing the Dougie, and my friend turned to me, smiled, and said, "Why does every black person have to dance when they hear that song?"

And now Hill Harper was letting us know that even the president of the United States knows how to do the Dougie. It wasn't as moving as the images, two years earlier, of Michelle Obama jumping double-dutch on the same lawn, because that carried the weight of nostalgia, but it was more thrilling because it seemed almost subversive—the black president of the United States doing the same dance as those random two black women in Miami, a connection that they have, that we all have, that he does not have with House Speaker John Boehner or even Vice President Joe Biden or Minority Leader Nancy Pelosi.

During his remarks, Hill Harper did not mention that, a few months before, M-Bone, who was one of the members of Cali Swag District, had been killed in a drive-by shooting in Inglewood, California, or that the Fox News Network had described the president's fiftieth birthday party as a "hip-hop barbeque."[72] It was not relevant to the occasion.

5

THE RACIAL METAMORPHOSIS OF JUSTICE KENNEDY AND THE FUTURE OF CIVIL RIGHTS LAW

Luis Fuentes-Rohwer

It's Justice Anthony Kennedy's country—the rest of us just live in it.[1]
—Noah Feldman

By the time the first African American president won re-election, it was clear that the future of our revered civil rights statutes was in jeopardy. A conservative majority on the Supreme Court seemed poised to strike down some of our most cherished laws. The warning signs were many. In his concurring opinion in *Ricci v. DeStefano*,[2] for example, Justice Antonin Scalia warned that the Court's resolution in *Ricci* "merely postpones the evil day on which the Court will have to confront the question: Whether, or to what extent, are the disparate-impact provisions of Title VII of the Civil Rights Act of 1964 consistent with the Constitution's guarantee of equal protection?"[3] A few years before, in *Georgia v. Ashcroft*,[4] Justice Anthony Kennedy similarly warned that "considerations of race that would doom a redistricting plan under the Fourteenth Amendment or § 2 [of the Voting Rights Act] seem to be what save it under § 5 [of the act]."[5] This was another way of saying that the Second Reconstruction was under reconsideration, and that the end may be near.[6]

The road to this unhappy moment was largely paved by Justice Kennedy. Such is the lot of the swing justice. At first glance, this seemed like bad news for civil rights litigants; the book on Justice

Kennedy is that he is hardly a friend of the civil rights community. His biography suggests as much, and his early voting on the Court easily substantiates the charge. As late as 2003, for example, he filed a caustic dissent in the Michigan University admissions cases, where he criticized the Court's decision to uphold one of the affirmative action programs under review.[7]

More recent evidence, however, seemed to muddy the waters. I have two particular cases in mind. The first was *LULAC v. Perry*,[8] where Justice Kennedy joined his moderate colleagues and struck down a congressional district in Texas that diluted the voting rights of Latino voters under federal law. The second was the school assignment case of *Parents Involved v. Seattle School District No. 1*,[9] where Justice Kennedy wrote an intriguing concurrence and staked out a position unlike anything he had written before. To be sure, this is not to suggest in any way that Justice Kennedy had become a member of the Court's left-of-center wing. The more recent *Bartlett v. Strickland*[10] and *Ricci v. DeStefano*[11] decisions readily tempered any suggestion that Justice Kennedy had become a reliably liberal vote. Analysis of the 2010 term was also strongly suggestive of Justice Kennedy's conservative bona fides, as evinced by his joining the Court's conservative bloc in fourteen 5–4 cases, an outcome that was not likely to happen by chance.[12] Rather, this is to suggest that Justice Kennedy appeared to be undergoing a racial metamorphosis of sorts.[13] Something seemed amiss.

This essay examines Justice Kennedy's recent race jurisprudence. It argues that the conventional wisdom is only partly right. Justice Kennedy is clearly the median justice on the Roberts Court—despite Chief Justice Roberts's controlling vote in the Affordable Care Act decision. But it is far more accurate to understand his position on the Court as that of a "super median."[14] This is because Justice Kennedy is both "crucial to the formation of majority coalitions"[15] within the Court as well as influential within these coalitions. For issues of great salience and where the Court splits along ideological lines, Justice Kennedy often holds the fifth vote for his preferred view. This is key and what distinguishes Justice Kennedy from median justices in general. A median justice must often compromise and find common ground with other justices. Median status only goes so far, especially when the justices are closely aligned ideologically. After all, to be a median justice is only to be the middle justice on the Court, the one member who occupies the fifth chair along the Court's ideological continuum. Justice Souter was once a median justice, for example, as were Justices Blackmun and Marshall,[16] and nobody would equate these justices with figures of much power and influence on the Court. But a super median can play a far more powerful role. A super median can let her true preferences and aspirations run free. In the case of Justice Kennedy, this is where we saw his idealism reflected in new and intriguing ways. This is what we saw in *LULAC* and *Parents Involved*.

This chapter is divided into three parts. The first part offers a brief jurisprudential sketch of Justice Kennedy. It explains how Justice Kennedy underwent a metamorphosis on questions of race. The second part argues that this metamorphosis can be explained in terms of Justice Kennedy's status on the Court as a super median. The third part examines the continued vitality of the Second Reconstruction as reflected in the constitutionality of Title VII and the Voting Rights Act (VRA). To be sure, these statutes raise very difficult constitutional questions. This chapter concludes that Justice Kennedy's evolution on questions of race reflects our society's general cultural ambivalence about these questions.

A BRIEF JURISPRUDENTIAL SKETCH

Since it was Justice Kennedy's actions that caused the Court to question the Second Reconstruction, it is imperative to pay close attention to his jurisprudence on race and equal protection, as it reveals how he has undergone a metamorphosis. The early cases—exemplified by his concurrence in the minority set-aside case of *City of Richmond v. Croson*[17] and his dissent in the *Metro Broadcasting v. FCC*, a racial inclusion case[18]—reflect a narrow and uncompromising color-blind stance on the use of race by the state. Upon Justice O'Connor's retirement from the Court, however, Justice Kennedy's approach changed.

Kennedy's Early Race Jurisprudence: DeGrandy's Proportionality

The uncompromising and formalistic nature of Justice Kennedy's early race jurisprudence is unmistakable. In *Croson*, for example, he wrote of the "imperative of race neutrality"[19] as the proper understanding of the equal protection clause. And in his dissent in *Metro Broadcasting*, he analogized the statute in question to Nazi laws and South Africa's apartheid laws, while comparing the Court's posture to that of *Plessy v. Ferguson* and *Korematsu v. United States*, the Japanese internment cases.[20] Many opinions could be added to this list, both in the constitutional[21] and statutory interpretation realms.[22] His concurring opinion in *Johnson v. DeGrandy*[23] discusses both realms.

In *DeGrandy*, the Court examined a redistricting plan from the state of Florida that sought to accommodate claims from various racial groups to political representation. As framed by the Court, the question in *DeGrandy* was whether a state must maximize the political representation of minority groups under section 2 of the Voting Rights Act or else face a challenge that it was diluting the political power of these groups. In a rather uneventful opinion, Justice Souter concluded for the Court that a state does not violate section 2 of the VRA when it fails to maximize the number of majority-minority districts. Justice Kennedy agreed with this conclusion on statutory grounds. But he also took time to highlight what he took to be "a more difficult question . . . whether proportionality, ascertained by comparing the number of majority-minority districts to the minority group's proportion of the relevant population, is relevant in deciding whether there has been vote dilution under section 2 in a challenge to election district lines."[24] Tellingly, he conceded that "the statutory text does not yield a clear answer."[25]

By looking to the Court's precedent, Justice Kennedy concluded that proportionality is a relevant consideration in section 2 inquiries. This is an uneventful conclusion. Far more important was his discussion of the statutory text, which reads as follows: "The extent to which members of a protected class have been elected to office in the State or political subdivision is one circumstance which may be considered [in determining whether there has been vote dilution]: Provided, that nothing in this section establishes a right to have members of a protected class elected in numbers equal to their proportion in the population."[26] Justice Kennedy paid close attention to this language, and its focus on the number of minorities elected to office, not on the number of seats where minorities constitute a majority of the population. These two propositions are not the same, according to Kennedy, and "it would be an affront to our constitutional traditions to treat them as such."[27] Curiously, his first argument on this point was an empirical one; it is simply not true that majority-minority districts elect only minority candidates or that majority-white districts elect only white candidates.[28] His second argument reflects his antiessentialist views. Citing his own language in *Metro Broadcasting*, he wrote that "on a more fundamental level, the assumption reflects 'the demeaning notion that members of the defined racial groups ascribe to certain "minority views" that must be different from those of other citizens.'"[29] The state must treat individuals as individuals and not as members of groups, racial or otherwise. To so stereotype anyone is demeaning and unconstitutional.

This portion of Justice Kennedy's *DeGrandy* concurrence reads as a gentle reminder of things we should already know. Justice Kennedy is not trying to persuade, much less argue, for his position. Instead, this is a statement of fact and not much else. This is why so much is missing from the discussion. Missing, for example, is any mention of the contextual background on section 2 and the concerns that gave rise to its implementation in 1965 and its amendment in 1982. Also missing is a discussion of the history behind the Voting Rights Act, or even of the history of voting rights in South Florida, where the case arose. Instead, the text of the law and the Court's own precedents do all the heavy lifting. Everything else is unnecessary.

This should have been the end of the matter. Before signing off, however, Justice Kennedy offered a warning to states, federal judges, and the U.S. Department of Justice that while proportionality plays a role, it must not be taken too far. To do so would raise serious constitutional questions. The discussion that followed was an ode to the antiessentialist principle that stood, for conservative justices, at the heart of the Equal Protection Clause. By way of an example, Justice Kennedy explained that a district court that orders as a remedy for a section 2 violation the creation of districts where minorities form a majority of the population would "tend to entrench the very practices and stereotypes the Equal Protection Clause is set against."[30] Justice Kennedy also placed much emphasis on *Shaw v. Reno*, the congressional redistricting case decided the prior term, where the Court asserted that "racial gerrymandering, even for remedial purposes, may balkanize us into competing racial factions; it threatens to carry us further from the goal of a political system in which race no longer matters—a goal that the Fourteenth and Fifteenth Amendments embody, and to which the Nation continues to aspire."[31]

At the heart of his constitutional vision was "the moral imperative of racial neutrality," which he described as "the driving force of the Equal Protection Clause."[32] His particular target was racial classifications, that is, the use of race by the state irrespective of context or history. His derision for racial classifications was palpable. He found support for this conclusion from familiar quarters, from *Croson* and *Shaw v. Reno* to *Power v. Ohio* and Alexander Bickel's *Morality of Consent*. These are canonical texts in the conservative assault on race-conscious measures. Justice Kennedy was thus in good company. He clinched his argument by turning to Justice Harlan's oft-cited dissent in *Plessy*. But his use of *Plessy* was quite telling, for he offered it at the end of a paragraph, as a "see also" cite unaccompanied by any text from the dissent. The case spoke for itself.

Justice Kennedy's *DeGrandy* opinion exemplifies his approach to questions of race. His interpretation of the language of the VRA was narrow and hard, formalistic in nature and unwilling to consider the very issues that gave the statute life. Even when he showed a willingness to consider empirical evidence, he sorted through the evidence selectively. His constitutional vision was similarly rigid and grounded on a principle of race neutrality. This is a vision where race may play a role only as a last resort, and where history and context play nary a role in the analysis.

Shifting Sands? *LULAC's* Essentialism

In more recent years, however, it seemed that Justice Kennedy's views on race had "softened."[33] The obvious example was his concurring opinion in *Parents Involved v. Seattle School District No. 1*,[34] the case where the Court struck down voluntary racial integration plans for the public schools in Louisville and Seattle. In a surprising concurring opinion, Justice Kennedy refused to take the hard line on race espoused by Chief Justice Roberts's plurality opinion. The following passage illustrates Justice Kennedy's newfound approach:

> This is by way of preface to my respectful submission that parts of the opinion by The Chief Justice imply an all-too-unyielding insistence that race cannot be a factor in instances when, in my view, it may be taken into account. The plurality opinion is too dismissive of the legitimate interest government has in ensuring all people have equal opportunity regardless of their race. The plurality's postulate that "[t]he way to stop discrimination on the basis of race is to stop discriminating on the basis of race" is not sufficient to decide these cases. Fifty years of experience since Brown v. Board of Education, 347 U. S. 483 (1954), should teach us that the problem before us defies so easy a solution. School districts can seek to reach Brown's objective of equal educational opportunity. The plurality opinion is at least open to the interpretation that the Constitution requires school districts to

ignore the problem of de facto resegregation in schooling. I cannot endorse that conclusion. To the extent the plurality opinion suggests the Constitution mandates that state and local school authorities must accept the status quo of racial isolation in schools, it is, in my view, profoundly mistaken.[35]

This is a surprising turn because it is in direct tension with Justice Kennedy's earlier positions on race. In case any doubt remains about the radical shift in Justice Kennedy's posture, his concurrence even questions Justice Harlan's color-blind aspiration in *Plessy*. Recall that a decade before, this canonical dissent warranted no more than a cursory citation devoid of any language or explanation. Yet in *Parents Involved*, Justice Kennedy explained that "in the real world, it is regrettable to say, it cannot be a universal constitutional principle."[36] The contrast with his use of Harlan's dissent in *DeGrandy* could not be any more jarring.

It is important to note that his concurrence in *Parents Involved* does not mark the beginning of Justice Kennedy's jurisprudential shift on race. The shift began a year earlier, in *LULAC v. Perry*,[37] the infamous middecade Texas gerrymander. In an opinion authored by Justice Kennedy, the Court struck down one of the challenged districts under section 2 of the VRA. This was district 23, a majority-Latino district formerly represented by Congressman Henry Bonilla. This was the first time that the Court struck down a district under section 2. For Justice Kennedy to author such an opinion is remarkable for at least two reasons. First, it is no secret that Justice Kennedy has long been skeptical about the constitutionality of the Voting Rights Act.[38] Yet, in *LULAC*, not only does he overcome his skepticism but he joins the moderate justices in striking down a congressional district under this same law. Indeed, no hurdle proved too difficult for him: not the lower court's findings and the clear error test[39]; not the actual words of the lower court's opinion[40]; and certainly not the constitutional concerns that occupied him in the past. The right of Latinos in district 23 to their district must be vindicated, and Justice Kennedy joined the moderates and happily put himself up to the task.

Second, in *LULAC* Justice Kennedy must confront his own antiessentialist critique of antidiscrimination law. This is the concept that individuals must be treated as individuals and not as members of groups. This is a position he developed in *Miller v. Johnson*,[41] where he wrote that "it takes a shortsighted and unauthorized view of the Voting Rights Act to invoke that statute, which has played a decisive role in redressing some of our worst forms of discrimination, to demand the very racial stereotyping the Fourteenth Amendment forbids."[42]

Yet in *LULAC*, Justice Kennedy worried that "the State took away the Latinos' opportunity because Latinos were about to exercise it." That is to say, Latinos, not Democratic voters, were about to achieve real political power, and only then would the state step in and ensure their minority status. In Justice Kennedy's words,

> Even if we accept the District Court's finding that the State's action was taken primarily for political, not racial, reasons, the redrawing of the district lines was damaging to the Latinos in District 23. The State not only made fruitless the Latinos' mobilization efforts but also acted against those Latinos who were becoming most politically active, dividing them with a district line through the middle of Laredo.[43]

This is a remarkable statement coming from a justice who explicitly derides the essentialization of voters of color in the name of a particular brand of racial justice. This is the same justice, after all, who wrote a decade earlier: "When the State assigns voters on the basis of race, it engages in the offensive and demeaning assumption that voters of a particular race, because of their race, 'think alike, share the same political interests, and will prefer the same candidates at the polls.'"[44] In the *Shaw* cases, to treat Democratic voters as black voters was to engage in demeaning stereotyping. In *LULAC*, to treat Latinos as Democratic voters was a cognizable harm under section 2. Reconciling the tension between the old Justice Kennedy and the new is difficult if not downright impossible.

Thus the question: what explains this apparent shift?

JUSTICE KENNEDY AS SUPER MEDIAN: OF DOMAINS, CONTEXT, AND CULTURAL WORLDVIEWS

Justice Kennedy's metamorphosis on race questions is best explained as a reflection of his status on the Court as a super median. According to Professors Lee Epstein and Tonja Jacobi, super medians are those swing justices who "(1) are crucial to the formation of majority coalitions and, thus, to the outcome of any given decision and (2) are influential in dictating the terms of the Court's opinion and, thus, to the formulation of any precedent it establishes, especially in consequential or otherwise high-profile decisions."[45] Both of these conditions make sense. In order for a swing justice to become a super median, she must be both a consistent member of the majority coalition and also an influential figure within that coalition. More to the point, the attainment of super-median status means that her colleagues on the bench must pay close attention to her preferences on any high-profile case. This is the quintessential role of a super median. But far more important than the influence that super medians derive from their positioning within the Court is the independence that attends to their super-median status. Such status allows them to enshrine their particular constitutional visions into law.

The example of Justice Kennedy is instructive. In the mid-1990s, he was considered both a reliable conservative vote on the Court as well as a justice whose ideology placed him—along with Justice O'Connor—somewhere in the middle of the Court's ideological spectrum. When he wrote his majority opinion in *Miller v. Johnson*,[46] another case where the Court struck down a majority-black voting district, he was not writing from a position of strength and independence: this was a 5–4 decision, and his opinion for the Court must preserve Justice O'Connor's vote as part of the majority. Notably, Justice O'Connor ultimately defected to the moderate side in the racial redistricting case of *Easley v. Cromartie*,[47] decided in 2001. The Justice Kennedy we see in 2006 is in a much stronger position. He is firmly in the Court's ideological center. Either faction, whether to his ideological right or left, has only four votes and needs Justice Kennedy's vote. As a result, Justice Kennedy is able to dictate the terms of vote and is free to assert his own views. This is what we see in *LULAC* and *Parents Involved*.

In order to appreciate how we arrived at a point where the Second Reconstruction was in danger, it is important to understand what lies at the heart of Justice Kennedy's shifting views. One piece of this puzzle is the concept of super medians. It is from this position of real independence that Justice Kennedy begins his jurisprudential shift. As for his views themselves, and their changing nature, we can understand them one of three ways. One understanding is proffered by Professor Pamela Karlan, who explains that Justice Kennedy's concurrence in *Parents Involved* reflects his particular cultural worldview as contradistinct from the cultural worldview of the justices in the majority.[48] As she writes, Justice Kennedy "saw racial separation as a persistent, and persistently constitutionally troubling, aspect of American society, while the majority saw the same facts on the ground as something beyond the reach of government."[49] There is, more importantly, a "gulf in language and sense of the world."[50]

Professor Heather Gerken offers a second understanding. This is the concept of constitutional domains. According to Professor Gerken, the way to explain Justice Kennedy's shift is to look to the domains where these cases arise. In *LULAC*, the domain is the First Amendment, political association, and political identity. In *Parents Involved*, the domain is public schools as sites where children learn to be good democratic citizens. Once he changes his filter, Justice Kennedy can then talk about race in far more interesting and helpful ways than when he focuses on race alone. Professor Gerken similarly explains Justice Kennedy's apparent embrace of the diversity rationale in *Parents Involved* not as a shift in his views but, rather, as "a more fine-grained approach to the educational domain than either O'Connor or Scalia offered in that case." This is also true of his switch from the *Shaw* cases to *LULAC*.

Professor Reva Siegel presents a third understanding, which she terms the "antibalkanization perspective."[51] This is a perspective grounded both in constitutional history and derived from the opinions of swing justices who have refused to ascribe to either of the conventional perspectives. In Siegel's words, an antibalkanization perspective "promote[s] social cohesion and . . . avoid[s] racial arrangements that balkanize and threaten social cohesion."[52] She finds support for this perspective in Justice Powell's controlling opinion in *Regents of the University of California v. Bakke* and Justice O'Connor's *Grutter v. Bollinger* majority. Professor Siegel situates Justice Kennedy's *Parents Involved* concurrence and *Ricci v. DeStefano* majority within this perspective. Her discussion of *Ricci*, where a group of firefighters challenged a city's decision not to use a particular employment test, is particularly illustrative.

In *Ricci*, Justice Kennedy's discussion draws a clear distinction between employer evaluations of the impact of an employment test before and after the test is administered.[53] The city of New Haven was well within its right and duties to inquire about the impact of the test on black and Latino firefighters. But what the city could not do, according to Justice Kennedy, was wait until administering the test to reach that conclusion. To be sure, this is not a conclusion devoid of criticism,[54] though I intend to neither defend nor criticize the opinion here. Instead, I am interested in how the antibalkanization perspective understands the distinction. According to Siegel "It might well reflect a context-attentive judgment about the different understanding of race produced by employer practices that attend to the racial disparate impact of employment tests before they are announced and administered—and after."[55] It is in this vein that *Ricci*, though often criticized, is in the tradition of *Parents Involved* and *Grutter*, among other notable cases.[56] Context matters, and so does one's sense of social cohesion as disrupted or fostered by the laws or regulations in question.

At their root, all three understandings lead us to the same place. This is because all three share an appreciation for the role that a super median plays in decision making. Whether it is cultural worldviews, or one's idiosyncratic sense of a particular domain or of social context, all three understandings concede what the attitudinal model[57] makes clear: personal preferences matter, and sometimes they matter a lot. This is where we found ourselves by the end of 2012. In Professor Noah Feldman's words, this is "Justice Anthony Kennedy's country—the rest of us just live in it."[58]

The question at that moment seemed to be how Justice Kennedy would understand the voting rights and employment discrimination contexts. Would he view the voting rights arena as a domain where states have dignitary interests,[59] or as a site where citizens must be accorded, yet have been long denied, equal personhood? Similarly, would Justice Kennedy understand the employment arena in pure market terms, as a place best left free to market forces, or as a domain where the state must play an important role in ensuring that structural imbalances in power do not perpetuate the inequalities that inhere in society with respect to traditionally disadvantaged groups? Relatedly, does the Voting Rights Act balkanize our society and threaten its social cohesion?

CHALLENGING THE SECOND RECONSTRUCTION

By the time Justice Kennedy emerged as the Court's super median, it was clear that the continued vitality of the Second Reconstruction was under serious threat. This had been true for many years, and written opinions by conservatives on the Court had made this threat explicit. Justice Kennedy, for example, raised questions about the constitutionality of the VRA,[60] while Justice Scalia had done the same for Title VII.[61] These are not easy constitutional questions. Two questions in particular bear close attention. The first is a question of congressional powers: could Congress declare illegal conduct that is not constitutionally prohibited as a way to enforce the Reconstruction Amendments? The second is a question about the special provisions of the Voting Rights Act: do the act's coverage formula and preclearance provision remain legitimate responses to the problem of racial discrimination in voting? The goal of this part is less to offer definitive answers to these questions than to suggest that any such answers are unavailing. Thus raising a question with which I conclude this chapter: how could we justify the role of one individual in shaping the framing and resolution of these important questions guided by his cultural worldview and idiosyncratic perspective and sense of context?

Enforcing Effects

The first question is harder than it looks. For context, consider the early history of the Voting Rights Act. In its original version, Congress intended section 2 of the act, its general prohibition of voting discrimination, as a codification of the Fifteenth Amendment, which prohibits any citizen from being denied the right to vote based on race, color, or previous condition of servitude. As a result, the constitutionality of section 2 never came under serious attack, because Congress left open the substantive question for the Court to resolve. That is, in enacting section 2 under its enforcement power, Congress was not dictating the substantive meaning of section 2, but rather, it was enforcing whatever interpretive gloss the Court would place on the Fifteenth Amendment in the future. And this is exactly what happened. In the mid-1970s, the Court decided in *Washington v. Davis* that the substantive provisions of the Fourteenth Amendment were only violated by intentional discrimination, and it extended this interpretation to the Fifteenth Amendment in *City of Mobile v. Bolden*.

Congress complicated the story two years later, when it amended section 2 to establish a test of discriminatory effect rather than of intentional discrimination. This is when the constitutional question arose in its sharpest form: could Congress enforce the substantive provisions of the Fifteenth Amendment—a provision that is interpreted by the Court as demanding an intent test—through the establishment of an effects test? In essence, this is to ask, could Congress enforce a substantive provision by changing what the provision means? The Court left this question open for many years, and in a sense, it has never answered it. But a recent case suggests an answer.

The case is *City of Boerne v. Flores*, which involved the Religious Freedom Restoration Act and Congress's power to enforce the Fourteenth Amendment.[62] In an opinion authored by Justice Kennedy, the Court explained that "Congress' power under § 5 . . . extends only to 'enforc[ing]' the provisions of the Fourteenth Amendment."[63] This is a "remedial power," and not a power to alter the substantive provisions of the amendment. This means that the power of Congress to enforce the Fourteenth Amendment is essentially a power not to define what the amendment means, but to enforce whatever substantive gloss the Court has cast over the amendment. To be sure, Kennedy recognized that the line between remedial actions and substantive changes in the law is not easily discernible, but this was not to say that the line did not exist. This is where the congruence and proportionality test came in. According to Kennedy, legislation must be congruent and proportional between the remedy that Congress seeks to address and the means chosen to address it. If the legislation is not so, then it "may become substantive in operation and effect."[64] This is something Congress may not do. In Kennedy's words,

> If Congress could define its own powers by altering the Fourteenth Amendment's meaning, no longer would the Constitution be "superior paramount law, unchangeable by ordinary means." It would be "on a level with ordinary legislative acts, and, like other acts, . . . alterable when the legislature shall please to alter it." Under this approach, it is difficult to conceive of a principle that would limit congressional

power. Shifting legislative majorities could change the Constitution and effectively circumvent the difficult and detailed amendment process contained in Article V.[65]

To grant Congress the power to enforce a substantive provision does not authorize it to alter the provision's substantive meaning. Justice Kennedy could not be much clearer than that. In the wake of *City of Boerne*, many federal "enforcement" statutes are now under threat.[66] The Voting Rights Act is one such statute, and so is Title VII of the Civil Rights Act of 1964. The constitutional argument to strike down these federal laws is not hard to discern. Consider in this vein then Justice Rehnquist's dissent in *City of Rome v. United States*, in light of the Court's conclusion in *City of Mobile v. Bolden*:

> After our decision City of Mobile there is little doubt that Rome has not engaged in constitutionally prohibited conduct. I also do not believe that prohibition of these changes can genuinely be characterized as a remedial exercise of congressional enforcement power. Thus, the result of the Court's holding is that Congress effectively has the power to determine for itself that this conduct violates the Constitution. This result violates previously well-established distinctions between the Judicial Branch and the Legislative or Executive Branches of the Federal Government.[67]

This is a powerful argument. It also tracks closely with Justice Kennedy's argument in *City of Boerne*. If the Fifteenth Amendment proscribes intentional discrimination, and there is no evidence on the record that a state actor has engaged in any such conduct, a finding that the state actor engaged in conduct that violates the Fifteenth Amendment is difficult to make. This is also Justice Scalia's point in *Ricci* and, earlier still, Justice Harlan's point in *Katzenbach v. Morgan*, an early case interpreting the Voting Rights Act.[68] The question for the future is whether Justice Kennedy will be persuaded by this argument in the voting rights domain.

The Federalism Revolution Meets Section 5 and the Coverage Formula

The constitutionality of the special provisions of the Voting Rights Act raises similarly difficult questions. The debate focuses on two particular aspects of the act. The first is the coverage formula, which determines which jurisdictions will be covered by the act's special and more stringent provisions. As enacted in 1965, the formula set two separate conditions for coverage: first, that the jurisdiction used a literacy test as a voting qualification; and second, that either the turnout rate for the 1964 presidential election or a registration rate in 1964 was below 50 percent. Subsequent Congresses extended the coverage to include data from the 1968 and 1972 elections.

The second and perhaps most controversial aspect of the Voting Rights Act, codified under section 5 of the act, is known as the preclearance provision. The controversy stems from the fact that this provision radically shifted basic legal burdens and presumptions. Under prior law, state and local laws were presumed constitutional unless and until the federal government could prove otherwise. Under the VRA, however, any voting law enacted by a covered jurisdiction was presumed to be unconstitutional until the federal government determined otherwise. Critics of the VRA object on both grounds. The coverage formula offers an easy target. At the time of enactment in 1965, critics objected that the formula was arbitrary and ultimately irrational, because it was both under- and overinclusive. The argument lingers. According to Justice Alito, "Wouldn't you agree that there [are] some oddities in this coverage formula? Isn't—is it not the case that in New York City the Bronx is covered and Brooklyn and Queens are not?"[69] The chief justice similarly queried why Congress chose not to extend coverage to Massachusetts, since the disparity in the state between Latino and non-Latino voting is larger than disparities in some covered jurisdictions.[70]

Critics also complained, then as now, that the formula violates the principle of equal sovereignty in treating the states unequally. And more recently, critics argue that the date that informs the formula is no longer reflective of the real world of voting rights at the state level. The date "is now more than 35 years old, and there is considerable evidence that it fails to account for current political conditions."[71]

The preclearance requirement has also had its share of critics. The most obvious charge is that the requirement treats covered jurisdictions as "conquered provinces."[72] More specifically, section 5 suspends all changes within covered jurisdictions, no matter how small these changes are, until they are precleared by federal authorities. This means that the VRA of necessity applies to conduct well beyond what the Fifteenth Amendment proscribes.[73] More recently, critics point to evidence that federal authorities object to very few changes—one-twentieth of 1 percent, according to Chief Justice Roberts.[74]

These arguments in hand, the stage was set for the Court to strike down the Voting Rights Act in *Namudno v. Holder*, a Texas case challenging the constitutionality of the act.[75] The conservatives on the Court finally had their majority, with Justice Kennedy casting the deciding vote. The oral argument led to no other conclusion. Instead, somebody blinked. Rather than tend to the constitutional questions on everybody's minds, the justices went out of their way to avoid the constitutional question and instead resolved the case by interpreting the VRA's statutory language in a way that made no sense at all. It is hard to know what happened, but we know this much: four justices—Stevens, Ginsburg, Breyer, and Souter—were prepared to uphold the constitutionality of the act, and four justices—Roberts, Scalia, Thomas, and Alito—were prepared to face the constitutional questions and strike down the law. From his middle seat it appears that Justice Kennedy proved unable to make up his mind. This is why the Court did the only sensible thing and avoided the constitutional question, waiting for the day when Justice Kennedy makes up his mind. This would not be the first time that Justice Kennedy has held constitutional doctrine hostage to his indecision.[76]

JUSTICE KENNEDY IN THE MIDDLE: LOOKING AHEAD

This is where we found ourselves. The Second Reconstruction hung in the balance, and Justice Kennedy held the deciding vote. This is precisely the role of a super median. One way to conclude this chapter would be to analyze where Justice Kennedy's newfound voice on race questions should have taken him. How should he understand the voting rights domain at the heart of the Voting Rights Act? How should his cultural worldview on employment discrimination questions inform his view on the constitutionality of Title VII? Or, similarly, how should the antibalkanization perspective and its focus on social cohesion help him better understand the role that the Voting Rights Act plays in American society?

But to focus on these answers would be to miss the richness and valuable implications of the role of Justice Kennedy on the Court. That is, it is a remarkable fact of American political life that one person, properly situated, can single-handedly be poised to bring down the Second Reconstruction. One way to understand this argument would be to ask whether Justice Kennedy should extend the logical import of his *City of Boerne* opinion to different facts and circumstances. But I think even this phrasing misses the real lessons of this story. Because in the end, the value of the story lies not in the fact that a justice might understand constitutional doctrine one way or another and might interpret a particular provision this way or that. This is fine as it goes, yet terribly uninteresting.

Instead, I close with two observations. First, it is useful to understand Justice Kennedy's ambivalence on the role that race may play in American society as tracking a general ambivalence in the culture at large. Public debates often exhort the virtues of racial equality, for example, and few disagree that this is a worthy goal, at least in the abstract. Yet, as Randall Kennedy writes, "less common, but badly needed, is acknowledgment that Americans share little consensus regarding what 'racial equality' entails or what landmarks or boundaries constitute that destination."[77] In fairness, this ambivalence is not new. Reconstruction-era debates over the concept of citizenship and its application to the freedmen, or the meaning of freedom as codified in our civil rights laws and Reconstruction Amendments, attest to how long the path to equality has been in question. This is a point worth remembering, especially when we grow impatient with the state of racial progress and equality today. This is not a new fight, nor an easy one. One lesson is thus that Justice Kennedy can be forgiven for reflecting these complexities in his jurisprudence. In this sense, donning judicial robes does not alter the fact that Justice Kennedy is subject to the same socializing forces that affect all of us.

Second, Justice Kennedy's role as a super median positioned him to bring down the Second Reconstruction all on his own on the basis of his idiosyncratic cultural worldviews and sense of social cohesion. This is a remarkable power. Alexander Bickel, in his classic critique of the power of courts to strike down legislation,[78] had it almost right. On Bickel's account, the challenge of constitutional theory lies in justifying this power when exercised by an unaccountable court. The story unearthed here raises a far more difficult challenge. How could we possibly justify bringing down the Second Reconstruction according to the views of a single justice? A more pressing question is one that brings to mind Derrick Bell's influential interest-convergence thesis, which argues that racial minorities will only win in court when their interests converge with the interests of whites.[79] Should persons of color accept as legitimate a decision striking down these revered civil rights laws? Maybe so. If the promise of American democracy means anything, however, such a decision demands a philosophical defense.

6

THE RIGHT KIND OF FAMILY

Silences in a Civil Rights Narrative

Jonathan Scott Holloway

How do we tell the story of the civil rights movement, which has now entered into the core narrative of American history, a generation after the events? For many of those who now write about the civil rights movement, it is a dim or nonexistent memory. The narrative of the civil rights movement is a heroic one, most often written by people who experienced it directly, or remembered it clearly. But a generation after the events, we find that it is difficult to separate memory from history. As we write the history of the movement from our own moment in history, we find that the separation between the past and the present constantly breaks down. This is the story of one example of such a collapse.

JAMES BALDWIN: *Black people need witnesses; in this hostile world which thinks, um, everything is white.*

INTERVIEWER: *Are you still in despair about the world?*

BALDWIN: *I never have been in despair about the world, I'm enraged by the world.*

INTERVIEWER: *Enraged, alright.*

BALDWIN: *I don't think I'm in despair. I can't afford despair. I can't tell my nephew, my niece; you can't, you can't tell the children there's no hope.*

—from James Baldwin, *The Price of the Ticket*

What do we tell our children? What stories do we pass along so that they know their past? For them to learn the past that belongs to the nation, that typically mythic narrative of exceptionalism and citizenship, is unavoidable. They will get this narrative in their school assemblies, through advertisements, via the media. The past that belongs to an aggrieved people—in James Baldwin's case and dare I say my own—is a different narrative. Of course, the African American past is no less exceptional than the mythic American narrative of belonging, but it is crafted in an often-cruel juxtaposition to that same notion of belonging. Stories of denial need to be passed along, to be sure, but it is important to ask when and how our children need to learn that the American narrative may not belong to them.

Baldwin's angry declaration that "you can't tell the children there's no hope" registers clearly at one end of a spectrum of citizenship denied. But for some African Americans, the notion of hopelessness and alienation is as strange to them as the American exceptionalist narrative that seemingly declares the entire nation was linked arm in arm with Martin Luther King Jr. when he marched for freedom (and jobs). I am talking here about the privileged classes of African America that for one reason or another actually did enjoy material resources unknown to most of the country, that did enjoy access to those things that embodied the American dream trumpeted in the news, in the advertisements, and on the radio and television.

But the question remains, indeed it has always remained: do you tell the children?

The question remains, of course, because race still has the potential to, at any given moment, strip away all the accumulated material and political privilege that well-placed blacks might enjoy. Our children—Baldwin's and my own—need to be prepared for a narrative in which they cannot see themselves, their past, or their future.

But when do you tell the children?

Leaving this to the schools means that we can wait for the primary and secondary school social science units that deal with the civil rights movement. Or, we can wait until February (and not coincidentally these two often line up). In either moment, determined parents have the opportunity to enhance the curriculum with stories about how their family fit into *that* narrative of American exceptionalism. Indeed, memoiristic opportunities abound at such moments; except, of course, when one's family feels it "can't afford"—to use Baldwin's construction—to tell even those stories.

What happens then? What happens when silence is the determining voice in a narrative about belonging?

Every spring I teach the introductory survey of the postemancipation black experience, African American History: Emancipation to the Present. It is a large lecture course by my university's standards, and I need a half dozen graduate students, most leading two sections, to cover the necessary number of discussion sections. In any given year I know most, but not all, of the graduate assistants assigned to my course. In this context, the start of the spring term 2010 was fairly unremarkable. My teaching fellows team was a mixture of those with whom I had already worked, those I had taught, and those who were my new acquaintances.

Shortly after our first meeting when we talked about the course expectations, what we each thought we would bring to the class and, more specifically, to each section, I received an e-mail from one of these new colleagues, Chris Johnson. Chris simply wanted to know if he had overheard correctly that I had grown up in Montgomery, Alabama. He had been raised in Lowndes County and Montgomery—both places, as it happens, that by the time we got to the mainstream civil rights history would figure prominently in the course I was about to lead. My response was fairly short but brimmed with the beginnings of many revelations:

Hi Chris,

I was just in Alabama for two years. My father was in the Air Force and taught at the Air War College in Montgomery— Maxwell-Gunther AFB. We lived on Lott Drive (wherever that happens to be).[1]

My memories of the area are slight—mainly focused on the worldview of a six-year-old. We're talking my pet hamster, the train that ran past the end of the development around my bedtime, and walking with my older brother and sister to the local 7–11 (although it wasn't that) to get candy.

Chris's follow-up was also short, but it pushed me down a surprising path of exploration and discovery:

It's incredible how many connections people have to Montgomery through Maxwell.
That's a nice neighborhood. One of the city's main tributaries, Vaughn Road, runs nearby. The area features some of the more expensive real estate in Montgomery— those homes that aren't locked inside gated subdivisions that is. I imagine that the neighborhood must have been newly developed then.
My father was a New York cop during the 1970s, but he would visit family in Alabama. He told me that the area near your childhood home was all farmland then, and he kicked himself for not investing when he had the chance.[2]

I read right past the relatively familiar phenomenon of the less than six degrees of separation that defines the lives of those African Americans who pursue a career in academia. Instead, I was simply mystified by Chris's residential assessment: my family lived in a nice neighborhood? How far was our home from the Air Force base? Was the sundry store still there? Did trains still rumble down the tracks? We lived in a nice neighborhood?

I sat down at the keyboard, navigated to Google Maps, and typed in "Lott Drive, Montgomery, Alabama." Simple enough. While I didn't doubt that Chris's assessment of Lott Drive was correct for at least *some* portion of the road, I thought I'd look to see where that road traveled and if the tell-tale signs of railroad tracks would help me figure out where I lived along what *had* to be a long road.

Lott Drive came up immediately. It was only two blocks long. I lived in a nice neighborhood?

On a lark I decided to try the street-view function in Google Maps. I knew it wouldn't work, but why not try?

It worked.

Not only did it work, but the image that filled the screen was of the house that I grew up in, or, more accurately, spent two years in during my early childhood. But perhaps this wasn't the house. Yes, we did live in a two-story, California stucco–style house, but there had to be more of the same in the development. It turns out that there weren't. My family lived in this nice neighborhood and owned this stylistically singular corner house. Everyone else lived in large, one-floor, brick ramblers. My first thought was that we must have been very conspicuous. As I would soon discover, we were conspicuous but not for reasons that immediately occurred to me, although they should have.

Still mesmerized by this discovery I zoomed out and began to look for other markers of my childhood. Right there! The railroad tracks. Satellite view tells me that they aren't in use anymore.

Our home on Lott Drive.

Perhaps they are turning into some sort of greenbelt that upwardly mobile professionals can jog along. But then again, perhaps not. In any case, one quick look at the tracks confirmed for me that my spatial sense was on target, though horribly skewed by a six-year-old's memory. The tracks told me where my home was, all right, but that long trek back from the break in the barbed-wire fence at the edge of the tracks to my family home wasn't quite two blocks. Lots of memories were made and lost in the meadow that separated the tracks from my bedroom window. I don't see the meadow now— just homes. For all I know they were there all the time.

What was a six-year-old doing near the train tracks and then wandering back home? I was following my older brother. Every so often we would go to the corner convenience store, buy some Lik-m-Aid or a *Mad* magazine or *Cracked* trading cards, and head home. But we didn't take the path back along the streets. Instead we'd go out the parking lot to the rear of the store and walk to the train tracks. If a slow-moving freight train came along, we would climb the ladder to a box car and ride there to the break in the barbed-wire fence. If the train was moving a lot faster, we'd put a penny on the track to watch it get flattened. The first to find the penny that had been shot off the rails in who knows what perilous direction would get to keep it. I still remember the warmth of the penny on that rare occasion when my brother let me find it. I can only hope that he let my sister or our cousins who lived nearby also have a fair shot at finding the penny. I'm pretty certain I was allowed to find the coin, since it was the best guarantee that I wouldn't tell our parents where we had gone or why.

Still marveling at these floods of memories, I went back to Google Maps' street view to see if I could find that convenience store. I knew exactly where to look. A few seconds browsing told me that the store was now gone and had been replaced either by a gas station or an Applebee's. I'm pretty sure my former source of empty calories and preadolescent gross-out humor is presently the gas station.

Now fully captured by the marvel of Google Maps, I decided to virtually walk my way back to the California stucco I called home—the legit way, not via the train tracks. I didn't make it a hundred electronic yards before I stopped in a different set of tracks. I *knew* that building. The second I saw it, I *knew* that building. Zooming out to satellite view provided confirmation. This was the private school, Montgomery Academy to be precise, for which I took an admissions test when I was about six. For years, my memory told me that I went to take that test with a few other kids from the neighborhood and that they, or rather, their parents, really wanted them to get in. I went along for fun. A few weeks or months later I realized that I must not have done well on that test since I never enrolled.

Some years later—maybe as many as another six or ten—I was talking to my mother about all of this, and she told me that my memory was wrong. In fact, I did quite well on the test, had gotten in, and the school really wanted me to matriculate. For reasons that still confound me, I have no recollection of what she said next, if anything.

All of this—the coincidence with Chris, the Google Maps discoveries, the truncated memory of my school admission—was still operating at the level of a neat story and nothing more. Wanting to share all of this with my brother, sister, and father (my mother had passed away four years earlier and with her went much of our family past), I sent them an e-mail and the URL for that two-floor California stucco.

Within minutes my brother responded.

My memory was correct, that was the house in which we lived. And, yes, those were the train tracks where we braved danger on innumerable occasions. After that, however, his story about those years in Alabama was markedly different than my own. We began to exchange e-mails as I discovered aspects of my family's history that simply weren't mine. The first e-mails were short; the latter, more expansive. Both astonished me but in wholly different ways.

The first rupture in my narrative of Montgomery, Alabama, revolved around the school. I had known for years that I had at least taken the school's entrance exam. My brother's e-mail—the first in our several days'–long exchange—parted these clouds:

*Actually, I don't know if you were ever told, when you, me and
Karen took that test and passed we were the first blacks ever to
pass the test [and] get in the Academy. Made the newspapers.
Too many Klan kids at the school. That's why we did not go.*[3]

"I don't know if you were ever told. . . ." The words lingered like
something simultaneously there and not there.

Though spectral, the story was clear: Brian assumed I knew that
we all tested for the school. This was news to me. More significant,
however, was the fact that Brian, Karen, and Jonathan Holloway
had been on the cusp of actually being part of "the movement."
That national narrative of American exceptionalism that I always
believed I was too young to have experienced was, it turns out, dra-
matically close to being my own lived history.

I grew up in a family that I understood to have benefited enor-
mously from the gains of the civil rights movement while never
directly engaging it. At least this is what my own gentle perusing
through family history could ever indicate. My father was a career officer in the United States Air Force. Although he had turned
down two commissions to West Point—something his father could
never understand—my father eventually joined the Air Force as
an officer. He had lived in seclusion for weeks with his squadron
during the Cuban Missile Crisis; flown KC-135 tanker-refuelers
during the Vietnam War; been chased by Russian fighter pilots
when his plane violated Russian airspace; was convinced for years
that he was under surveillance by the Air Force for reasons he never
fully divulged, beyond saying that he took on a lot of "extra mis-
sions" to secure better pay; and had refused to let my mother attend the March on Washington for fear of her safety *and* his security
clearance.

My maternal grandfather had been in the struggle as a member
of Franklin Roosevelt's Black Cabinet and then as the first executive
director of the United Negro College Fund, but somewhere along
the line the struggle faded from view.

All of this is to say, it was quite a shock to discover that I was on the verge of being part of the movement myself, only to be yanked back to my safer world, where I worried about a short-lived hamster, securing candy from the convenience store, and hopping slow-moving freight trains back home.

My brother's follow-up e-mail—the one generated by my almost-frantic entreaties for more information and seeking affirmation that our potential integration actually made the local news—provided a little more detail:

> Made all the newspapers.
>> It was a big deal.
>> This place was a target for all civil rights activist [sic].
>> When we all passed it was a BIG DEAL!
>> And mom and dad were afraid now that we were in the
> newspapers.
>> Didn't want to become the next posters for the next
> Klan rally.[4]

In another e-mail, immediately following this one, Brian went on at greater length and in more evocative detail:

> It was a very wierd time.
>> Not steppin in the neighbors yard was no joke.
>> Living in that neighborhood was no joke.
>> You were one of the neighborhood darlings, so young, you
> would go up and speak to Klan folk and they got all nervous
> and jerky because they liked you and you were so cute.
>> screwed them up.
>> over them, the other kids were allowed to play in our yard.
>> the only neighbors that we could visit were the ones from
> the military—which oddly enough lived behind us and across
> the street.
>> we had all sorts of joy, every day.
>> when karen and i went to school we would get chastized,
> harassed, intimidated and [ostracized] by the blacks.

*we were the only ones who did not have [a] lunch voucher,
and could actually pay for our lunch.*

That made it worse.

And we got on the bus with all the white kids after school.

*Trouble started when we would actually do our homework
and raise our hands in class. Pretty soon, I just stopped
talking.*

*The biggest event in school was when Hank Aaron hit
715 HR, black teachers cried silently because it was too
dangerous to celebrate. There was such a joy in all the blacks
eyes, the lunch room servers, the janitors, etc. Everyone was
smiling with their eyes and saying nothing. It was like "We
did it!"*

*I did not see that again, until Gramma cried when Tiger
won the Masters. It was one of those moments.*

White teachers were pissed and angry.

Never forget that day.[5]

Given the various shorthands and typographical errors that are
endemic to e-mail communications, I'm comfortable assuming my
brother meant to say, "I will never forget that day" or "Never forgot
that day." However, taking creative license when I read that line, I
actually see my brother closing the e-mail with literal directions to
me: "Never forget that day." Naturally, this assertion, even fabricated
as an assertion, is an impossibility since none of what my brother
had to offer was part of my recollected past. Well, I did remember
the neighbors behind us and across the street. They were both in the
Air Force as well and I *only* remember them. It never occurred to
me that there might have been a larger reason behind this. (It also
never occurred to me that because my mother "looked" white, the
neighbors I never got to know were probably pushed to the edge of
their sensibilities for all manner of reasons.)

I followed up with my sister and father. Was Brian right?

Karen responded that because Brian was two years older, he
simply had a different set of recollections than she did. But as she

thought more about it, the general ambience of the time sounded true. She wrote,

> *I was called names myself at Cloverdale—"oreo"—and I
> had no knowledge of what it meant. The military kids were
> definitely ostracized. You could try out for teams and stuff but
> there was a townie flavor to decision making. . . . I remember
> mom saying that it blew them away when cousins (Brian,
> Pam, and I) could perform at the highest levels. Unheard of!*[6]

Although less detailed in the retelling than my brother's e-mail, this was sufficient sibling confirmation. My father, unfortunately, was a different story altogether. This was a man who has never been one to look backward. Rather, this was a man who sprinted. Sprinted to get ahead and always sprinting to leave his past behind.

It was worth a shot, though. Certainly he had something to say about all of this. I remember being very excited when his e-mail

The only neighbors I ever knew. I'm on the far left.

arrived. The excitement lasted all of a few seconds, as it took that long to read the entire note:

> *That was really something to view the old home and to relive all the things that happened during that time in our lives. So many things and so many moments!!!! Remind me to tell you the story of how we bought the home.*[7]

That was it. But still, there was something there.

Too excited about the e-mails that kept coming in from my brother and sister and too intrigued by the closing sentence in his e-mail that suggested a powerful story about busting racial covenants, integrating neighborhoods, or engaging in some quietly subversive civil rights action, I decided to pick up the phone and press my father on the issues.

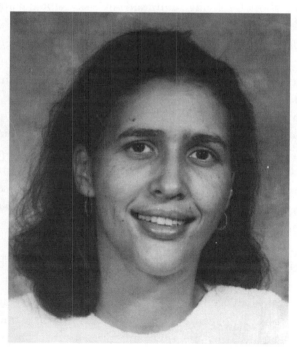

My mother.

The housing story was something of a bust. It turns out that my father went with one of the leading real estate firms in the city, Blitz and Golinsky. (My father made the conscious decision to go with a real estate firm that had a Jewish surname. He felt that this firm would show him a full range of properties and not just point him in the direction of Montgomery's black enclaves.) To their credit, the Blitz and Golinsky agents said they'd be happy to work with him to find a place to buy, and in short order he was under contract for a home three doors down from Montgomery's mayor.

Since we didn't move into that house, I assumed there was a great story to be told about race, housing, integration, privilege, and access. If the story is there (and, really, how could it not be?), it's lost to time. My father simply recalls that the sellers wanted to change the closing cost distribution after the contracts were signed. They argued that my father was getting a good deal and shouldn't be "bitching" about the change. Blitz and Golinsky kept at it and found the place that would become our home.

Reaching out to my father to find out what really happened with the Montgomery Academy was also something of a disappointment. My father recalled that we took the exam and that "something" ran in the newspapers, but he insisted he had no memory of why the Holloway kids never enrolled. But just when I felt I had run into a dead end with him, he started to talk in greater detail about Montgomery Academy and even the neighborhood where we lived.

"It was all part of a greater strategy," he said. "Montgomery Academy was the place where Montgomery's power elite sent their children: the bankers, the politicians, the doctors, the lawyers, and the generals at Maxwell [Air Force Base]." He continued:

The generals had a plan for me. You see, I was the first black to teach at the Air War College and they wanted to make me a general. I had been a line officer, meaning I hadn't spent my career pushing paper around on a desk somewhere but had actually risked my life time and time again. They really wanted to change the face of the Air Force and part of that was finding the right kind of officer and, with him, the right kind of family. Our family was tall, your mother looked right and came from the right background, you kids were all doing well in school and could probably cut it at Montgomery Academy. The generals met with the other leaders at the school and made the case that you three should take the test and, if you passed, be admitted. That's really all I remember about Montgomery Academy. For them and their small way of looking at the world, we were the right kind of family.

But I didn't want any of that. I didn't want to be their poster child. I didn't want to be a general. I just wanted to get out of the Air Force. They had taken enough of me.[8]

When we hung up, my mind was reeling. Part of the dislocation was certainly due to the frustration that my newly imagined place in the grand civil rights narrative was being denied by a father who couldn't remember the most important detail in the story. What was more disorienting, however, was that my father *could* confirm the immense challenges of the era—soldiers coming home from Vietnam and suffering further degradation and isolation due to their role in that catastrophe, the constant burden of racial tightrope walking—and that all of this was news to me. Granted, I was approaching my seventh birthday when my family left Montgomery, and so, in a very real way, I should be excused from knowing these histories then. But *never* knowing these things? Never understanding that my father actually broke a color line and made a measure of military history? Never knowing that the reason I could only remember children whose parents were in the military is that these were the only people who would deal with us? How could this be possible?

I understand the desire to protect a young child from a certain ugliness in life, but erasure was a different phenomenon altogether. But, then, in a coincidental moment that one could only describe as cheaply cinematic, just a few days after this part of my family's past was reconstructed and while I was still processing why it was unknown to me (especially given my professional pursuits and the fact that my family knew I was working on a book concerning memory and identity), I came across a box of our mother's possessions that my brother had put together and sent to me for Christmas. I hadn't ventured near the box since it had arrived a month earlier, avoiding the emotions that were going to accompany opening this archive.

I had actually forgotten about the box, even though I practically stepped around it every day when I went to my closet. Perhaps emboldened, perhaps excited, I opened the box and started tracing my own childhood through report cards, pictures, and crude art projects my mother had kept. And then I stumbled across a document that I had never seen before. It is dated July 4, 1968, and addressed to "My dear son." I wasn't quite one year old at this point, so before the end of the first line I knew that I wasn't the "dear son" in the letter.

July 4, 1968

My dear son,
    You recently questioned me as to "why" I would take the time to fight for America when this same America has placed so many troubles in the path of black men. I know that my answer has been long in coming but your question was so honest, so full of deep, pointed thought! I must confess, an answer seemed very hard to find and even harder to express. But as I worried about your throwing fire crackers against my orders and reflected on my thoughts of the deadly "firecrackers" we Americans are using to kill and wound an enemy, I found your answer. I only hope that you can understand a little of what I am saying and wishing for you in my "answer."
    Son, I am here because I belong here! The black people of America have been there during all of the many crises that

have faced this most magnificent, most lovely, most confusing country! We have shared these crises with our blood and our strength. It is our continuing heritage to be a part of the building of America, and a part of her strength. We must share in her hope of freedom for all men, everywhere!

I believe that through my sacrifices this year, I can guarantee a little better chance for you to realize the full benefits of a free country! Just as I eagerly joined in the fight for the right to vote, to have a chance to cast my free ballot, freely, so too must I fight for the right of other men to cast their ballot. And son, the thousands of other black men here realize too, that this fight for a free ballot is equally a fight for a free country. To fight for one, you fight for the other . . . guarantee one, and you guarantee the other! We know that the sound of free ballots being cast is the beautiful sound of freedom that we so want for our children and the children of all people wherever they might live.

You must realize that the sacrifice you are making in having your dad away and the sacrifices of the thousands of other black men and white men are forcing the dream of freedom forward.

> *Yours in love and understanding,*
> *Dad*

Having recently discovered how Google Maps could refresh my own understanding of my family past, I went straight back to Google and began to enter in phrases from this letter. I knew it wasn't Baldwin, but it was in the tradition of the letter to his nephew that prefaced *The Fire Next Time*. Nothing came up no matter how many different ways I searched for the original author. And then I found myself coming to an inescapable, if unbelievable, conclusion: my father might actually be the author.

My brother, the best family historian we have left, wasn't sure of this himself. It seemed right to him given everything that was going on in the world and in our home, but he didn't remember the letter. I called my father back, and he confirmed, without going into any details, that it sure sounded like a letter he wrote. He didn't recall giving it to Brian though, but I simply had to understand that his memory wasn't what it used to be and, after all, it was such a challenging time.

I was left with one question: whose father was this? I now understood that he broke barriers at the Air War College and that the generals there wanted him to break even more. I had long known that he didn't want his family, especially his wife, to be too conspicuous for fear of some sort of professional or political backlash—a fear that he felt was substantiated by the fact that immediately after he left the Air Force, his taxes were audited for five straight years. But, in the privacy of letters that he wrote and maybe never sent, was my father some sort of militant patriotic race warrior? Was his personal silence on these issues something that he felt the need to pass along to his children? Is that what made us the right kind of family? And, if so, what were the costs of being that kind of family? What did we give up, if anything, by living a life of structured silences?

Yes, I lost my (highly romanticized) chance to be a civil rights warrior like the brave souls in places like Little Rock or Birmingham, but since I had no idea that this was even a possibility, I never felt any sort of remorse or loss about this when I was growing up. But now that I know about it, what am I to make of it? The clinical assessment might be that my father insisted on letting the movement's frontline activists pass my family by and that my family simply rode their coattails to a life of material comfort and advantage. Being the right kind of family certainly allowed for that kind of advantage taking.

But maybe I should make of this something that is much larger than a single narrative of a single family in the civil rights era. In the time since Chris Johnson asked me if I grew up in Montgomery, I've had plenty of opportunity to ponder the significance of this found history. Putting aside the exceptionalism that the Montgomery

Academy represented and that the Air Force generals desired, what we are left with is a fairly typical story of a family struggling to find a way to fit into a viciously poisoned social and political climate. It is, perhaps, a mundane story of parents working hard to protect their children in the way they thought best, hoping to leave for them a better future than the present and past they had known. Put another way, it is a story of not telling stories with the faith that being the right kind of family would pay dividends that extended beyond a child's ability to imagine a heroic past.

7

JOHN HOPE FRANKLIN

The Man and His Works

Orlando Patterson

John Hope Franklin passed away in 2009, an era very different from that in which he was born. His passing provides an occasion to look back at the body of his scholarly work, to help understand our own present experience of race relations. It also provides an opportunity to think about how a historian with a deep understanding of America's racial past might have understood the challenges of race relations in a world very different from both the one he was born into, and the one in which he produced his most famous works.

My respect and admiration for his work go back to my high school days in Jamaica when I first read his then newly published, and now classic, textbook on African American history. With time, that admiration deepened into a sense of academic affinity. For although we have never met, our intellectual and personal paths have crossed in various critical and, for me, formative ways.

Intellectually, I share Franklin's passion for history and historical understanding, even if from different disciplinary perspectives. Substantively, I have, following in his footsteps, focused much of my academic interest on the study of slavery. I also share Franklin's preoccupation with the nature of race and racism and the ways in which the past, especially the slave past, incubated and permanently shaped both the social cancer of racism as well as other tragedies in the African American, and Euro-American, experiences. It was thus a proud moment for me when I read the following passage in the glowing *New York Times* obituary on Franklin: "Dr. Franklin's discussion of racial ambiguity pioneered a new form of scholarship that questioned familiar categories and foreshadowed the work of later scholars like the social scientist Orlando Patterson who continue to examine the complex realities of race in an increasingly plural world." [1]

The only correction I would offer is that Franklin not only foreshadowed but influenced my own thinking on the problem of race and its historical roots, both here and in the world at large. I am honored to acknowledge Franklin's influence and happy that others have recognized it.

With this in mind, I have three objectives in this essay. First, to write briefly about Franklin the man and his times; second, to reflect on his role and achievement as a historian; and, third, to comment on the changes in American race relations over the course of Franklin's long life, ending with Franklin's own rather surprising closing appraisal of where we are now on this stubborn national problem.

THE MAN AND HIS TIMES

Franklin was blessed with a very long life and a mind that stayed alert right to the very end. Born in 1915 in Rentiesville, Oklahoma, he grew up in the South, but spent most of his working life in the great cities of the North—in Washington D.C., New York, Chicago, then in his final decades back in the South at Duke University. His was an American life. He lived through the worst and best of times and places for black folks in this country, and he personally experienced some of the worst aspects of racism as well as the nation's finest effort at eradicating this social scourge.

Franklin was a witness to a good part of the very history he did so much to illuminate. He was therefore thoroughly justified in seeing his life as a "mirror to America," as he so aptly titled his autobiography, published shortly before his death. It was, indeed, a life that reflected America in all its protean complexity. One can do no better than to quote from his autobiography's opening passage, which skillfully foreshadowed all that was to follow:

Living in a world restricted by laws defining race, as well as creating obstacles, disadvantages and even superstitions regarding race, challenged my capacities for survival. For ninety years I have witnessed countless men and women likewise meet this challenge. Some bested it; some did not; many had to settle for any accommodation they could. I became a student and eventually a scholar. And it was armed with the tools of scholarship that I strove to dismantle those laws, level those obstacles and disadvantages, and replace superstitions with humane dignity. Along with much else, the habits of scholarship granted me something many of my similarly striving contemporaries did not have. I knew, or should say know, what we are up against.[2]

Without self-pity, but with a calmly controlled sense of outrage, Franklin documented from his own experience the all-pervasive nature of race and racism in the America in which he grew up. We learn how, at age six, he and his mother were tossed off a train for sitting in the wrong, white-only car; how his family was traumatized and dislocated by the Tulsa race riot of 1921; how at age twelve, proud to be a boy scout and attempting to do his good deed for the day, he offered to guide a blind white woman across the street, but who, on discovering halfway across the intersection that he was black, screamed at him to take his filthy black hands off her, preferring to be left stranded in the middle of the road. And we learn how, in 1945, after a commencement ceremony, he was forced to stand jammed together with other blacks in a hot, sweltering segregated car of the train, while four white men lounged in an otherwise empty car. Incredibly, these four men were German POWs.

His recollection of his experiences at Harvard as a graduate student is painful for me to read, having spent most of my life as a professor there, a place that I have come to love and call home. It was typical of Franklin that he was as appalled by the anti-Semitism at Harvard as he was by the casual, antiblack racism of a professor he admired sometimes making "darky-jokes."

A day, and often an hour, didn't go by without my feeling the color of my skin—in the reactions of white Cambridge, the behavior of my fellow students, the attitudes real and imagined struck by my professors. However well Currier had equipped me to meet the demands of Harvard's course work, race precluded my enjoying the self-assurance to which most of my colleagues, along with affluence and influence, were born.[3]

At the same time, there was much in Franklin's life that led him to a full recognition of the complexities of race in America. Chief among these were the Euro-American men and women who behaved with great decency and kindness toward him and, in several cases, played decisive roles in his career. The most important of these was his teacher and lifelong friend at Fisk University, Theodore Currier, an almost saintly figure from Maine who monitored Franklin at Fisk and was not only responsible for getting him into graduate school at Harvard, but actually loaned him money for his school fees there.

Franklin's greatest influences, however, were his parents. His father, a lawyer, was an outstanding role model; his mother a fountain of wisdom and love. One story about his mother, told to a writer, captures her warmth and influence: "My mother and I used to have a game we'd play on our public. She would say if anyone asks you what you want to be when you grow up, tell them you want to be the first Negro president of the United States. And just the words were so far-fetched, so incredible that we used to really have fun, just saying it."[4] It was this remarkably supportive emotional environment, combined with the good fortune of unselfish mentorship and, of course, his own exceptional intellectual gifts and calm, resolute personality, that saw him through the worst postemancipation era of America for blacks and accounted for his success.

And what a successful life it was! Franklin was to achieve the highest honors his profession and nation had to offer: he was the first black historian to become president of the American Historical Association; the first to present a paper to the segregationist Southern Historical Association; the first African American to chair one of the nation's preeminent history departments, that of the University of Chicago; the first to hold an endowed university chair at Duke; the third recipient of the John Kluge Prize for lifetime achievement in the humanities, in 2006; and, to top it all, President Clinton awarded him the Medal of Honor, the nation's highest civilian honor.

FRANKLIN'S WORKS

Although he was always an engaged scholar, "determined to be as active as I could in the fight to eradicate the stain of racism that clouded American intellectual and academic life even as it poisoned other aspects of American society,"[5] and in his mature years Franklin was to become actively involved in civic affairs—most notably in his chairmanship of President Clinton's Initiative on Race—it was as an academic historian that he won recognition. From the very beginning, he wrote, "the goal I sought was to be a scholar with credentials as impeccable as I could achieve." What he achieved was the status of a scholar's scholar. Meticulous and exhaustive in his research methods, dispassionate in his assessments, bold and ambitious in his research goals, yet morally engaged with his subject, he became a model for generations of scholars of all ethnicities and, as my own case illustrates, from many nations, including even my own little island. At a deeper level, Franklin saw no real tension between his role as an academic historian and one engaged in civic life, because he firmly believed that "the historian, as the servant of the past, is in the best position to provide a rational basis for present actions."[6]

Franklin published more than twenty books. They ranged in subject from the study of the freed people in North Carolina[7] (his first major work) and the Reconstruction era[8] to the psychocultural foundation of racism in the South (his masterwork)[9] to slave revolts[10] to biographies of former African American historians[11] to studies of the color line and modern racism.[12] It was typical of Franklin that one of his earliest refereed papers, published when he was still a second-year graduate student, was on the nineteenth-century

Euro-American novelist and critic Edward Bellamy,[13] and one of his finest books was about antebellum white southern travelers to the North, in which he adroitly analyzed their fascination and repulsion with their strange and distant countrymen.[14] In addition to his published works, from his youthful academic years he took a keen interest in the history of women.

The work for which he is best known is, of course, his history textbook, *From Slavery to Freedom*, first published in 1947 and always in print, having gone through nine editions, the last extensively and admirably revised by Professor Evelyn Brooks Higginbotham.[15] As is so often the case with eminent scholars, the work for which he is best known is not necessarily his best. *From Slavery to Freedom* is an important textbook (and remains so), which brought black history to generations of young minds. Franklin drew on the many distinguished historians that preceded him, such as Carter Woodson, W.E.B. DuBois, and George Washington Williams. He integrated an impressive body of secondary literature and primary sources to produce a new highly readable and coherent account of the African American past that lent authority and dignity to the subject and helped to lift it out of its isolation in the historical profession, especially in the way it was taught in colleges. For Franklin, this was not just a scholarly endeavor, but something he felt passionately about; a history he wanted the world to understand and to care about. In writing this work the historian as witness and voice of the voiceless victims of the past was more important than the scholar trying to unearth something original. In a moving passage in his autobiography he recalled what drove him to write it:

> In the planning and writing of my work, I had witnessed more than five hundred years of human history pass before my eyes. I had seen one slave ship after another from Portugal, Spain, France, Holland, England, and the United States pile black human cargo into its bowels as it would coal or even gold had either been more available and profitable at the time. I had seen them dump my ancestors at New World

ports as they would a load of cattle and wait smugly for their pay for capture and transport. I had seen them beat black men until they themselves became weary, and rape black women until their ecstasy was spent leaving their brutish savagery exposed. I had heard them shout, "Give us liberty or give us death," and not mean one word of it. . . . I had seen them lynch black men and distribute their ears, fingers, and other parts as souvenirs to the ghoulish witnesses. I had seen it all, and in the seeing I had become bewildered and yet in the process lost my own innocence.[16]

Nonetheless, however great it was as a pedagogic work, we do it a disservice by making extravagant claims about it as a work of original scholarship. Franklin never intended it to be that, given the relatively short period of time he spent writing the first edition. It never attempted, and did not do, what Kenneth Stampp's classic work *The Peculiar Institution*[17] achieved, which was to transform scholarship on American slavery and topple the previously established authoritative general interpretation of the subject, that by the racialist, southern historian at Yale U.B. Phillips.[18] Instead, it splendidly realized what it set out to do: to tell the story of African Americans from African to modern times, drawing on the best available scholarship, in graceful prose that appealed to college students and the general educated layman.

It is in his other works that Franklin excelled as a scholar and academic model, especially in his masterpiece *The Militant South*, which is one of the best accounts of the origins of racism and especially of the honorific and belligerent culture of the Old South. This is not the place to write a detailed assessment of Franklin's works—one would need a small volume to do such a task justice. Instead, I wish to emphasize what I consider three of the most defining and influential features of his works.

The first of these is his insistence on the centrality of slavery for any understanding of both the African American and the broader American past and present. Many today might think this obvious;

only after becoming cognizant of the many revisionist wars in the study of American slavery can one truly appreciate how important this lifelong academic stance of Franklin was. Slavery has gone through a bizarre set of reinterpretations, in which both white and black historians, often for different reasons, have relentlessly attempted to downplay the influence of slavery on both the African American and broader American past and present. For Euro-American historians, the reasons for downplaying the impact of the slave and Jim Crow past are all too obvious; some, such as U.B. Phillips went so far as to argue that slavery was a net gain for blacks in that it exposed and enculturated primitive Africans into enlightened westerners. Black historians, especially those who most influenced Franklin, including the eminent historical sociologist E. Franklin Frazier, a colleague at Howard, strongly rejected this interpretation. While applauding the achievements of black people in spite of their oppression, they made no mistake in highlighting the tragic negative effects of three centuries of enslavement on black life, all vividly summarized in Malcolm X's bitterly pithy comment: "We did not land on Plymouth Rock . . . Plymouth Rock landed on us." [19]

However, when the civil rights movement entered its black identity phase, many African Americans, in their search for what some have called a "usable past," began to emphasize the positive side of "the black community" during slavery and to play down or neglect the deleterious effects of slavery and Jim Crow on black life, especially in gender and familial relations. Indeed, some even came to condemn any discussion of the role of the past in explaining the present plight of black Americans as racist and reactionary blaming of the victim. In this they were joined by a chorus of revisionist Euro-American historians, including many on the left, such as Herbert Gutman and Eugene Genovese. Between these two well-meaning but sadly misguided views of the black past—one in search of a glorious, triumphant heritage, the other desperate to explain the current dilemmas of black Americans purely in terms of current structural factors and white racism—the historical and social science community pretty nearly ended up writing the slave master and the horrific impact of the holocaust of slavery and the slave trade (external and internal) on its black victims right out of the history and sociology of black American life.[20]

Franklin would have none of this. Throughout this revisionist distortion, he kept a cool and balanced scholarly head, recognizing and celebrating the triumphs of black life and culture, but never losing sight of the tragic negative impact that "the heavy hand of history," as he described it, dumped upon the African American present, one that still had to be confronted and overcome. Speaking of the tragic plight of incarcerated black men and troubled youth, he had no doubt that

> it was the nation's slave policy, even before it was a nation, that sealed their fate and the fate of the nation. It was the nation's erection of an apartheid society after slavery that made them pariahs of the land. . . . It was a national economic policy that withheld from them opportunities to train for jobs requiring technical skills and special responsibilities that modern America could provide. . . . And it was national policy that permitted its citizens to badger them, goad them, and humiliate them to the point that they could not be easily reached.

For Franklin, the harm of bad and neglectful policies must be understood in conjunction with the effects of slavery and past evil policies and attitudes that so undermined the worldview and dispositions of many African Americans that they have become difficult to help.[21]

Franklin's second major contribution as a scholar is that he was among the first academic historians to explore in depth the role of racism as a solidifying agent in southern life, preserving the system and the socioeconomic inequalities among whites at the expense of the degradation of blacks. Racism created a bond of solidarity among all whites in giving even the lowest and poorest of whites a sense of racial superiority, in this way not only securing their strong support for the system but leading them to blindness about their own poverty and exploitation by elite southern whites both during the era of plantation slavery and Jim Crow. Franklin has not been given due credit for helping to excavate and reveal this very important herrenvolk principle of American life. In a masterful paper, "Slavery and the Martial South," he wrote:

> The racial basis of slavery gave southern leaders an effective means of solidifying the economically divergent elements among the whites. At the same time, it strengthened the ardor with which most white southerners were willing to fight to preserve slavery. The sharp cleavage between slavery and freedom was made even sharper by the factor of race. All slaves belonged to the degraded, "inferior" race; and, by the same token, all whites, however wretched some of them might be, were superior. In a society where race was so important, the whites at the lowest rung could satisfy themselves because they could identify themselves with the most privileged of the community. "Color alone is here the badge of distinction, the true mark of aristocracy," said Thomas Dew, "and all who are white are equal in spite of the variety of occupation." [22]

It is important to note that this pathbreaking paper was published in the *Journal of Southern History* in 1952, when very few thought of whiteness as a social construction having major consequences for whites as well as blacks. [23]

The third defining feature of Franklin's work is his mainstreaming of black history. What I am getting at is best summarized by Franklin himself in his elegantly rendered account of his craft as a historian:

> My field of concentration has been the South, where I have studied intensively the two great racial groups, black and white, the principal actors in the drama of southern history.

At times during my studies the focus was on free Negroes and those slaves who were virtual free. At other times I gave attention to the relationship of slavery to certain attributes of white southerners, such as their apparent predisposition toward militancy. I was also interested in the expansionist tendencies of southerners, which also seemed related in some ways to slavery. These forays into various aspects of southern history had as their principal objective a better understanding of *the entire South and all of its people*.[24] (emphasis added)

This passage beautifully condenses his main intellectual mission. Note, first, that his aim was to explore the black historical experience as an integral part of southern life and development: not as an aberration, as most white historians of his early years would have it, nor as a thing apart, as many black historians would prefer to write it, but as southern history. This mainstreaming of black history within southern history set the model for the later integration of the African American experience as an essential part of American history.

THE WORLD HE LEFT BEHIND

I come, finally, to the issue that bothered Franklin during his last years: the paradoxical world of race in America at the start of the twenty-first century, what he sometimes referred to as America's two worlds of race. For all the changes brought about by the civil rights movement, which Franklin documented superbly and was clearly proud of, he was nonetheless surprisingly pessimistic, even bleak, in his assessment of American race relations during his last days. Significantly, he remained so even after the historic election of the first black president, an event quite unimaginable for most of his life, or imagined only as the source of humor. "I didn't think it would happen in my lifetime," he said of President Obama's election. "It's an indication of the willingness, as well as the ability of this country to turn a significant corner toward full political equality." Note, however, the very measured tone in which he spoke, and the qualifier—political equality. The truth is that Franklin remained extremely disappointed until the end of his life about the state of inequality in America and especially about African American inequality. "I don't see enough that is different from what I experienced X number of years ago," he told a journalist not long before he died, and added: "The big picture is still the subtleties and the sophistication that characterize the maintenance of the status quo."[25]

One paradoxical element in our present racial situation that greatly distressed him was the persistence of racial segregation, in spite of all the progress—a segregation that includes the black middle class. Having grown up in the segregated South, Franklin had no doubt about the damage that this does to both whites and blacks, and he had little patience with blacks who romanticized the supposedly cohesive and supportive black community that existed under Jim Crow. "We point with pride to the historical congressional legislation and Supreme Court decisions against racial discrimination," he wrote. "But racial discrimination and even racial segregation continue in blatant as well as subtle forms."[26]

However, what most disappointed and deeply saddened Franklin was the desperate condition of black youth, particularly young African American men. The bias against black men, he frequently pointed out, goes deep into the nation's history, and tragically, some African Americans have internalized it. Thus, he observed bitterly that his maternal grandfather sent all his daughters and none of his sons to college and that his own father was the only educated male among his many siblings. Instead of the number of blacks in middle-class positions, he proposed another index of progress: "I believe a much more accurate measure of American progress toward justice and fairness is in the number of young adult African American men detained in various stages of the criminal justice system as opposed to those in, say, higher education."[27]

Franklin also had very mixed feelings about the cultural productions of successful black youth and the examples their producers set. Indeed, he very presciently anticipated the revival of sociological discourse on the significance of culture[28] in understanding the problems of black youth and made clear where he stood on the subject, a position not guaranteed to endear him to those who dismiss all cultural explanations as irrelevant or blaming the victim: "Those who became wealthy established impossible goals for most of their peers, thus adding to their frustrations and encouraging further misconduct. I have come to regard most of these success stories as millionaire wastrels, spending their fortunes on huge mansions and custom-built automobiles, with little thought of their fellows in the ghettos, from which many of them came."[29]

Franklin confesses that he has "had these angry, disappointing musings challenged," but by his refusal to answer them, or even state what they were, it is clear that he did not think much of them. Instead, he ended his great autobiography with challenges of his own, to the nation that had both honored and disappointed him, and to the group and class to which he belonged. Both sets of challenges reflect the compassion and appealing humility of the man, as well as the wisdom of a scholar who could penetrate to the hard core of truths. To America he proposed a modest moral dictum: "The test of an advanced society is not in how many millionaires it can produce, but in how many law-abiding, hardworking, highly respected, and self-respecting loyal citizens it can produce."[30] And to his fellow middle-class African Americans he pleaded that they "could do much to rescue young African Americans from the brink of dismal failure if only they would be willing to take the time."[31]

This, finally, was the mirror he held up to America, like a skilled, proud African American barber at the end of a haircut showing how a well-groomed head should look. He asked nothing grandiose of his nation: only that it should fulfill its part of the social contract that would, in turn, enable and motivate its citizens to be loyal, honorable, and productive. And he asked no more of his fellow, successful African Americans than that they should do what his glorious generation of leaders had done: take time to help in rescuing those who have yet to overcome.

8

THE PUZZLES OF RACIAL EXTREMISM IN A "POSTRACIAL" WORLD

Jeannine Bell

Commentators from a wide variety of locations on the political spectrum hailed the election of a black man to the presidency of the United States as a definitive sign of racial progress.[1] Some claims of racial progress were quite far-reaching. For instance, Bob Herbert, a columnist for the *New York Times* wrote, "The nation deserves to take a bow. This is not the same place it used to be."[2] There was of course a range of opinion regarding the depth of the racial change that President Obama's election represented. While some heralded the election as evidence of a "postracial" society,[3] others did not see it as a fundamental break with the past.[4] Part of the conservatives' argument that America had transcended race had to do with their desires to end progressive policies like affirmative action.[5] Supporters countered by raising the persistent racial inequality that African Americans continue to face.[6]

It was not just commentators and pundits who saw the election as significant. Surveys administered by Gallup immediately after the election in November 2008 indicate that seven of every ten individuals surveyed believed that race relations would improve as a result of Obama's election.[7] In these surveys, respondents were asked whether as the result of Barack Obama's election race relations had "gotten a lot better, gotten a little better, not changed, gotten a little worse, or gotten a lot worse." Thirty-nine percent of non-Hispanic whites and 53 percent of blacks surveyed cited improvement in race relations as a result of Obama's election.[8] Although that optimism has been tempered somewhat by the challenges that beset him during his first term in office, it is still common to assert that his victories in two presidential elections are an unmistakable sign that race prejudice no longer plays a significant role in American life.

The broadest claims of postracialism have been widely debunked,[9] but in some cases the rush to respond to those who claim that America's postracial status signals the end of race-specific policies results in a failure to acknowledge the significant racial progress Americans have made in a relatively short period of time. For instance, in 1954, the year that *Brown v. Board of Education* was decided, surveys conducted by researchers at the National Opinion Research Center (NORC) revealed an even split between respondents who felt that black and white students should attend the same and not separate schools.[10] There were steady increases in support for integrated schooling, and by 1995, 94 percent of respondents supported integrated schools.[11] Though there is still room for increasing tolerance, social scientists studying the improvement in whites' racial attitudes over time described the improvements as "sweeping and robust," demonstrating favorable shifts not just in significant areas but rather "in fundamental norms with regard to race."[12]

Another trend indicating improved racial equality appears in how individuals view interracial marriage. American views of intermarriage are seen as thresholds for expressing local racial attitudes. In 2011, a record number of Americans told Gallup pollsters that they approved of interracial marriage, with 86 percent (96 percent of blacks, 84 percent of whites) indicating that they approve of marriage between blacks and whites.[13] An even greater measure of acceptance is the actual interracial marriage rate, which has increased steadily since the 1970s. A Pew Research Center report on intermarriage found that in 2008 nearly one in seven marriages was interracial or interethnic, a rate more than double that of the 1980s and six times the intermarriage rate in the 1960s.[14]

THE TOLERANCE-VIOLENCE PARADOX: RACIAL VIOLENCE IN THE ERA OF OBAMA

Despite the increases in tolerance over the last forty years that allowed many in the white electorate to support the election of a black man as president of the United States, violent expressions of racism—cross burnings and other extreme mechanisms of racist terror—remain all too common, as I describe below. I call the existence of violent racism occurring in the same space and time as such significant increases in racial tolerance the "tolerance-violence paradox." While many eras in American history have had moments of racial progress occurring in the midst of violence, I submit that in this particular moment—the 2000s—violent expressions of racism are all too present, and especially seem to defy logic.

Racism Directed at Candidate and President Obama

Close watchers of the manifestations of racial violence saw it even during the early days of the 2008 presidential campaign. According to some reports, Barack Obama was threatened more times than any presidential candidate in history.[15] During the campaign, the Secret Service followed up on more than 500 death threats against the candidate. Some of these cases involved racial extremists, like the two neo-Nazi skinheads arrested for their conspiracy to assassinate candidate Obama.[16]

Somewhat surprisingly, given the power associated with the job for which he had been chosen, overt racism directed at President Obama did not evaporate. In fact, some reacted to the election of a black man as president, even one who has acted in a racially neutral way, as an assertion of black power and a danger to whites. As such, whites vehemently opposed to Obama's person, or his policies, responded with extreme bitterness,[17] uncharacteristic lack of respect,[18] and racialized rhetoric. One of the most prominent, relatively mainstream purveyors of racialized rhetoric in response to President Obama is the Tea Party. Darrel Enck-Wanzer has extensively documented the many manifestations of racism by members of the Tea Party in a variety of formal and informal mechanisms—for example, at Tea Party rallies, on Facebook, and e-mail. Tea Party rhetoric depicting Obama as a racial threat to the nation included:

> Visuals such as (A.) the "Obama care" poster featuring a dark "witch doctor" with Obama's face digitally sutured to the image, (B.) the "Barack the barbarian" cartoon featuring Obama as a hard body barbarian wielding a bronze age axe directed at a scantily clad white woman with long blond hair, and (C.) the iconic "socialism" poster featuring Obama in Joker makeup.[19]

These were not random depictions, of course. Such racialized images are deployed to mark Obama as a threatening, uncivilized, racialized "other" without ever using the term "black" or using race.

In keeping with the notion that because Obama is black, he is dangerous, attacks on Obama also included the characterization that Obama's policies pose danger to whites. Signs at Tea Party rallies read: "Obama's Plan: White Slavery" and "The American Taxpayers Are the Jews for Obama's Ovens."[20] Enck-Wanzer argues that the goal of such racist stigmatization is to construct Obama as a racialized other, who is both a black racial threat and an antiwhite racist who poses a danger to white America.[21]

Making claims having to do with Obama's otherness that are similar to the Tea Party's are the "birthers," so called because they demanded that Obama release a copy of his birth certificate to prove he was born in the United States. The suspicion that they articulated was that he was not born in the United States and was therefore ineligible to be president.[22] Though the birther movement included at least one mainstream figure (Donald Trump), many of those insisting that Obama had not been born in the United States were from the far right, including the Council of Conservative Citizens, a white nationalist group which contends that blacks are a retrograde species of humanity.[23] After a long-standing refusal to justify the birthers' arguments with a response, Obama elected to release his long-form birth certificate in July of 2011. This did not end the birthers' complaints however. Several in the birther movement insisted that the long form released by the White House was a fraud. Joseph Farah, sponsor of the "Where's the birth certificate?" billboards, said, "It would be a big mistake for everyone to jump to a conclusion now based on the release of this document, which raises as many questions as it answers."[24]

Extremist and Other Bias-Motivated Violence Directed at Ordinary Folks

It is not just the power of a black president that has generated an extremist response in this post–civil rights era. The Southern Poverty Law Center (SPLC), which tracks extremist activity, identified 1,002 separate hate groups—groups that have beliefs or practices that attack or malign entire classes of people, generally for immutable characteristics—that were active in the United States in 2010. Such groups were located throughout the United States, in nearly every state, and were engaged in activities ranging from leafleting and publishing to criminal acts, such as race-based arson.

In addition to keeping track of extremist hate groups, SPLC also scans news reports and other media sources for bias-related activities to compile its catalog of hate incidents. The organization's list includes more than 3,000 incidents occurring between 2003 and 2011. These incidents range from vandalism—slurs or epithets scrawled on someone's house, car, or religious institution—to bias-motivated murder. The SPLC catalog only scratches the surface of bias-motivated crime. A much more comprehensive list of bias-motivated incidents is compiled each year by the Federal Bureau of Investigation (FBI) from reports submitted by law enforcement agencies serving in cities and towns around the United States. In 2009, law enforcement agencies reported some 3,816 racially motivated bias crimes to the FBI. Nearly three-quarters of these incidents (71.4 percent) were motivated by antiblack bias.[25]

The Systemic Nature of Contemporary Bias Crime
and the Parameters of "Move-in Violence"

Bias-motivated crime is, of course, not new. Looking more closely at the individual incidents of bias-motivated crime reveals much about the contours of such violence. Close analyses of patterns of bias-motivated crime are one of the first steps in explaining why such violence occurs even in the midst of increasing tolerance. A more detailed examination of some of the bias-motivated incidents that have occurred in recent years reveals a pattern of violence in one particular context—violence directed at racial and ethnic minorities who have moved to white neighborhoods. Such violence is historically so common that scholars have coined a term—"move-in violence"—to describe incidents of harassment directed at racial and ethnic minorities who have moved to or are in the process of moving to white neighborhoods. Since violence can occur weeks, months, or even years after moving in, I use the term "anti-integrationist violence" to describe the acts of violence and harassment directed at minorities who moved to white neighborhoods. Most of the incidents that fit the anti-integrationist-violence label occur immediately after the family moves in. But sometimes this is not the case. As I describe below, even if the violence occurs weeks or years after the family moves in, the perpetrators' intent is clear—they want the family to leave.

My analysis of newspaper stories published since 1990 reveals more than 400 explicitly race-based incidents targeted at minorities moving to majority-white areas across the country in the 1990s and 2000s.[26] Incidents of anti-integrationist violence run the gamut in severity, including arson and firebombing, cross burning, harassment and verbal threats, murder, racial epithets, racist graffiti, and vandalism. Some of these are serious crimes, like murder and arson; while others, like the use of racial epithets, fall into the category of behavior that most likely can only be criminalized if it fits the legal definition of harassment.

Such incidents can be prosecuted under a variety of types of state and federal civil rights law, and also under criminal law.[27] The most common type of incident prosecuted in cases of anti-integrationist violence is cross burning, but individuals have also been convicted for attempting to drive minorities out of the neighborhood with threats, gunshots, arson, vandalism, firebombing, and beatings.[28] Perhaps surprisingly, perpetrators of anti-integrationist violence are frequently *not* skinheads, members of the Ku Klux Klan, or involved with some other hate or extremist group. In fact, as with hate crimes in general, most of the incidents involve those unaffiliated with any sort of hate or extremist group. Jack Levin and Jack McDevitt, experts on hate crimes, write, "Hate crimes are more often committed under ordinary circumstances by otherwise unremarkable types— neighbors, a coworker at the next desk, or groups of youngsters looking for 'bragging rights' with their friends."[29] The vast majority of individuals targeted by the violence are African Americans who have moved to white neighborhoods, though several cases involve individuals of other races, including cases targeted at interracial couples and people who have nonwhite children.[30]

One common assumption is that contemporary racial violence is largely restricted to the southern United States. In fact, the incidents I identified were not limited to any particular geographic area of the country and occurred in cities in every region of the country. Over the twenty-year period between 1990 and 2010, fewer than ten incidents were identified in twenty-seven states. Instead, the vast majority of incidents seem to be concentrated in just eight states,[31] with the largest number of incidents occurring in California (48), followed by Florida (40). The region of the country with the greatest concentration of incidents is the southern United States, followed closely by the midwestern United States. Perpetrators in just four states—Ohio, Missouri, Illinois, and Pennsylvania—were responsible for 23 percent of the total number of incidents countrywide.

In addition to occurring in nearly every area of the country, no particular type of neighborhood setting is immune. Incidents of anti-integrationist violence occurred in big cities, towns, and rural areas during this period. The affluence of either the neighborhood or that of the family moving to the neighborhood does not provide immunity against such violence. Incidents occur in working-class white neighborhoods as well as affluent neighborhoods and upscale developments.[32] In fact, one of the most costly residential fires in Maryland history, estimated at $10 million in damage, was an act of anti-integrationist violence.[33] On the night of December 6, 2004, arsonists set fire to a number of homes in Hunters Brooke, an upscale development in Indian Head, Maryland. Ten homes were destroyed and sixteen others were damaged. Many of the families moving into the Hunters Brooke development were black. One of the men, who pled guilty to the arson, said the development had been targeted because many of the new residents were black.[34]

As in the Hunters Brooke arson, in the vast majority of anti-integrationist-violence cases, there is evidence that the perpetrator is not happy with the integration of his or her neighborhood, and his or her actions are aimed at scaring the new family so that they will leave the neighborhood.[35] Though the majority of the cases in which individuals are federally prosecuted for acts of anti-integrationist violence involve African American victims, a few of the cases involve whites, and also members of other racial and ethnic minority groups. When members of other ethnic minority groups are attacked, the perpetrators have a similar motive to rid the neighborhood of individuals of that particular background.

In cases of anti-integrationist violence involving people of color who are not African American, the defendants' desire to preserve their whites-only space was crystal clear. For instance, the incidents that led to the government prosecution in *U.S. v. Nichols* involved an attack on a group of Hispanics who had moved to a white neighborhood in Bessemer City, North Carolina.[36] Minorities—in this case, blacks and Hispanics—had begun to move into the formerly all-white neighborhood of Michael Nichols and Shane Greene, two white men. Nichols and Greene had complained about the neighborhood's changing demographics, indicating that they had a problem with "niggers" and "spics" living in Bessemer City.[37] Witnesses also heard Nichols and Greene spewing racial epithets at African

Americans and Hispanics who lived in the neighborhood.[38] On July 30, 1999, Nichols and Greene approached Julio Sanchez while he and a friend were sitting on Sanchez's front porch. One of the men assaulted the friend and tried to hit Sanchez. Nichols and Greene left and then returned with an iron pipe, which they used to break all the windows in the front of the house, in addition to the windows of vehicles parked outside the house.[39]

One undercurrent running through these incidents is that the offenders do not want minorities in their neighborhoods because they feel that the very presence of minorities, particularly African Americans, ruins the neighborhood. Perpetrators have expressed the fear that the presence of minorities will lead to the ruin of the offender's white neighborhood. In some cases, whites who commit crimes against African American neighbors attribute problems they've seen in the neighborhood to the nearest member of a minority group. In these incidents, African Americans and, in some cases, other minorities constitute an undifferentiated mass, and a crime directed at one may be viewed by the perpetrators as helping to solve the problem. As the perpetrator in *Nichols*, described above, was vandalizing the Latino target's home and car, a witness testified that Nichols had screamed, "Go back to Mexico, you done got all our jobs."[40] Sanchez, as the target of Nichols, had invaded Nichols's white neighborhood, and his very presence symbolized white unemployment.[41]

The Impact of Incidents on Targets

Ironically, increasing tolerance nationwide makes the incidents that targets experience all the more difficult. For many contemporary targets of racial violence in the post–civil rights era who encounter the violence firsthand, the very existence of such violent hatred is stunning and shocking. Frequently, multiple incidents may have to occur before the family even realizes someone has a problem with their presence.[42] Such was the case for the Defoe family. The Defoes, a Jewish family, moved from New England to Gilbertsville,

Pennsylvania, in 2004. Mr. Defoe had been transferred, and Jocelyn Defoe indicated that she expected their life in Pennsylvania to be as uneventful as the life they lived in Massachusetts.[43] This proved impossible. After they moved into their house in Pennsylvania, it was vandalized multiple times. Less than three months after they moved in, Richard Rick, who lived less than five minutes from the Defoes, tried to burn a cross on the family's front lawn.[44] After the attempted cross burning, the Defoes prepared themselves for further incidents. "I didn't know what to say. I thought, what the heck did we do to deserve this?" said the clearly upset Jocelyn Defoe.[45]

Neighbors are similarly taken aback by acts of anti-integrationist violence. When asked to comment on a cross burning, racist graffiti, or other incidents, neighbors and others express amazement. In reacting to acts of anti-integrationist violence directed at two black women in Cleveland, for instance, the executive director of the local NAACP commented, "Something like this is not supposed to happen in 2007. . . . Those are things that we had to deal with back in the 50s and 60s and we should not have to deal with it today and the NAACP refuses to let that happen on our watch."[46] The surprise publicly expressed by those interviewed in the wake of acts of anti-integrationist violence is in line with what one might expect given the current levels of racial tolerance expressed in survey research. Disgust and shock was not the reaction of white neighbors who witnessed similar crimes in the 1950s and earlier. From the 1920s, when African American moves to white neighborhoods began to be controversial, until the late 1960s, when the Fair Housing Act was passed, angry, often stone-throwing mobs gathered in front of homes of blacks who had moved to white neighborhoods.[47]

Explaining Racial Extremism

So how can we explain contemporary racial extremism in this post–civil rights era? One explanation put forth by scholars, the averse racism theory, suggests that conflicting views, such as those suggesting equal treatment for all regardless of race and racial bias, may coexist within a particular individual.[48] Because such views are contradictory, averse racists subconsciously suppress their negative views and will not discriminate unless they can ascribe nonracial reasons to their perspectives. One method of testing such hidden racial bias is the Implicit Association Test (IAT). The IAT measures the speed of individuals' computer responses to concepts of race (black or white faces) when paired with evaluative attributes ("pleasant" or "unpleasant").[49] Researchers assume that racially biased individuals will take longer when forced to respond to a pairing that reflects a view they do not hold, for example, white=unpleasant; black=pleasant.[50] With respect to whether there has been change as a result of Obama's presidency, measures of racial bias using IAT responses taken before Obama's announcement of his candidacy for presidency and four months after Obama's first inauguration showed little evidence of change.[51]

Political scientist Vincent Hutchings obtained similar evidence regarding the lack of progress on racial change by examining the black-white divide during Obama's first presidential campaign and then after his election. Hutchings found significant divisions by race. National exit polls administered postelection revealed significant correlation between Americans' (or voters') race and the candidate they supported in the presidential election. Exit polls showed that 95 percent of blacks and approximately two-thirds of Latinos and Asian Americans voted for Barack Obama. Whites however are a much different story—the majority, some 55 percent, voted for Senator John McCain, with only 43 percent supporting Obama.[52] While 43 percent of the white vote exceeds the percentage gained by Jesse Jackson in his 1998 presidential primary (11 percent), it nevertheless still represents a black-white racial divide that exceeds 50 percentage points. Hutchings also examined surveys detailing racial policy preferences in surveys administered in 1988 and 2008 and found little change in the significant racial divides on blacks' and whites' views of fair job treatment, aid to blacks, and racial preferences.[53] Hutchings concludes that there is little "Obama Effect": "There is little evidence . . . that White liberals, defined as respondents identifying as either extremely liberal, liberal or slightly liberal, are more likely to support racially egalitarian policies in 2008 compared to 1998."[54]

Neighborhood Violence and the Tolerance-Violence Paradox

Not only are many of those who commit acts of anti-integrationist violence not extremists, many claim to not even be racists.[55] It is easy to claim to not be a racist when one articulates a nonracial reason for not wanting minorities in their neighborhood. Frequently, and this is clear from many of the perpetrators' words, the nonracial reason articulated by the perpetrators is that they feel that minorities moving in will harm their property values. The problem of African Americans moving in and destroying property values was explicit in the case of Cassandra and Edward Terry, an African American couple who moved with their two children to the Country Club of Arkansas neighborhood in Maumelle, Arkansas, in February of 2007. Within two weeks of moving in, Cassandra Terry discovered the following note in her mailbox:

> Just a note from ALL your new neighbors in the new neighborhood. This Ls [sic] a white neighborhood and if you have to choose to live in a white neighborhood ACT white not like nigger. Keep your children contained in your house and not riot [sic] hanging out in the street like gangs. You really hurt the property value of the neighborhood. We so appreciate that. Please keep to your selves . . . and not disturb anyone else. It's embarrassing enough.
> —Concerned people in the Country Club[56]

Though the note had been signed to reflect several neighbors, it was written by Shawn Simone Hardin, the Terrys' next-door neighbor, who was later indicted on federal charges.[57] As in other contemporary cases of anti-integrationist violence, there was little evidence that the Terrys' moving in affected the neighborhood's property values. They had respectable jobs (as a mental health professional and a member of the Arkansas National Guard) and received support from their neighbors after the note was publicized.[58] The neighbor who left the note claimed to have written it because the Terry clan had drifted onto her lawn when they were outside. Hardin also said she was worried about the fact that the Terry's twelve-year-old son had come over to play with her eighth-grade daughter.[59] When interviewed by the local paper she indicated that she shouldn't have said what was written in the letter, "but I was just so scared for my daughter."[60]

Though it is not always expressed as graphically as it was in the Terrys' case, perpetrators in cases of anti-integrationist violence are asserting their neighborhood—and all of the houses in it—as a white person's space. As one of the neighbors of Kelvin Williams, who was harassed by his white neighbor in Independence, Missouri, in 2005, told a police officer investigating the harassment, "This is a white man's neighborhood and he did not want any niggers living around him."[61] In the Williams and Terry cases, the perpetrators acted alone and their neighbors did not go on record as supporting the violence. This is typical, since frequently the perpetrators of such actions act alone, and their neighbors disavow connection with the incidents. In cases involving neighborhoods that have a history of segregation, where segregation is enforced by reputation and anti-integrationist violence, the idea that the neighborhood is a whites-only space may be shared by many in the neighborhood, even if they do not participate in the violence.[62] Such was the case with Sean Jenkins, who moved to a white neighborhood in the Port Richmond area of Philadelphia in 2007. Largely unbeknownst to Jenkins, the neighborhood had a history of anti-integrationist violence. Before Jenkins could move into the row house, vandals broke in, shattering the windows and defacing the walls with epithets.[63] "All niggers should be hung," said one.[64] A young white man later accosted Jenkins's girlfriend in front of the house saying, "Y'all niggers taking over the neighborhood."[65] After this incident, the couple decided not to move in.

The belief that nonwhite professionals will destroy a neighborhood seems more rational given the intense separation of private life that most whites experience today. According to analyses using 2010 census data, the average non-Hispanic white person lives in a neighborhood that is 77 percent white. Statistically, for whites then, predominately white neighborhoods are very much the norm. Even though on the face of it many workplaces may be racially integrated, workplaces are not the same as neighborhoods, which individuals may see as a private space, or sanctuary.

How can white preferences for white neighborhoods exist in light of survey responses demonstrating many whites' stated preferences for an interracial lifestyle? Research on whites' racial segregation and isolation suggests that predominately white neighborhoods exist at least in part because many whites, including white liberals, choose them. One such piece of research, conducted by Eduardo Bonilla-Silva and David Embrick, using surveys conducted as part of the Detroit Area Study (DAS), explored the disjuncture between respondents' abstract views on social distance issues and the lives that respondents were actually living. Though a large number of the respondents expressed racially tolerant views, their daily lives did not reflect this: "When students were asked for the five people with whom they interact with most on a daily basis, 67.7 percent stated that none of these five people were black."[66] Such was the case for other measures of social distance—having close black friends (87 percent indicated that none of their three closest friends were black); having invited a black person to lunch or dinner recently (67.7 percent said no); and ever having had a romantic relationship with someone black (89 percent never had).[67] The racial isolation of whites was confirmed in interviews, with only four of the forty-one individuals interviewed having lived in neighborhoods with a significant black or minority presence (defined as a neighborhood where at least 20 percent of the residents were nonwhite).[68] Whites' separation from people of other racial backgrounds, the authors argue, helps create a sense of racial solidarity (i.e., "we whites").[69]

TAKING OFF OUR ROSE-COLORED GLASSES

With respect to housing integration, the America we talk about is quite different from the one experienced by minorities, who either find themselves confined to minority neighborhoods or harassed while attempting to integrate white neighborhoods. When will Americans' idealized notions of race relations change? It may not happen anytime soon. Postracial America is the dream that we would prefer to believe, and the one that many would rather see depicted.

The events surrounding the 2005 ABC television "reality" show *Welcome to the Neighborhood* are one example offering a snapshot of this postracial ideal and commitment. The show examined the process by which three white, conservative Christian families in Austin, Texas, evaluated seven minority and nontraditional families for a position as their neighbor.[70] The family selected would win a suburban house.[71] Six episodes of the show were taped. According to press reports, though there were moments of bigotry over the course of the episodes, in the end the neighbors overcame their prejudices and selected a gay white couple with an adopted black child.[72]

Even though it showed the mildest version of the difficulties that can occur when housing is racially integrated, *Welcome to the Neighborhood* was canceled before it even aired because civil rights groups threatened the network with a housing discrimination lawsuit.[73] Those civil rights groups were correct; selecting one's neighbors based on invidious characteristics may be a violation of the Fair Housing Act. The cancellation of the show, however, leaves most Americans with no picture of some of the troubling truths. The too-little-traveled road to racial integration can be fraught, and may be marred by discomforts and harassment. Minorities who have traveled this road and their supporters may ultimately have found more protection in being forewarned.

9

AN OFFICER AND A GENTLEMAN

Angela Onwuachi-Willig

Conscious racism—a person's surface racial attitudes as well as the actions that result from those attitudes—has undoubtedly diminished over the past generation. This decrease in conscious racism has led many to contend that our society has moved beyond its old racial divisions and to make such claims without acknowledging the harm of unconscious or implicit biases. Unconscious racial biases are those prejudices and stereotypes that people are unaware they hold and that, in many cases, do not comport with their own values and beliefs regarding race and equality.

Our failure as a society to confront our own unconscious biases has prevented us from truly improving our nation's race relations. This essay exposes the ways in which we can begin to move beyond racism by acknowledging, confronting, and analyzing our own unconscious racial biases. Specifically, this essay examines the 2009 arrest of Henry Louis Gates Jr., a fifty-nine-year-old black professor at Harvard, by Sergeant James Crowley, a white officer who had lectured about the harms of racial profiling, as a means of demonstrating how Crowley, a man with considerable antiracist credentials, could have responded to Gates with actions that seem to manifest race prejudice.

A TALE OF TWO CITIZENS

On July 16, 2009, Crowley arrested Gates at his home in Cambridge, Massachusetts.[1] Crowley was responding to the report of a possible break-in at a Harvard-owned home. When Crowley arrived at the house, he questioned Gates about his presence in the home. Gates responded with his concerns about being targeted because he was black. Gates also showed Crowley his Harvard identification card and his driver's license. In the end, Gates was booked, placed in handcuffs, and brought to jail for "exhibiting loud and tumultuous behavior."[2]

Other than these facts, the two men's reports of the arrest diverged completely. Crowley contended that he approached Gates at the house because a female caller told him that "she observed what appeared to be two black males with backpacks on the porch." According to Crowley, Gates responded with impassioned charges of racism. Crowley also wrote, "While I was led to believe that Gates was lawfully in the residence, I was quite surprised and confused with the behavior he exhibited toward me." According to Crowley, after Gates showed him his identification, he radioed his findings, called for backup, and began to leave; but Gates continued to yell at him and ask him for his name, within public view. As a result, Crowley explained, he arrested Gates because of the "tumultuous" behavior he exhibited in public.[3]

Gates's version of the event differs from Crowley's in important respects. According to Gates, when Crowley approached him, he told Crowley that he was a Harvard faculty member who lived in the house. According to Gates, Crowley then asked him whether he could prove that he lived there and taught at Harvard. Gates handed the officer his Harvard University identification, which includes his photograph, and his Massachusetts driver's license, which includes both his photograph and address. Thereafter, Gates indicated that he made several requests to Crowley for his name and badge number, but that Crowley did not provide any of the requested information. According to Gates, when he stepped onto his front porch, Crowley handcuffed him and placed him under arrest.[4] Gates denied any loud and tumultuous behavior.

Later reports revealed that Lucia Whalen, the person who made the 9-1-1 call, indicated that the two men on Gates's porch could be residents who were trying to push open a stuck door and, more so, did not identify the men as two black men with backpacks. Only when prompted by the 9-1-1 operator did Whalen mention race or ethnicity at all, and even then, mentioned only that one of the men may be Hispanic.

THE BLACK AND WHITE OF IT

The Gates arrest elicited numerous responses from the public, ultimately resulting in the police department's description of the incident as "regrettable and unfortunate" and the department's decision to drop all criminal charges against Gates. Still, Crowley refused to apologize to Gates for what he referred to as doing his job, and Gates refused to apologize to Crowley for what he referred to as asserting his rights in his own home. People of all races expressed outrage about the arrest, just as many others, specifically whites, expressed support for Crowley's actions.

The General Public

Public responses diverged along racial lines. Many blacks and Latinos expressed their belief that Gates's arrest reflected a broader problem of police harassment, profiling, and targeting based on race. For example, S. Allen Counter, a black professor at Harvard Medical School, stated, "[Gates] and I both raised the question of if he had been a white professor, whether this kind of thing would have happened to him, that they arrested him without any corroborating evidence. . . . It brings up the question of whether black males are being targeted by Cambridge police for harassment."[5] Counter had been stopped in 2004 by police, who had mistaken him for a robbery suspect as he crossed Harvard Yard and threatened to arrest him when he could not produce identification.

On the other hand, many whites expressed support for Crowley or expressed concern about jumping to conclusions regarding the role of race in the arrest. Whites, who often have a different level of trust for the police than blacks and Latinos,[6] could not understand why Gates questioned the officer at all. For instance, as Huffington Post writer Martha St. Jean noted in her article "Race in America: Comments on the Arrest of Henry Louis Gates Jr.," one man on Boston.com blamed Gates for the arrest, even pointing to Obama as a reason to believe that race was a nonfactor. The man wrote, "Enough of throwing down the race card. . . . We have a Black President now, so that tired old ship has sailed. The guy got indignant like any self-important Harvard professor does, pulled the old 'Do you know who I am?' routine, and got arrested as a result."[7] Another white person rejected race as a factor, too. He declared on Aol.com: "I am WHITE and if I did what Gates did I would have been arrested also. I am tired of the RACE CARD being played EVERY time a black person is arrested/questioned or ANYTHING else that happens with the police. I am not saying that there aren't 'BAD' cops but this is getting ridiculous."[8]

The Powers That Be: Obama Adds His Voice

Public officials even chimed in. For example, Deval Patrick, the governor of Massachusetts, explained, "In some ways, this is every black man's nightmare and a reality for black men."[9] Patrick, who is black, also asserted, "You ought to be able to raise your voice in your own house without risk of arrest."[10]

Even the president of the United States, Barack Obama, offered his opinion. While indicating that he had no idea what role race played in the arrest, President Obama asserted that the Cambridge police "acted stupidly" in arresting Gates in his own house *after Gates had proved that he lived there.* Obama stated:

Now, I don't know, not having been there and not seeing all the facts, what role race played in that. But I think it's fair to say, number one, any of us would be pretty angry; number two, that the Cambridge Police acted stupidly in arresting somebody *when there was already proof that they were in their own home*; and number three, what I think we know separate and apart from this incident is that there is a long history in this country of African-Americans and Latinos being stopped by law enforcement disproportionately. That's just a fact. . . .

And even when there are honest misunderstandings, the fact that blacks and Hispanics are picked up more frequently and often time for no cause casts suspicion even when there is good cause. And that's why I think the more that we're working with local law enforcement to improve policing techniques . . . the safer everybody is going to be.[11]

Obama's words sparked a firestorm. Many people expressed their outrage at Obama's comments, and, as suggested by a Pew Research Center poll that focused solely on the opinions of whites toward Obama and the arrest, those divisions fell across racial lines. By a two-to-one margin—45 percent to 22 percent—whites of all political affiliations disapproved of Obama's handling of the situation.[12]

Obama later apologized for his choice of words, but still continued to receive flak. The Cambridge Police Department insisted that Obama apologize, even as Crowley refused to apologize to Gates. Ultimately, Obama scheduled a private outing at the White House (now known as BeerGate), where he, Gates, Vice President Joseph Biden, and Crowley could meet, drink a beer, smooth matters over, and try to put the incident behind them.

In all, many citizens shied away from discussing the Gates arrest as an incident with potential racial implications. More than that, and in line with an emerging form of postracial racism that denies the reality of differing experiences based on race, many people refused to acknowledge that race may have influenced how individuals, including both Gates and Crowley, saw and interpreted the Gates arrest. The fact is that black and brown people, because of their personal experiences, are less likely to trust the police and the criminal justice system than white people are. This distrust extends back to the days of unruly mobs, which were often led and protected by police as the mobs ignored the law and lynched black and brown men. It continues all the way to today's "random" stops and searches of black and brown people on highways and roads, in airports, on the border, and in their homes.[13]

A Gallup survey conducted the year before Gates's arrest captured such differing perceptions of police fairness by race. In that survey, when asked how much confidence they had in local police to treat whites and blacks equally, only 45 percent of blacks said they had a fair or great deal of confidence compared to 81 percent of non-Hispanic whites.[14] Another study by the New Jersey attorney general revealed that blacks and Latinos represented 77.2 percent of searches on highways and roads.[15] Related to that finding, another study found that these high percentages for searches of blacks and Latinos are less likely to yield evidence of criminal activity than the less-frequent stops of whites. Specifically, the study found that, in Los Angeles, frisked blacks are 42 percent less likely than frisked whites to be found with weapons, 25 percent less likely to be found with drugs, and 33 percent less likely to be found with other contraband.[16] Surveys in Massachusetts, the home of the Gates arrest, found that 45 percent of whites felt that race relations had improved in the last five years, while only 16 percent of blacks agreed.[17]

Yet, as far as the Gates arrest was concerned, a number of whites insisted on ignoring these racial differences, an insistence that resulted in the loss of yet another opportunity to have an honest conversation about racism. As a society, we failed to confront and challenge our own conscious and unconscious biases and, as a result, we lost an important chance to really begin to overcome our nation's troubled racial past (and present).

LAW AND ORDER: A SPECIAL VICTIM

On top of the refusal to see the Gates arrest as likely influenced by racism via unconscious bias, many went so far as to reframe the incident to mark Crowley as the victim. Commentators pointed to Crowley as a victim of a society that had become too politically correct—as someone who had been unfairly targeted as racist. Most of all, the various reactions from many white supporters of Crowley deprived our society of a "teachable moment" that could have shed light on many significant topics, including (1) the role of unconscious bias in the disproportionate racial profiling and targeting of blacks and Latinos; (2) the underlying assumptions and biases, both conscious and unconscious, in the defenses of Crowley; and (3) the impact of racially influenced targeting and arrests on the lives of black men in the United States.

White Man's Burden

First, the focus on Crowley as a victim who had been wrongfully tagged as racist deprived the public of an important lesson concerning the role of unconscious bias and of how everyone, including people with good intentions who consciously believe in racial equality, can fall prey to unconsciously internalized stereotypes. In other words, societal reluctance to view the Gates arrest as influenced by race prevented us from learning about and understanding the powerful impact of unconscious stereotypes on all of us, even those of us who profess a commitment to racial equality. As Professor Angela Harris has explained, "We carry [stereotypes] in our heads. . . . Asian men are seen as smart with no social skills. Black men are seen as violent criminals. And people act and respond, based on those stereotypes."[18] Similarly, in her research, Professor Mahzarin Banaji has found that whites more quickly associate black faces with negative adjectives and white faces with positive adjectives and that whites also more quickly associate black faces with harmful weapons than white faces. That Crowley may have acted on such unconscious biases in arresting Gates does not make him a rac-ist in the Jim Crow, segregationist sense; it just means that he, like so many of us, may have internalized racial stereotypes that "can nega-tively and nonconsciously affect [his] behavior toward blacks." [19]

In fact, there is no reason to think that Crowley is anything other than what he suggests—a good man who does not harbor preju-dice against black people. There is no reason to think that he is the "monster or the bigot or racist that [some] portrayed [him] to be," [20] but like so many people, he may harbor unconscious thoughts that conflict with his conscious beliefs.

Given the pervasive, negative images and stereotypes about blacks as criminals in the media, it would be difficult for Crowley, without explicit resistance, not to be exposed to such negative images and implicit stereotypes and then act upon them in performing his job. More important, as Professor L. Song Richardson has explained, "In the policing context, implicit stereotypes can cause an officer who harbors no conscious racial animosity and who rejects using race as a proxy for criminality to unintentionally treat individuals dif-ferently based solely upon their physical appearance. . . . Even when officers are not intentionally engaged in conscious racial profiling, unconscious biases can lead to a lower threshold for finding identi-cal behavior suspicious when engaged in by blacks than by whites." [21] The critical problem in the Gates arrest was that due to racial ste-reotypes Gates was not given the same benefit of the doubt that a similarly situated, fifty-nine-year-old white professor (with a cane) would have been given. Professor Michael Eric Dyson explained this problem well, stating:

> Had Gates been a white professor trying to get inside his home, and called on his driver to help him jar his door open, he probably wouldn't have as readily aroused the suspicion of neighbors. And when police arrived to check out the prem-ises, they probably wouldn't have been nearly as ready to be-lieve the worst about the occupant of a home who clearly wasn't engaged in a criminal act.

Whatever one believes about what happened, Gates clearly wasn't the beneficiary of the benefit of the doubt, a reasonable expectation since he posed no visible threat.[22]

Many empirical studies support this argument, confirming that individuals, even children, evaluate blacks more negatively than whites who are engaged in the exact same behavior. For instance, Professor Richardson reported in one study, "black and white school-age children rated an ambiguous bump in the hallway as more aggressive when performed by a black actor rather than a white actor," and in another study "using buttons labeled 'shoot' and 'don't shoot' as a weapon's trigger, the nonconscious activation of negative black stereotypes caused individuals more quickly to shoot a potentially hostile black than a potentially hostile white."[23] Even Crowley's own words suggest that he did not give Gates the benefit of the doubt during their interaction, despite having reviewed two forms of identification. Crowley explained, "I was not aware of who [P]rofessor Gates was. And when I read the name off the card, it wasn't like I said, 'Oh wow, that's [P]rofessor Gates.'"[24] It thus appears that Crowley did not take Gates's possession of a Harvard University identification card with a photograph as a sufficient basis for assuming he was who he said he was.

Furthermore, because of our fear of confronting our own racial demons and the resulting resistance to discuss race honestly, we as a society failed to fully comprehend how unconscious biases against blacks in this country could have influenced the arrest, leaving Crowley to expect Gates to be more deferential to him precisely because of his race. To say that Gates's arrest was merely the act of an overzealous cop may not sufficiently explain the full power dynamic here. It could have been that Crowley unconsciously reacted to Gates because he was not remaining in his expected place as a black man and was perceived as uppity. Moreover, as Professor Frank Cooper explains in his article "Who's the Man? Masculinities and Police Stops,"[25] race often intersects with masculinity in a police stop, resulting in a masculinity contest, meaning, "a confrontation where one person will boost his internal or attributed masculine esteem at the expense of the other."[26] For example, with regard to race, Crowley may have questioned Gates longer, even after seeing proof of residence, because Gates appeared racially out of place as a black man in a nice house in Cambridge. Moreover, as Cooper suggests with an example of one type of masculinity contest, Crowley's ultimate reaction to Gates may have "stem[med] from the need to dominate other men in general and to denigrate contrast figures [such as black men] in particular."[27] Gates, in turn, may have responded as he did to Crowley to reassert the masculinity that he, a black man, felt deprived of within his home precisely because of the encounter.

Finally, what we as a society failed to learn was how understanding unconscious biases can help to fill in gaps about what ultimately caused Crowley to arrest Gates for "exhibiting loud and tumultuous behavior" in a period of time that could have been no longer than six minutes. After all, the 9-1-1 call came in around 12:45 P.M., and by 12:51 P.M., Gates was being led to jail. As journalist Bob Herbert explained, "If Professor Gates ranted and raved at the cop who entered his home uninvited with a badge, a gun and an attitude, he didn't rant and rave for long. . . . Gates was never a danger to anyone. At worst, if you believe in a police report, he yelled at Sergeant Crowley."[28] The obvious question, then, is: did Crowley, as a result of unconscious bias, view Gates's resistance as more threatening or disorderly because of his blackness? Again, Richardson's work on implicit bias and police stops is instructive. As she has explained:

When officers approach an individual to confirm or dispel their suspicions, implicit biases can cause officers to behave aggressively without realizing it. The confronted individual may respond in kind, fulfilling officers' beliefs that the individual is suspicious and aggressive. . . . All the while, officers will be unaware that the behavorial effects of their implicit bias triggered the entire chain of events.[29]

In essence, Crowley's unconscious biases may have affected how he approached Gates, which in turn affected how Gates responded, which ultimately led to Gates's arrest, public outrage, and an ending without serious discussion and reflection at BeerGate.

For most Americans, there is no dispute about whether we should work to undo the negative stereotypes and images of blacks that have been internalized in our hearts and minds, but unlearning those stereotypes and images first requires acknowledging them, including how they can be unconsciously held. The knee-jerk reaction of many white Americans to insist that race could not have influenced the arrest and to defend Crowley as one who is uninfluenced by racism deprived us of a good chance to see the consequence of unconscious bias and, more so, the real need for all of us—who are mostly nonracist, well-intentioned people—to unlearn them.

What's Wrong with a Black Mouth?

In fact, the defenses of Crowley as a white victim of political correctness came with their own set of biases that failed to challenge unconscious racism or acknowledge its power. Take, for example, the claim that Crowley could not have acted upon racism in arresting Gates because he had performed CPR on Reggie Lewis, a black professional athlete who died during a basketball practice, and because Crowley "put his mouth on" Lewis.[30] Of course, the first question that should spring to mind is: what's wrong with a black mouth? After all, Crowley, like many police officers, must be a brave man who works to save the lives of others. His job is to protect and serve, and there is no doubt that he and other police officers are heroic in these feats.

But why is it not enough to assert that Crowley performed CPR on Lewis to save his life? Why the need to also indicate that Crowley *"put his mouth"* on a black man's mouth?[31] The act of performing CPR on a black mouth is only noteworthy if one has an unconscious or even conscious bias in thinking that there is something extraordinary or even profane about being willing to put one's white mouth to a black mouth, especially given that the very act is implicit in noting that someone performed CPR at all.

Similarly, the defense of Crowley's actions as nonracist because of his work in teaching a new-cadet course about racial profiling lacked reflection. There was no close examination of how a good officer like Crowley—one whose actions indicate a commitment to eliminating racial profiling—may nevertheless fall prey to unconscious racial biases. Again, think back to Crowley's report of the arrest, where he indicated his surprise at Gates's reaction to him. In his report, Crowley wrote, "While I was led to believe that Gates was lawfully in the residence, I was quite surprised and confused with the behavior he exhibited toward me."[32] But given Crowley's knowledge of racial profiling, it is surprising that he could not understand the frustration of Gates, a law-abiding and extremely successful fifty-nine-year-old black man with a cane, at being questioned about potential criminality in his *own* home. At the very least, one would expect that an officer who teaches about the harms of racial profiling could put himself in the shoes of a black man who believes he is being unfairly racially profiled. It is even more surprising that Crowley then called for more backup, even though he had seen Gates's identification cards, believed that Gates lived there, and indicated that he was leaving the house. Rather than viewing Crowley's teaching experience as evidence to absolve him of any claims of racism, one must wonder why journalists did not engage in a more complex view of the arrest, one that noted the power of unconscious racial biases in our society such that even a good officer like Crowley, who knew enough to educate others about the dangers of racial profiling, could not escape their grip.

Additionally, the defense of Crowley's actions as free of racism based on the presence of a black police officer, Sergeant Leon Lashley, at the scene was simplistic at best. Such a defense is based on the mistaken belief that racism is acceptable or implicitly sanctioned when a member of the oppressed and targeted group is physically present but silent. Moreover, this defense failed to unearth not only the complexities of racism but also the way in which racism, especially in team work environments, provides incentives for blacks to distance themselves from other "troublemaking" blacks. For one thing, that particular defense fails to acknowledge that blacks also discriminate against blacks. Like whites, blacks internalize negative stereotypes about themselves, and in fact, in group settings, may have greater incentives than whites to distinguish themselves from "troublemaking" blacks in order to avoid ostracization from their work group.[33] Such incentives are especially high in the police department, where blue is viewed as the most important color in the unit.

Finally, our reluctance as a society to acknowledge the role that race may have played in the Gates arrest left us with no means for learning how unconscious bias may have affected what Crowley heard in Lucia Whalen's call for help. As Richardson has explained, studies show that just "thinking about crime can trigger nonconscious thoughts about blacks, which in turn activates negative black stereotypes. . . . Disturbingly, not only does seeing a black individual bring negative racial stereotypes to mind nonconsciously, but simply thinking about crime triggers implicit thoughts about blacks in police officers and civilians alike."[34] The insistence that Crowley was simply doing his job in settling down an unruly citizen made it such that we as a society never fully interrogated Crowley's police report claim that Whalen identified "two black men with backpacks" on the porch of Gates's residence when she called. Instead, newspaper articles simply noted the contradictory facts between Crowley's police report and Whalen's 9-1-1 call. While the media reports cleared the name of Whalen, who had been accused of engaging in racial profiling herself, they did not ask why Crowley had indicated otherwise in his official police report, and they rarely searched for any meaning between the two differing factual accounts.

In the best-case scenario, these differences between Whalen's 9-1-1 tapes and Crowley's written police report expose Crowley again as someone who is unconsciously influenced, like so many of us, by racial stereotypes. If his merely thinking about a potential crime unconsciously triggered an image of black men in his mind, that information is critical to know, as only through acknowledgment can we undo such effects of bias. More important, these differing factual accounts provide important insights into the disproportionate number of law-abiding black men who are stopped, questioned, arrested, and, in the worst cases, shot by the police. The fact is that Crowley's report suggests that he went to Gates's house, without any suggestion or prompting, with the image of two black men in his mind. That kind of presumption has huge implications for the administration of justice or injustice by police. Our failure as a society to acknowledge it represents a lost opportunity for a huge teachable moment.

Critical Masses

In addition, general public resistance to discussing the Gates arrest as an event influenced by race left us without any opportunity to explore deeper issues concerning the experiences that black men without Gates's status routinely face. The fact remains that many black men who experience racial profiling and harassment by the police will not have the resources of Gates. Gates had the best protection that prominence and money can buy. Gates was picked up from the police station by Lawrence Bobo, another prominent Harvard professor; had first-rate legal representation from renowned Harvard Law professor Charles Ogletree; and received nationwide attention as a result of his arrest.

For the vast majority of black Americans, however, the ultimate result of profiling, harassment, and arrest based on unconscious and, at times, conscious racial bias is much more severe. The end result has been the hyperincarceration of black and brown men, who have been linked to criminality with prevalent media images and social stereotypes. As Georgetown University professor Paul Butler proclaimed, "A black man born in the 1990's can expect, statistically, that he will be arrested at some point in his life. For many, it's the start of a downward cycle that includes unemployment and a broken family. . . . Cops don't encourage respect for the law when they treat even law-abiding citizens like criminals."[35]

Blacklash

Finally, the strong reaction by some whites against acknowledging the Gates arrest as an event influenced by race, including unconscious bias, deprived our society of the opportunity to further eliminate existing racial divides through understanding and honest conversation. Take, for example, the public outrage at President Obama's comment that police "acted stupidly" in arresting an *older, disabled gentleman* at his own house *even* after he had produced sufficient identification. This reaction exposed the manner in which racial minorities are, unlike whites (who also belong to a racial group), viewed as interested and biased, especially in their roles as public leaders.

Because Obama is black, when he spoke about the Gates arrest, he was not viewed simply as a leader whose moral guidance had been sought on an issue of public concern (or even just as someone who is biased in favor of his friend), but instead was accused by many whites of taking sides based solely on race. For Obama, his comments about the arrest marked him *first* as a black man, then as the president. Unlike his predecessors, Obama, because he is black, simply could not condemn Crowley's actions in arresting Gates without being identified as racially biased. The public reaction to Obama's comment revealed that our society has not moved beyond race, even in how it sees its president. In fact, it reflected some whites' anger at the fact that Obama's presence in the White House could stand for more than a symbol of our sordid racial past overcome—that it also could mean that the president, who has lived a different set of racial experiences than his forty-two predecessors, may actually understand certain facts and events from a distinctly different lens in part because of his race. The fact is that Obama, a black man, has likely been racially profiled in his lifetime and may have had some awareness, whether stated or not, that race could have played a role in the interaction between Gates and Crowley. The reaction to Obama's comments demonstrates, in part, why so many of us are afraid to engage in honest discussions about race and racism: we don't want to endure the extremely negative reactions from others. As journalist Bob Herbert contended, "The message that has gone out to the public is that powerful African American leaders like Mr. Gates and President Obama will be very publicly slapped down for speaking up and speaking out about police misbehavior, and that the proper response if you think you are being unfairly targeted by the police because of your race is to chill." [36]

CONCLUSION

In all, when the Gates arrest exploded onto the scene, we failed as a society to use it as a moment to move closer toward becoming a truly postracial society by actually acknowledging and truthfully discussing race and racism. We should strive for better. Striving for better means that we face fears of our own conscious and unconscious racial biases and that we work hard to combat them. Achieving better means admitting that we are not living in a society that has put race prejudice behind it—that racism, both conscious and unconscious, is alive and well. Doing better means understanding that each of us carries stereotypes in our heads; accepting, rather than rejecting, what we score on the Implicit Bias Tests at https://implicit.harvard.edu/implicit/; and resisting the impulse to allow our fears to enable us to miss one more moment in which we can learn about and from ourselves, others, our country, and its racial legacy. We would expect no less from an officer and a gentleman, and we should expect no less from ourselves. As Harvard University president Drew Gilpin Faust declared, "Legacies of racial injustice remain an unfortunate and painful part of the American experience, and inform our views, our actions, and their consequences. As President Obama has remarked, ours is an imperfect union, and while perfect justice may always elude us, we can and must do better." [37]

Thanks to Dean Gail Agrawal and the Kierscht family for their research support. My research assistants, Christie Canales and Matt McMurrer, provided invaluable assistance. I also thank Shanna Benjamin, Frank Cooper, Karla Erickson, Aya Gruber, Kevin Johnson, Lakesia Johnson, Michelle Nasser, and L. Song Richardson for conversation and comments. Finally, I give special thanks to my husband, Jacob, and our children, Elijah, Bethany, and Solomon.

10

OBAMA IS NO KING

The Fracturing of the Black Prophetic Tradition

Glenn C. Loury

In breaking through the skin-color barrier in American politics, does Barack Hussein Obama bring with him a distinctive African American moral vision—does he somehow embody an alternative version of American history? Some say so. They anoint the ascendancy of President Obama with world-historic significance linked to his race: a black man, an African American, a son of Africa has risen to occupy the highest office in the land! Hallelujah!

At Obama's first inauguration, the soaring close of the Reverend Joseph Lowery's benediction had the new president smiling and applauding. This famed black preacher, and longtime leader of the Southern Christian Leadership Conference after Martin Luther King's death, exalted the humble in America's history—its minorities, black, brown, yellow, and red—and humbled the exalted. He dared to hope that "white will embrace what is right."[1] Joseph Lowery nearly stole the show on that day in January 2009, confirming for many the glow of a blessing on a new era. Now that President Obama has won re-election, the iconic character of his ascendancy has been given an official seal of approval by the American people. We are living, for better or worse, in the Age of Obama.

Have we, in fact, entered a new era? More pointedly, do the election and re-election of Barack Obama constitute some kind of fulfillment of Martin Luther King's famous dream? I think the answer to this question must be a resounding "No!" Obama's election has neither fulfilled King's dream nor does it usher in any sort of new era.

In what follows I argue that the prophetic tradition of critical political thought and faith-based moral witness out of which the Reverend Dr. Martin Luther King Jr. emerged, and which he embodied, is radically at odds with both President Obama's electoral ambitions and his exercise of the powers of office. Neither is this tradition compatible with the president's rhetoric concerning the moral significance of his ascendancy. For the tradition of social criticism that emerged over the generations from the suffering of the slaves, and that gathered strength from the unrequited hopes of the freedmen, has always and necessarily been keenly aware of the moral ambiguity of the exercise of American power in the world. No mere politician—not even one as gifted at oratory as Obama—can afford to give public voice to such critical skepticism about the American project. And yet, to achieve the historical rightness of national conduct for which King gave his life, it is essential to challenge publicly the prototypically American boast that this nation stands as a moral exemplar.

First, I want to acknowledge the truly historic nature of Obama's election and the powerful hope for the possibilities for real change that he has brought to our nation. It is often said that the United States of America is a country defined not by kinship, ethnicity, religion, or tribal connection, but by ideas—ideas about freedom, democracy, and the self-evident truths that "all persons are created equal, and are endowed by their creator with certain inalienable rights," to quote from Thomas Jefferson's Declaration of Independence.

Another plain fact, too often forgotten, is that America is, always has been, and always will be a nation of immigrants. So, in November 2008 this nation of immigrants elected a son of Africa—a black man whose father was born in Kenya and who goes by the name Barack *Hussein* Obama—to be our forty-fourth president. "Historic" hardly begins to describe just how momentous, how remarkable, and how improbable is President Obama's achievement. From now on, whenever Europeans complain to me about the flaws of American society—and there are many—I can respond by saying, "No, America is not perfect. But, please, can you show me your black president (or prime minister)?!"

As a black man who grew to maturity on the South Side of Chicago in the 1960s and who was inspired by the words and deeds of King, I could not help but feel a sense of personal joy at Obama's triumph. Something profound has happened in America, of this there can be no doubt. Also, I will confess something: I was one of those cynics who didn't believe it possible—who thought the "audacity of hope" was just an empty phrase. Even as I witnessed millions of believers rallying around this cause, even as I saw people of all races bending themselves to this historic task, even as I observed the vast increase in voter registration in African American communities and among the young all across the land—I nevertheless remained doubtful. It did not seem possible to me that the deep structure of American power would permit the ascent of this son of Africa and America to its pinnacle. But, I was wrong, thank God.

So, notwithstanding the somewhat caustic nature of what I argue in this essay, I celebrate the fact that America has twice elected this eloquent and brilliant young black man, this representative of the Chicago neighborhoods that I have known so well, this usurper of power from a complacent establishment, this proponent of "change," as president of the United States of America. Whenever I reflect on this fact, I just want to shout, "Hallelujah!"

Nevertheless, I worry about what Obama's personal success could imply for the future of the black prophetic tradition. Moreover, I am skeptical about the claims of this president of the United States—who happens to be an African American—to a connection with that tradition. I speak here not about his personal views, as a black man and/or as a Christian believer, but rather about his role as the occupant of a very special, very powerful office, with all of the awesome responsibilities which that entails. I rather doubt that these are commensurate matters at all—the black prophetic tradition on the one hand, and the exercise of executive power on the other. I doubt that they are denominated in the same units of currency, so to speak. That is, I doubt whether the black prophetic tradition has much to do with the exercise of the powers of the office of the presidency.

What do I mean by "the black prophetic tradition"? And, how

does Obama's ascendancy "fracture" it? To see what I am getting at here, consider the following quotations from two speeches, one given by King in 1967 and the other by Obama in 2009.

First, here is Obama in Oslo accepting the 2009 Nobel Peace Prize:

> We must begin by acknowledging the hard truth: We will not eradicate violent conflict in our lifetimes. There will be times when nations—acting individually or in concert—will find the use of force not only necessary but morally justified. I make this statement mindful of what Martin Luther King Jr. said in this same ceremony years ago: "Violence never brings permanent peace. It solves no social problem: it merely creates new and more complicated ones." As someone who stands here as a direct consequence of Dr. King's life work, I am living testimony to the moral force of non-violence. I know there's nothing weak, nothing passive, nothing naïve, in the creed and lives of Gandhi and King.
>
> But as a head of state sworn to protect and defend my nation, I cannot be guided by their examples alone. I face the world as it is, and cannot stand idle in the face of threats to the American people. For make no mistake: Evil does exist in the world. . . . To say that force may sometimes be necessary is not a call to cynicism—it is a recognition of history; the imperfections of man and the limits of reason. . . . But the world must remember that it was not simply international institutions—not just treaties and declarations—that brought stability to a post–World War II world. Whatever mistakes we have made, the plain fact is this: The United States of America has helped underwrite global security for more than six decades with the blood of our citizens and the strength of our arms.[2]

By contrast, here is King denouncing the Vietnam War at Riverside Church in New York City on April 4, 1967:

As if the weight of such a commitment to the life and health of America were not enough, another burden of responsibility was placed upon me in 1964. And I cannot forget that the Nobel Prize for Peace was also a commission, a commission to work harder than I had ever worked before for the brotherhood of man. This is a calling that takes me beyond national allegiances. But even if it were not present, I would yet have to live with the meaning of my commitment to the ministry of Jesus Christ. To me, the relationship of this ministry to the making of peace is so obvious that I sometimes marvel at those who ask me why I am speaking against the war. Could it be that they do not know that the Good News was meant for all men—for communist and capitalist, for their children and ours, for black and for white, for revolutionary and conservative? Have they forgotten that my ministry is in obedience to the one who loved his enemies so fully that he died for them? What then can I say to the Vietcong or to Castro or to Mao as a faithful minister of this one? Can I threaten them with death or must I not share with them my life? . . .

This I believe to be the privilege and the burden of all of us who deem ourselves bound by allegiances and loyalties which are broader and deeper than nationalism and which go beyond our nation's self-defined goals and positions. We are called to speak for the weak, for the voiceless, for the victims of our nation, for those it calls "enemy," for no document from human hands can make these humans any less our brothers.[3]

So, here we can see the two greatest African American leaders of the past half century as they address themselves to the gravest public question of our time—that of war and peace. My, what a difference forty years can make!

King is a black American prophet standing squarely within the tradition of social criticism that I wish to defend here. Obama is not. This difference, I will argue, matters a great deal.

I see the black prophetic tradition as embodying an outsider's and underdog's critical view about the national narrative of the United States of America. It is, to be concrete, a historical counternarrative—one, for example, that sees the dispossession of the native people of North America as the great historic crime that it was; one that looks back on the bombing of Hiroshima with feelings of horror and national shame. It is an insistence that American democracy—which of course has always been a complicated political compact, often serving the interests of the powerful at the expense of the weak—live up to the true meaning of our espoused civic creed. It is an understanding that struggle, resistance, and protest are the only ways to bring this about. And it is the recognition that even in the late twentieth and early twenty-first century, America has yet to fully do so.

The black prophetic tradition is antitriumphalist vis-à-vis America's role in the world, and it is deeply suspicious of the "city on a hill" rhetoric of self-congratulation to which American politicians, including President Obama, are so often inclined. It is a doggedly critical assessment of what Americans do, an assessment that sympathizes in a deep way with the struggles of those who are dispossessed: the stateless Palestinians in the Middle East today, for instance, or the blacks at the southern tip of Africa three decades ago. This is a tradition of moral witness within American historical experience that I associate with the antislavery movement of the nineteenth century and the civil rights movement of the twentieth century. It is a tradition that views "collateral damage"—where civilians are killed by U.S. military operations—as not simply the unavoidable cost of doing the business of national defense in the modern world, but rather as a deeply problematic offense against a righteousness toward which we ought to aspire. What I am calling the black prophetic tradition also reflects a universal theory of freedom—one with a strong antiimperialist, antiracist, and antimilitarist tilt.

What, then, is President Obama's relationship to this tradition? What, in this regard, are we entitled to expect from him? I have concluded that *as president* his connection to this great moral tradition is tenuous, at best. More crucially, we would be foolish to expect much at all from him in this vein. President of the United States is an office. The office has its own imperatives quite apart from an individual's personal beliefs. When one is sitting with military advisers and is told that a Predator drone operation against a "terrorist" operative in the tribal regions of Pakistan awaits one's authorization, then one has to make that call. Such a moment as that is no time to be quoting Martin Luther King or Frederick Douglass, or to be talking about the tradition of critical political thought which has been nurtured by black people in America for centuries.[4] Rather, at a time like that, one simply has to decide whether or not one is going to kill that person. The person who is the commander in chief of the United States of America, regardless of his individual biography, when placed in that position and forced to carry out those acts, needs to be viewed with clear-eyed realism for who and what he is: namely, in the context of the example at hand, the commander in chief of the largest military force in the history of human experience. Such a person ought not to be viewed through a rose-tinted glass, with some romantic and unrealistic narrative.

So, the question I wish to pose is this: what does the tradition of black protest and struggle in America have to do with the exercise of the powers of the office of the presidency? I suspect that the answer to that question is, very little at all. Romantic idealists argue that surely his biography, his history, even his skin color informs the man who is now president. But that merely shifts the question to an inquiry about the extent that personality and individual morality can exert real leverage over the exercise of such an office as the American presidency.

Here is an analogy to ponder: a woman rises to the position of CEO at a large corporation—for instance, Exxon-Mobil or Bank of America. What real difference should we expect this to make—for matters like the environment, or economic equity, or corporate governance? At the end of the day that job is about making money for the shareholders. It is not about anything else. It is not about saving the planet, or integrating the workforce, or ending poverty. It is about making profits for the shareholders. Now this woman—with her unique experiences and inspiring biography—may approach the exercise of her responsibilities in that office with a slightly different style than would a man. But she will not be the chief executive officer for very long if she fails to continue making profits for the shareholders. The leverage she has for doing good in the world is small, relative to the imperative of sustaining her company's financial performance at a high level.

Similarly, if someone is the chief executive officer and commander in chief of the largest military in the world—if someone has a military officer always nearby carrying a nuclear "football," as the U.S. president does have, allowing one to signal the special codes to authorize the release of nuclear weapons so as to incinerate untold numbers of persons—then the imperative of that office is to "make profits for the shareholders." The imperatives of office in the position of the American presidency are, essentially, to further the interest of the American imperial project, not to criticize that project. If one were to engage in too much of the latter, then one will not be running the show for very long. Yet, if the history of blacks in America teaches us anything, it is that *the American imperial project must be criticized.*

I am not attacking Barack Obama, the man. I admire him greatly. My assessment of Barack Hussein Obama, the man—given all I know about him, the books he's written that I have read, the speeches he's given that I have heard—is that he is compassionate and possessed of a deep historical sensibility. Left to his own devices, I feel confident in saying, he would always stand on the right side of history. King was fond of saying that "the arc of the moral universe is long, but it bends toward justice." In 2010, President Obama had a rug installed in the Oval office with King's quote—one of Obama's favorites—embossed upon it.[5] It is at least arguable that the rise of Obama represents one way in which that moral arc is, indeed, bending toward justice. He is someone who has more room within his own philosophy for concern about the dispossessed than anyone who has held that office. He is, I believe, aware of the imperfections of American democracy and of the inflated character of some of the rhetoric that he himself has had to use as a matter of political expediency. But the office has its own imperatives. Those of us who have been clamoring for change, and who so far have been sorely disappointed, must take account of this plain fact.

Another crucial point to consider revolves around "the narrative," and how the ascendancy of Obama to the presidency has affected our national discourse on issues of race and social justice. I recall that there was a heated discussion on this matter during the 2008 campaign, when candidate Obama gave his big speech on race—a speech made necessary by the uproar that had been created when some inflammatory comments of his former pastor, the Reverend Jeremiah Wright, came to public light.

The speech was very well received at the time, but I remember having been singularly unimpressed by it. "The best speech and the most important speech on race that we have heard as a nation since Martin Luther King's 'I Have a Dream' speech," one gushing TV talking head pronounced, breathlessly.[6] I recall thinking that a shocking degree of historical amnesia/ignorance had been revealed in the press commentary on Obama's race speech. People were confusing personality with a kind of politics that would be capable of making institutional reforms. As I listened to Obama's speech, my thoughts turned not to MLK, but to LBJ—and I compared, unfavorably, Obama's "race talk" with LBJ's commencement address at Howard University in 1965. Unlike Obama, LBJ staked out a political position that has had consequences.[7] This kind of stand-taking was the very last thing candidate Obama wanted to do, for obvious reasons of electoral survival. Still, I found, and still find, the contrast to be instructive.

LBJ's position was that the people of the United States were obligated to undertake a massive expansion of social investment for the disadvantaged in American society, and that this obligation rested at least in part on the historical necessity that we act so as to reduce racial inequality in our country. What LBJ had to say on that late-spring afternoon forty-three years prior—about race, history, policy, and social obligation—has echoed down through the decades.

Of course, nobody could have expected Obama to argue for a return of the Great Society. Still, I thought at the time of Obama's Philadelphia race speech in the spring of 2008 that his views about race and American social obligation—whatever their merits—were not in the same league with LBJ's, not even close.

This matters greatly, for there is tremendous social inequality along racial lines in the United States even today, and there remains a great need for effective political advocacy on behalf of more egalitarian and more humane policies. To see what I am getting after here, consider the following brief survey of the facts on the ground.

Percent of Native-Born Non-Hispanic Men and Women Aged 25 to 59 Who Were Employed from 1968 to 2007

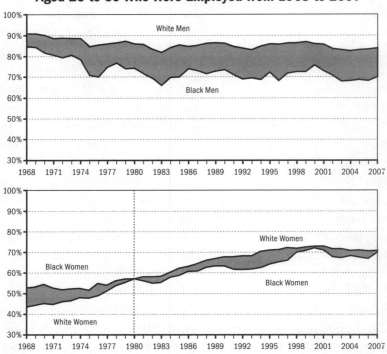

Reynolds Farley, "The Kerner Commission Report Plus Four Decades: What Has Changed? What Has Not?" Population Studies Center Research Report No. 08-656, 2008.

Percent of Native-Born Non-Hispanics
Below the Poverty Line from 1968 to 2007

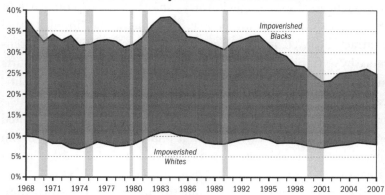

Reynolds Farley, "The Kerner Commission Report Plus Four Decades: What Has Changed? What Has Not?" Population Studies Center Research Report No. 08-656, 2008.

Men's Risk of Imprisonment by Ages 30–34

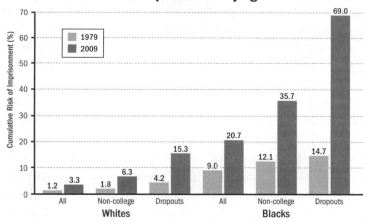

Bruce Western, Punishment and Inequality in America (New York: Russell Sage Foundation, 2006).

173

I also came to think during his first campaign that this black presidential candidate, Barack Obama, did not really have the standing to renegotiate the implicit American racial contract on behalf of *my* (i.e., African American) people. What might that "implicit racial contract" be? Well, in a word, it is the broad recognition and acceptance by governing elites in this country—in the press, in the courts and legal establishment, in the academy, and in the broader political culture—that structural impediments exist to the equal participation of blacks in American life, and that government-sponsored initiatives (like affirmative action at public universities, but by no means limited to this) are an appropriate vehicle for redress in this situation.

It is the recognition that, despite the huge social transformation occurring in this society under the pressures of immigration, globalization, and rising economic insecurity—which are, as Obama has frequently pointed out, changes affecting all of us, regardless of race or ethnicity—we nevertheless have unfinished business here on the race front. It is the willingness to constantly interrogate our institutions as to whether their actual practices are consistent with our professed ideals concerning equality and social justice. It is an acknowledgment that, imperatives of personal and communal responsibility notwithstanding, the American nation-state nevertheless bears a collective, political responsibility for the social disasters and the human suffering that are unfolding, and that can be so readily observed in the centers of our cities.

This responsibility extends to immigrants who have joined our society in recent decades no less so than to those with American ancestry extending back many generations. Just as present generations—immigrants and natives alike—are obligated to service a national debt incurred by their predecessors, so too are those who prosper within our social order obligated to contribute to the fair resolution of social problems deeply rooted in the nation's historical experience. This unfinished racial business, I would argue, is a part of what you inherit when you become an American.

While there has never been unanimity on these matters, there nevertheless has been a consensus view. This consensus has been under attack for a generation. And it is, in effect, being renegotiated by Obama as a consequence of his political ascendancy. I am not accusing Obama of being soft on affirmative action. Furthermore, some will object that Obama has shown through words and deeds his appreciation of the structural bases for racial inequality in this country. They will say that his views are nuanced, pragmatic, and historically well informed.[8] This is all true, and I do not deny it. Still, the question that matters is not whether Obama knows anything about history or sociology. The question is, what are the American people prepared to do next, if anything, about these matters? And how will Obama's vision promote progress?

Yet another key element to evaluate regarding the limits of reform and the importance of maintaining a sober realism when discussing the current American president, has to do with American foreign policy and, in particular, U.S. policies toward the conflict in the Middle East. When I have spoken in the United States about these matters, some people are perplexed by my evocation of the spirits of long-dead African American figures—practitioners of the black prophetic tradition—and by my connecting them with present-day moral concerns raised by the plight of the dispossessed, stateless Palestinians. How does this even come up, they seem to be asking, as if I pulled this subject out of thin air—as if it is somehow a real stretch to inject the conflicts of the Middle East into a discussion about race and American politics.

What I claim is that the moral legacy of these past, heroic warriors against white supremacy—the critical, subversive, prophetic, outsider's voice that I associate with their legacy—stands in danger of being lost or, at least, severely attenuated. Obama's "bargaining" with segments of the American people over such matters—as he strove to preserve his viability within the American political system in the midst of a presidential campaign and in the aftermath of his former pastor's offending public remarks—could have the effect of counteracting this critical voice. Furthermore, one of the issues, among others to be sure, where this development could have practical consequences has to do with how the experience and political voice of blacks would be inflected within the ongoing, broader American national dialogue over the conflict in the Middle East. I stand by these claims.

For example, many may not remember how Louis Farrakhan became a nationally recognized figure. It occurred in the aftermath of Andrew Young's resignation in 1979 from his position as Jimmy Carter's U.N. ambassador, because Young had unauthorized contact with representatives of the Palestine Liberation Organization, contrary to official U.S. policy. Jesse Jackson had been forthright in defending Young and had traveled to Palestine to show solidarity with Young, and with Yasser Arafat. Five years later, during Jackson's historic first run for the White House in 1984, a firestorm erupted after Jackson, in an unguarded moment of banter with reporters, referred to New York City as "Hymietown"—a remark by which many Jews, and others, were (rightly) offended. As Jackson fell under attack, Farrakhan spoke out before black audiences in Jackson's defense, making a number of anti-Semitic remarks which were seen (again, rightly) as deeply offensive by many Americans.

Now, there is nothing new to the American experience about the notion that an ethnic group's historically conditioned sensibilities might inform how members of that group come to construe, react to, and advocate about events taking place abroad—whether in South Africa, or Ireland, or Cuba, or Taiwan, or Palestine. I can say with some degree of certainty that Rev. Wright's views—about the plight of the Palestinians and their victimization at the hands of what Wright has called U.S.-sponsored "state terrorism"—are not the least bit unusual, within the context of the black experience as lived, for instance, on Chicago's South Side. That a person steeped in Wright's social world could find himself reminded by events in today's Middle East of the anticolonial and antiracist struggles of an earlier time can come as no surprise to anyone who has bothered to walk the streets of that community, to sit in its barber shops and beauty salons, or to spend more than a passing moment in the vicinity of a black church (or mosque) in the community that Obama represented in the Illinois state legislature for a decade. You can be sure that, no matter what he may say about the matter, these views were no revelation to Obama himself.

Take a look at what Obama actually had to say about this matter in his Philadelphia race speech on March 18, 2008:

> But the remarks that have caused this recent firestorm . . . expressed a profoundly distorted view of this country—a view that sees white racism as endemic, and that elevates what is wrong with America above all that we know is right with America; a view that sees the conflicts in the Middle East as rooted primarily in the actions of stalwart allies like Israel, instead of emanating from the perverse and hateful ideologies of radical Islam.[9]

Again, I have to insist: the fact that a black Muslim or, for that matter, a black Christian religious leader, ministering to a huge flock in Chicago's black ghetto, would fail to see the Palestinian-Israeli conflict as being due to a purportedly "perverse and hateful" Muslim ideology hardly certifies that said religious leader has a "profoundly distorted view of this country." Such a claim is just propaganda, pure and simple, and it can serve only one purpose—to delegitimate criticism of American foreign policy by means of some not-so-sophisticated name-calling. One may agree or disagree with Wright's (and, for that matter, Farrakhan's) reading of the situation in the Middle East, but one cannot fairly characterize those views as deluded, unfounded, irrational, or un-American. In the sentence quoted above, acting on behalf of his own ambitions (and perhaps articulating sincerely held views), Obama nevertheless denied any space within the legitimate American conversation for an important dimension of the historically grounded, authentic African American political voice. In my considered opinion, he has not earned the right to do so.

I will conclude with a story about a friend of mine, Tony Campbell. The Reverend Anthony C. Campbell served as minister in the

Boston University chapel during the summers for over a decade, until his death a few years ago. An African American who had for many
years been pastor of a large church in Detroit, and who was a close
personal friend of then B.U. president John Silber, Tony preached
in the university's chapel nearly every Sunday during the summers,
while serving as preacher-in-residence and professor of preaching
in the university's school of theology. His sermons were broadcast
throughout the New England region on the university-sponsored
public radio stations.

As it happens, Tony's father had also been a well-known Baptist
minister. The family hailed from South Carolina, and Tony had an
academic bent. Though a Baptist by birth, he was also very familiar with the Anglican and Episcopalian traditions. He had preached
at Westminster Abbey and Canterbury. Indeed, before his death he
preached sermons from pulpits in a dozen countries throughout the
world. He was an elegant, beautifully poetic preacher. No ranting
and stomping in the pulpit from him. He was always understated.
His voice tended to get lower, and slower, as his sermons approached
their climax. My son and I once traveled to New York from Boston
for the sole purpose of hearing Tony preach at the Riverside Church,
because it was such an honorific thing for him. On that occasion he
once again hit it out of the park with achingly beautiful and profound reflections on Christian teaching.

Less than two weeks after the events of 9/11, Tony preached his
final sermon of the summer at Boston University. I was there. The
title he gave for that sermon was "A Reversal of Fortune." His text
was based on a teaching in the New Testament about the figure of
Lazarus, not the one who was raised from the dead, but the wealthy
man who ignored the beggars sitting in front of his door throughout his blessed life. When he died, said Lazarus was sent to roast in
the fires of hell and upon asking for relief from the angel of the Lord
was denied it, being told that he had had his chance on earth. When
he asked that word be sent back to his brothers, lest they fall into the
same condition, he was told, in effect: "They didn't listen to Moses

and the prophets, why would they listen now? Let them roast along with you."

The late Reverend Anthony C. Campbell, heir to a great tradition of prophetic black preaching—an urbane, mild-mannered sophisticate—started his sermon with that scripture. This is a man who did not have a radical bone in his body—a Baptist with high-church pretensions who had preached at Canterbury. He was as thoroughly American and as committed a Christian as one could imagine. And he argued, in the wake of our country having been attacked by terrorists, that the United States was now in the position of the Lazarus figure of that biblical tale. We were, in effect and to some degree, he argued, reaping what we had sown. Those were not his words, of course. He was far too eloquent and subtle a preacher for that. But that was his message, and there really could be no mistake about it. He argued that we live now with the consequences of our neglect of complaints against injustice, our contempt for decent world opinion, our arrogance, our haughtiness, and our self-absorption.

The point of this extended closing anecdote is to explain and defend my assertion that the African American spiritual witness—for Christians, the teachings of the Gospel of Jesus Christ as refracted through the long generations of pain and suffering and disappointment and hopelessness endured by millions of the descendants of slaves in this country—has a prophetic message for the American people. In my humble opinion, Barack Obama has not earned the right to interpret that message to suit his political needs of the moment. More important, he certainly ought not to be allowed to denigrate or to marginalize it. With respect to the application of this tradition to moral problems raised by the plight of the Palestinians, this is precisely what he did during his campaign for the presidency.

As I ponder these questions, I am reminded of the work of the African American political scientist Martin Kilson, who is professor emeritus of government at Harvard and was a tenured professor at Harvard in the late 1960s and early 70s when student protest caused the university to establish a department of African American studies. Marty Kilson was a critic of that advocacy. He believed that African Americans needed to advance through the disciplines, coming up and earning their spurs just like anybody else. He didn't want a separate department. But his thinking evolved. There is a book that he has been promising to write for years that was subtitled *Neither Insiders Nor Outsiders*. African Americans were neither insiders nor outsiders. Not insiders for the obvious reasons. Our noses are effectively pressed against the candy-store window. We do not quite have equal opportunity. But neither are we outsiders, because we are an indigenous American population going back six, eight, ten generations—sons of the soil, as American as anybody could possibly be. So, therein lies the conundrum, the paradox—neither insiders nor outsiders.

The central theme of American racial politics over the past quarter century is that outsiders are becoming insiders. Thus, the question arises: just what kind of insiders are we going to be? That, indeed, is *the* question. President Obama has given us one kind of answer. I wonder, is this the only one available to us?

11

FREE BLACK MEN

Elizabeth Alexander

Along with millions of others, I spent exorbitant amounts of time considering, analyzing, fretting, and exulting over the two presidential campaigns of Barack Obama and the difficulties he has encountered during his time in office. Obama is one of the most visible emblems of black masculinity we have before us today in the mainstream U.S. media. As a close reader of texts of various kinds, and as one with particular interest in African American iconography, I apply those tools of analysis to thinking about Obama in terms of symbols and symbolic power. The American president is the monarch in the following sense: he gives us an immediately available symbol, every single day, of who he is and thus who we (the body politic) are and might be. Let's accept, for the sake of argument, that symbols actually do bear power. We have no imagistic precedent for understanding what it means for an Obama to be president and for Michelle Obama to be First Lady. What is instantly rewritten when a black woman is for the first time at the highest levels of our nation's imaginary, at the head of the category of "lady"? Policies, appointments, and issues are all of obvious import. But my analytic focus is on how Obama *means*, which I hope is also an avenue to think about the immeasurable impact he has had on so many communities and how he helps us imagine what I call "free black men."

What do I mean by "free black men"? My father is a free black man, and once you have been inculcated in that worldview there is no acceptable alternative. There have been free black men as long as there has been American history, from nineteenth-century exemplars, such as Frederick Douglass, David Walker, Nat Turner, and Joseph Cinqué, who were "free" when they were not literally free, to the twentieth-century likes of W.E.B DuBois, Marcus Garvey, Martin Luther King Jr., Ossie Davis, A. Philip Randolph, and Malcolm X, black men whose superbad words and deeds operate according to a logic utterly outside of supplication. Even if we understand the ways racism and classism and sexism have clipped our wings and our tongues and our imaginations; even if we know the literal and metaphorical violence black men are up against on a daily basis; even if we recognize the straitjackets of stereotype and its consequences, we must also know black men who teach us how to think outside the proverbial box, even as they know how to delineate the parameters of the box, who can imagine what the poet Robert Hayden called "something patterned, wild, and free," which is to say black selves beyond the reach of the pernicious roadblocks to our full and flourishing personhood.

I am always watching for free black men, in the public arena and up close, and I know them when I see them. I had a colleague once who would proclaim out loud, "This is BORING!" in his meetings with his all-white colleagues at an elite university talking infinitely about the supposed superiority of European culture. He didn't meet their arguments with measured reasoning, with footnotes. He didn't clench his jaw, clear his throat, sip from a lukewarm glass of water, and later implode. No, he rejected the terms of their assertions and gave them not one second of his own considerable intellectual energy. He merely dismissed them: *This is BORING!* He thrilled and empowered me beyond measure: this man had said the emperor had no clothes! How liberating to say, maybe they're not that smart and maybe they're not that fascinating. Like Muhammad Ali's "I'm so pretty," which signaled a global beauty writ large, meant to make black male beauty displace all the other kinds of overly vaunted beauties in the world.

During the 2008 primary season, efforts to substitute Obama's actual history and body with stereotypical ones was textbook and predictable. Youthful, Afroed drug-dabbler; turbaned colored other; darkened and more "sinister" black man, à la O.J. Simpson on trial; Farrakhan-loving, arm-waving black radical preacher. But what is interesting is that none of those images really stuck; the comparisons ultimately seemed absurd in the face of Obama himself. We passed through either a moment of actual shift or an anomalous moment wherein the power of false images could not override the power of the thing itself.

In its primary endorsement of Hillary Rodham Clinton, the *New York Times* called Obama "incandescent if still undefined."[1] Incandescent: artificial light, as in incandescent lightbulb. Not the sunshine. Blinding. Magical, mystical, hoodoo, conjurer, evanescent, inconsequential, evaporative. An optical illusion. Literally, substanceless. Light. Lightweight. In the act of conjuration, a form of deception. Not to be trusted. Don't believe your eyes. Don't trust it. Incandescent also refers to something called "black body radiation"; in physics, a black body is an object that absorbs all light that falls on it. The light emitted by a black body may be incandescent—black body radiation. I riff on this word choice to surface both "magic negro" stereotypes that floated around candidate Obama, and also the way he confounded those who beheld him with such wonder. This type of imagery was muted during Obama's second presidential campaign but it lay just below the surface.

How do iconographically unprecedented representations of black men suggest something new underfoot in the present? The images of John Lewis, Andrew Young, and Jesse Jackson at the groundbreaking for the King memorial on the Mall are something we have rarely seen, grown black men weeping in public, holding each other's bodies up as they weep. And why did they weep? There are so many potential answers, many things true at once. In the intense last year of the first Obama presidential campaign we saw Obama's friend Marty Nesbitt listening to Obama's so-called race speech in Philadelphia; Obama himself, crying at the end of almost his final campaign appearance after speaking of the death of his grandmother on the eve of the election; and then, Jesse Jackson in Grant Park after Obama had been named president—once again, so many unknowable feelings behind those tears.[2] These men cry at moments of extraordinary progress, but their expression of "we've come so far" is not merely celebratory; it must hold simultaneous with triumph a memory of struggle and travail. They cry, it seems to me, for Gordon the slave who did not, and for the Medgar Everses and Fred Hamptons and Martin Luther Kings who gave their lives along the road to something hopefully better.

The Reverend Jesse Jackson comforts former UN ambassador Andrew Young during the groundbreaking for the Martin Luther King Jr. Memorial in Washington, D.C., on November 13, 2006.
Lawrence Jackson/AP

Andrew Young speaks about the significance of the Reverend Martin Luther King Jr. Also present is Georgia representative John Lewis (leaning on shovel).
Lauren Victoria Burke/AP

Tears flow down the face of
supporter Marty Nesbitt as
Democratic presidential
hopeful Senator Barack
Obama speaks about race
during a news conference
in Philadelphia on
March 18, 2008.
Alex Brandon/AP

Democratic
presidential nominee
Senator Barack
Obama cries while
speaking about his
grandmother during a
rally at the University
of North Carolina,
Charlotte, on
November 3, 2008.
Joe Raedle/Getty

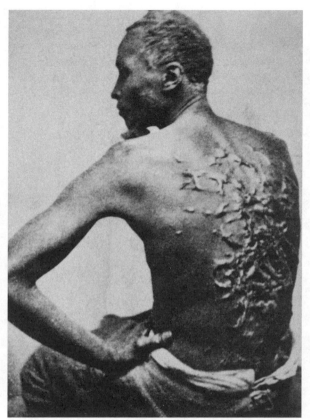

Gordon, a freed slave in Baton Rouge, Louisiana, displays his whip-scarred back in 1863.
Corbis

The Reverend Jesse Jackson reacts after projections show that Senator Barack Obama will be elected to serve as the next president of the United States during an election night gathering in Grant Park in Chicago on November 4, 2008.
Joe Raedle/Getty

Derrick Bell, free black man. Harry Belafonte, free black man. Amiri Baraka, free black man, not only because he is a born genius, but also because he adapted contentious critique as his mode in his poetics and in his public utterance. Even when he is wrong, he is free. Free black men who are loud, free black men who are quiet. The brother I see kissing his son goodbye every morning at school, those kisses standing out from the other black fathers I see, free black man. Most black jazz musicians, listening for their own strange, unprecedented, and historical selves in the sometimes powerfully nonrepresentational musical language—resisting the straitjackets of representation—and offering it to us. I invite you to imagine the free black men in your communities. It is an enlightening exercise.

Free black men. Among some of the things my father taught me: always carry "F-you money" and keep some in the bank, no matter what, so that you have your own money *on you*, so you can always walk away from the man, the job, the situation—that you had to put yourself in. A situation where lack of funds would not cost you your life, your health, your dignity. This philosophy went beyond the dime for the emergency phone call, and it wasn't about the amount of money. The point was that no white man's job was worth your mental health. Period. He instructed me to always speak up for what you knew was right, even when absolutely no one in the room would sign on with you, because you never knew who would be listening, and someone was always listening. He taught me to ignore fools, simply ignore them, call them fools, reject their paradigms and render them irrelevant, even if they had power over my very livelihood. This is not always practical advice but it is soul saving. Even when you don't act according to those dicta, to have them in your arsenal is crucial and enabling. Seeing yourself relative to the always-dominant paradigm is a soul-killing game; my father taught me that if we evaluated black people in terms of those paradigms, we would forever come up short and supplicating.

He saw his mother work, like most black men. Her name was Edith McAllister Alexander. She was a righteous warrior who taught him things like memorizing badge numbers of Harlem police officers in the 1930s and 40s and then reporting them for their abuses against black children. This abuse of authority first happened for my father when he was eight. She organized a successful campaign against New York City newspapers to get them to stop identifying only black alleged criminals by their race. His own father was a quieter man who taught my father much about kindness and decency, diligence and honor. But I am quite sure it was his mother who taught him how to fight and who made him free; I extend this argument to say, free black men cannot exist without black feminists. Free in this context doesn't just mean having accomplished the seemingly impossible. It doesn't just mean being outspoken. It means, to borrow from Langston Hughes, being "free within ourselves," but in a way which is discernable to and legible by those in his community. "You never know who is watching you when you stand up, even if nobody tells you they support you."

Is Barack Obama a free black man? When he refuses to hew to party lines about black and white, when he is cool in the face of month after month of racial bait, as he articulates a nuanced identity without being cute about being "black" or "biracial," when he respects his listeners by presenting ideas in the best language he has, understanding that words are what we live in and they have true power, and when he displays his evident intelligence and cool dignity, I think he expands the mainstream imaginary under the sign of "African American man" and a free black manhood that does crucial, sometimes surreptitious work. During the 2008 primary season, when pundits repeatedly called for Obama to get angry, to fight back against the Clinton campaign's trickery, I thought of the battle royal scene in Ellison's *Invisible Man*, and the protagonist's subsequent discovery that the letter of introduction he'd taken with him to seek employment in fact read "Keep this nigger boy running."

At a campaign rally in October, Obama pulled a clever one by using the words "hoodwinked" and "bamboozled" to a mostly black audience from which he knew he'd get an amen. He slyly conjured Malcolm X, without having to actually become visibly angry or "radical." His words alluded to Spike Lee's film *Malcolm X* ("You've been had. You've been took. You've been hoodwinked. Bamboozled. Led astray. Run amok."), which is perhaps even more media savvy than quoting Malcolm himself. And indeed, when the literally, visibly angry black man was before us as an Obama surrogate in the figure of the Reverend Dr. Jeremiah Wright, African-dress wearing and growling with passion in the same clips looped incessantly on television, that angry black male body became horrifying for the same liberal white commentators (Anderson Cooper, Chris Matthews) for whom Obama was their cool black roommate in college just a few days prior. "Anger" at American inequality is a tarring brush. That wish for a visible and discernable kind of ire was a wish for a spectacle. A black man with power engorged with the might of anger is a terrifying sight we have rarely seen in public. Middle-class black men who are in the public eye tend to experience a kind of implosive anger that has, as we know, taken its toll on their health in the disproportionate deaths from asthma, cardiovascular disease, and other ailments that kill not incrementally but rather cataclysmically (disproportionate rates of prostate cancer among black men being the exception to this point). And homicide. Or, rather, the increments are not visible, only the cataclysm. What would a brief flash of visible rage have done to the campaign? I see Obama's cool not as masking rage but rather as an expression of profound discipline and an African philosophy of cool.

The success of the first Obama presidential campaign brought out the worst in mainstream white feminists. Gloria Steinem's much-discussed op-ed in the *New York Times* ("Women Are Never Front-Runners," January 8, 2008) essentially argued that in the race and gender hierarchical sweepstakes it was women's (read: white women's) turn to become president, implicitly before black men. Her strategic reminder to readers that black men got the vote before white women—as though that made them equal players in American society—echoes the deep rift in the white feminist movement that opened in the late 1860s. Outraged that black male suffrage could be accomplished without enfranchising women, vaunted white feminists such as Susan B. Anthony, Carrie Chapman Catt, and Elizabeth Cady Stanton affiliated themselves with white supremacy and made comments such as Anthony's: "If intelligence, justice, and morality are to have precedence in the Government, let the question of the woman be brought up first and that of the Negro last." Stanton said, "As the celestial gates to civil rights is slowly moving its hinges, it becomes a serious question whether we had better stand aside and see 'Sambo' walk in the kingdom first." Nearly fifty years later, Catt stated plainly, "White supremacy will be strengthened, not weakened, by women's suffrage."

During that presidential primary season, former vice presidential candidate Geraldine Ferraro repeatedly stated, "If Obama was a white man, he would not be in this position. And if he was a woman of any color, he would not be in this position. He happens to be very lucky to be who he is. And the country is caught up in the concept."[3]

Black women are nowhere in these pictures, either in the vision of female electoral power that mainstream white feminists envisioned in 1868 or in 2008. That they cannot imagine a black male candidate as being in their best interest overextends the idea that we should vote for people "who look like us." Obama, by the way, never made any kind of gender-based critique of Clinton. If someone had asked him, "How do we beat the bitch?"—which was asked of John McCain during the campaign in reference to Hillary Clinton by a very blonde, older woman in a headband, pearls, and an accent sometimes described as "Locust Valley lockjaw"—Obama certainly would have responded quite differently from McCain, who laughed a little nervously and then said, "That's an excellent question."[4] Obama came of age in family contexts where the full participation of women was a given, so much a given as to be unworthy of extended comment. This is something else that separates him from previous generations of black male leadership and also undergirds the liberation of mind that would characterize a free black man. "It's our turn," white feminists intoned during the primaries, implicitly, explicitly, and with increasing bitterness, as though no allegiance can ever be made across race or gender, as though "I" is the most important unit of thought, as though tit for tat is the way to make things right, as though black women do not exist. That belief system is the cancerous center of what's wrong with that kind of feminism. Even privileged black feminism is not tit-for-tat feminism. I think of Elsa Barkley-Brown's essay "Negotiating and Transforming the Public Sphere: African American Political Life in the Transition from Slavery to Freedom," which describes African American men's votes as being the joint or family vote, decided on together, with many black women accompanying their husbands to the voting booth with shotguns hidden in their aprons.[5] That kind of *we are not playing* pragmatism is a hallmark of black feminism, understanding as we do that we must navigate and negotiate the realities of disenfranchisement and partial emancipation, and most important, that our fates as black men and women are intertwined.

And what do free black men owe to black feminism? If Obama can be a free black man, it is at least in part because of the black woman he is married to, who gives forty-five-minute speeches without notes and without smiling, telling us things like "Power is hard," "Never give up your power," "You have to fight for your power every single day," "Change is hard. It will always be hard. And it doesn't happen from the top down," and so forth. Her persona is tough, demanding, and pragmatic. And she says "black things," with a very savvy understanding of what might not be so successful coming from him.

When Barack and Michelle Obama first appeared on *60 Minutes* in a dual interview, their performance was a model of what a free black manhood intertwined with black feminism might look like.[6] You saw their proximity, their overlapping heads, the way her words seem almost literally to emanate from his, but his mouth is closed. Her surrogacy was made almost explicit with the glance they gave each other before she answered questions, and then after, with his wry smile of both assent—endorsing the truth of the message, and the identity it confers upon him—as well as endorsement of his forthright wife speaking in the familiar truth-telling directness that is a particular rhetorical hallmark of black women. She closes the fused circle of the two-as-one when she says, "We just weren't raised like that," their dual upbringings now one. In many speeches she performs a similar rhetorical strategy when she moves from "people" to "a man like Barack Obama," the singular "I" in service to the communal "we."

Black feminism, in the form of Michelle Obama, took black Americans through their own skepticisms about her husband. Remember, at the beginning of his first presidential campaign he did not enjoy the level of black support he now has. The conversation about "Is he black enough?" though I think manufactured by white people, was nonetheless relevant. Michelle Obama repeated her story of first encounter with her husband-to-be: "I've got nothing in common with this guy. He grew up in Hawaii! Who grows up in Hawaii? He was biracial. I was like, okay, what's that about? And then it's a funny name, Barack Obama. Who names their child Barack Obama?"[7] She acts as the surrogate chorus for so many black people, working us out of our racial and class litmus testing.

She was called "emasculating" by Maureen Dowd and many others.[8] I don't want to reprise all of the ways in which Michelle Obama was painted as the stereotypical "angry black woman." Conservative websites abounded with "angry Michelle" photographs; mainstream internet comments vibrated with the viral throb of racist and sexist invective, such as Fox News's Bill O'Reilly's response to a caller who claimed she knew Michelle Obama to be "angry" and "militant" with, "I don't want to go on a lynching party against Michelle Obama unless there's evidence, hard facts, that say this is how the woman really feels. If that's how she really feels—that America is a bad country or a flawed nation, whatever—then that's legit. We'll track it down."[9] That still hasn't received the kind of attention it should have, showing the ways in which the safety of black women is often overlooked or subsumed under the idea that we are so "strong" that we don't need defense or protection, let alone a pedestal. This is just some of the thinking that Mrs. Obama as First Lady has pushed back against.

ELIZABETH ALEXANDER

"Angry Michelle" to me is the black women going to the polls with their men with shotguns in their aprons. Michelle Obama showed us black families, where the woman has never been on a pedestal nor has the man, where we eschew the kind of tit-for-tat heterosexual feminism that my black sisters and I decry in our equally privileged white sisters. She can say Barack didn't put the butter away or Barack didn't pick up his socks because we understand the bigger picture. Just like we understood before we had the vote that the black man's vote was the precious family vote, so too we understand that our struggles are greater than butter and socks. Here is another quotation, from a campaign luncheon on April 16, 2007:

But the reality is that my husband is a man who understands my unique struggle and the challenges facing women and families. It is not just because he lives with me, someone who is very opinionated and makes my point. I am not a martyr so he hears it. It is because he actually listens to me and has the utmost respect for my perspective and my life experience. It is also because he was raised in a household of strong women who he saw struggle and sacrifice for him to achieve his dreams. He saw his grandmother, the primary breadwinner in their household, work her entire life to support their whole family. He saw his mother, a very young, very single-parent trying to finish her education and raise two children across two continents. He sees his sister, a single-parent trying to eke out a life for herself and her daughter on a salary that is much too small. He sees it in the eyes of women he meets throughout the country, women who have lost children and husbands in the war, women who don't have access to adequate healthcare, to affordable daycare or jobs that pay a living wage. Their stories keep him up at night. Their stories, our stories, are the foundation of what guides Barack throughout his life. . . . But we need you to join us, because, you know what? Barack, as I tease, he's a wonderful man,

193

he's a gifted man, but in the end, he is just a man. (laughter) He is an imperfect vessel and I love him dearly. (laughter and applause) In all seriousness, he is going to get tired. He is tired now. He is going to make mistakes. He will stumble. Trust me, he will say things that you will not agree with all the time. He will not be able to move you to tears with every word that he says. You know? (laughter) But that is why this campaign is so important, because it is not all about Barack Obama. It is about all of us. It is about us turning these possibilities into action.[10]

This is a kind of black feminist talk that feels resonantly cross-generational to me, stand-by-your-man rhetoric as told by black women: that love is fierce and demanding and often uncute and unsmiling; that even as they are protectors, black men also need to be protected by the women who love them; that all of us are vulnerable; that we only thrive collectively; that we can disagree and still be allied. Because black women have not occupied the pedestals of femininity; because black women have historically worked; because black women understand the many meanings of "pool your resources"; because conventional gender roles have already been deconstructed for us. There is liberatory space in these negations.

Free black manhood must articulate its visionary-ness as something that names the disproportionate burdens black women carry, that names the continued experiences of being the detail people, the cleanup women, not always seen or imagined as the leaders we are or can or should be. Black women have fathers and brothers and husbands and sons; black men have mothers and sisters and daughters and wives. Our fates are intertwined, and so must the strengths of our bodies of knowledge, ideologies, and wisdoms be intertwined. The candidate has become the president of the United States, and the question of how anyone can be free within the strictures and demands of the job on the world stage is one I am not equipped to answer.

John Hope Franklin and Evelyn Brooks Higginbotham, *From Slavery to Freedom* (New York: McGraw-Hill, 2010).

The great historian John Hope Franklin's legacy and memory inspired this essay, so here I conclude with a read of the cover of the ninth and latest edition of his foundational African American history textbook, *From Slavery to Freedom*, prepared by Harvard professor and chair of African American studies, Evelyn Brooks Higginbotham.[11] As the book came out, the publisher could not resist putting the first African American president on the cover. A color image of Obama faces a black-and-white image of the Negro bonded, visually marking the distance from the American past to the present, "from slavery to freedom." The American flag is the background, its symbolic glory and possibility restored. The book that was written by a black scholar who did some of his early research inside a small room that segregated him from white researchers has moved from margin to center; the book is written from an African American studies department at Harvard University. A "triumphal" version of American history now dominates. African American history has been visually moved to the center, in the person of the first black president.

But what's wrong with this picture? I resist thinking that we ever come to the triumphal end, nor should we desire it. So I take interest in the fact that Obama's back is turned in this image and that his face cannot be seen, so symbolic freedom is still, in part, unknowable, or knowable only in pieces and through the slow work of two steps forward, one step back. We are not, as viewers of this book cover, given the satisfaction of smiling back at a perhaps smiling Obama, and the implacable faces he faces are not altered to respond to what they see, either. Their gaze is skeptical and direct, as though the historical Negro will not be charmed nor cheered by the triumphal present. That looking and attempting to see things as they really are with the unflinching critical eye is the way black people have strategized and survived. The will to the triumphal is understandable in African American studies, as it is among any people who have suffered more than their share of oppressions. But the lesson of African American studies is that the call to the triumphal is a siren song. And so I hope that the ways in which the humanities forwards the racial conversation in this country—thorny, difficult, unsettled—will direct us to think in terms of process rather than finish line, and will leave us ever more open to the complexities of America's racial story.

Not so long ago the president began airstrikes against Libya in an attempt to avert massacres of the Libyan people led by the unpredictable dictator Muammar al-Gadhafi. More recently, in the case of massacres and violence in Syria, he hesitated. Faced with myriad impossible choices as president, Obama toggles daily between the devil and the deep blue sea. I persist in dearly wanting—perhaps reading into—Obama's presence to be empowering for black people. "He's a wartime president as far as I'm concerned," said my father, a free black man who deeply loves and supports the president.

Can the first black president be a free black man?

ACKNOWLEDGMENTS

Sincere thanks to Marsha Sukach for superb research assistance; Dean David Levi for sponsoring the conference on John Hope Franklin; Marc Favreau and Tara Grove of The New Press for believing in the manuscript and Tara especially for shepherding it to publication; and my wife, Lisa Jones, for her encouragement and critical engagement with the central message of *The New Black*, which helped make the volume immensely better.

—K. M.

Thank you to Michelle Huang and Kate Dickinson-Varner for outstanding research assistance; Lisa Musty and Briana Brake for their assistance with preparing the manuscript; Dean David Levi for his supporting this and many other projects; in appreciation to my wife Lora and kids Brie, Alex, and Mateo for their continued love and support. Thanks also to Ken for his tremendous work on this volume.

—G.-U. C

Thank you also to the participants at the conference "From Slavery to Freedom to the White House: Race in 21st Century America." This conference was held at Duke Law School on April 8–10, 2010, in honor of Dr. John Hope Franklin. We are grateful to Michelle Adams, Elizabeth Alexander, Richard Banks, Jeannine Bell, Lawrence Bobo, Eugene Borgida, Khalihah Brown-Dean, Tomiko Brown-Nagin, Paul Butler, Jennifer Chacon, Dalton Conley, Luis Fraga, Luis Fuentes-Rohwer, Lani Guinier, Melissa Harris-Perry, Jonathan Holloway, Vincent Hutchings, Sherrilyn Ifill, Michael S. Kang, Randall Kennedy, Taeku Lee, Glenn Loury, Angela

Onwuachi-Willig, Orlando Patterson, Richard Pildes, Cristina Rodríguez, Daria Roithmayr, Brent Staples, Ray Suarez, Patricia Sullivan, and Gerald Torres for making the conference a success, and for inspiring us with your wonderful ideas and scholarship to begin working on this book.

—K. M. and G.-U. C.

CONTRIBUTORS

Elizabeth Alexander is a poet, essayist, playwright, and teacher. She is chair of the African American Studies Department at Yale University and the author of six books of poems: *The Venus Hottentot: Body of Life; Antebellum Dream Book; American Sublime,* a finalist for the Pulitzer Prize; *Miss Crandall's School for Young Ladies and Little Misses of Color,* a young adult collection co-authored with Marilyn Nelson; and *Crave Radiance: New and Selected Poems 1990–2010,* which won the Paterson Prize for Poetry. Her two collections of essays are *The Black Interior* and *Power and Possibility,* and her play, *Diva Studies,* was produced at the Yale School of Drama. In 2009, she composed and delivered the poem "Praise Song for the Day" for the inauguration of President Barack Obama.

Jeannine Bell is a professor of law and the Louis F. Niezer Faculty Fellow at Indiana University's Maurer School of Law. A nationally recognized scholar in the area of policing and hate crime, she has written extensively on criminal justice issues. She has authored or edited several articles and three books including *Policing Hatred: Law Enforcement, Civil Rights, and Hate Crime* and *Hate Thy Neighbor,* which explores hate crime in integrating neighborhoods. Her research is broadly interdisciplinary, touching on her work in both political science and law. She has served as a trustee of the Law and Society Association (LSA), as treasurer of LSA, and as a member of the American Political Association's Presidential Taskforce on Political Violence and Terrorism.

Paul Butler is a professor of law at Georgetown University Law Center. He teaches in the areas of criminal law and race and the law.

Prior to joining Georgetown's faculty he was Associate Dean for Faculty Development and the Carville Dickinson Benson Research Professor of Law at George Washington University Law School. Professor Butler is one of the nation's most frequently consulted scholars on issues of race and criminal justice. His book *Let's Get Free: A Hip-Hop Theory of Justice* received the Harry Chapin Media award. His scholarship has been the subject of much attention in the academic and popular media. His work has been profiled on *60 Minutes, Nightline,* and the ABC, CBS, and NBC evening news, among other places. He lectures regularly for the American Bar Association and the NAACP, and at colleges, law schools, and community organizations throughout the United States. Prior to joining the academy, Butler served as a federal prosecutor with the U.S. Department of Justice, where his specialty was public corruption. He is a graduate of Harvard Law School and Yale College.

Guy-Uriel Charles is the Charles S. Rhyne Professor of Law at Duke University and the founding director of the Duke Center on Law, Race and Politics. Previously he was a professor of law at the University of Minnesota Law School, where he was named Teacher of the Year for 2002–2003. Charles is a frequent public commentator on constitutional law, election law, campaign finance, redistricting, politics, and race. A co-founder of the Colored Demos blog, he has authored several published articles and was the founder and first editor in chief of the *Michigan Journal of Race & Law* while a law student at the University of Michigan. Charles has clerked for the Honorable Damon J. Keith of the United States Court of Appeals for the Sixth Circuit and is a past member of the National Research Commission on Elections and Voting.

Luis Fuentes-Rohwer is a professor of law and Harry T. Ice Faculty Fellow at Indiana University's Maurer School of Law. His scholarship focuses on the intersection of race and democratic theory, as reflected in the law of democracy in general and the Voting Rights Act in particular. Fuentes-Rohwer is interested in the way that institutions—especially courts—are asked to craft and implement the ground rules of American politics. His dissertation, "The Rise of a Concept: Judicial Independence in the American National Context, 1787–1833," examines the way that the concept of judicial independence gained traction soon after the U.S. Constitution came into being as a necessary counterpoint to the rise of political parties. His most recent work focuses on the political and constitutional status of the commonwealth of Puerto Rico under American rule.

Lani Guinier is the first woman of color appointed to a tenured professorship at Harvard Law School (1998) and is now the Bennett Boskey Professor of Law. Before her Harvard appointment, she was a tenured professor at the University of Pennsylvania Law School. Educated at Radcliffe College and Yale Law School, Guinier worked in the Civil Rights Division at the U.S. Department of Justice and then headed the Voting Rights Project at the NAACP Legal Defense Fund in the 1980s. Guinier has published many scholarly articles and books, including *The Tyranny of the Majority* and *The Miner's Canary: Enlisting Race, Resisting Power, Transforming Democracy* (with Gerald Torres). In her scholarly writings and op-ed pieces, she has addressed issues of race, gender, and democratic decision making, and has sought new ways of approaching questions like affirmative action while calling for candid public discourse on these topics.

Jonathan Scott Holloway is a professor of African American studies, history, and American studies at Yale University. He specializes in postemancipation United States history with a focus on social and intellectual history. He is the author of *Confronting the Veil: Abram Harris Jr., E. Franklin Frazier, and Ralph Bunche, 1919–1941* and the editor of Ralph Bunche's *A Brief and Tentative Analysis of Negro Leadership* and *Black Scholars on the Line: Race, Social Science, and American Thought in the Twentieth Century* (with Ben Keppel). In 2009, Holloway won the William Clyde DeVane Award for

Distinguished Scholarship and Teaching in Yale College. He is the recipient of an Alphonse Fletcher Sr. Fellowship and a nonresident fellow at the W.E.B. Du Bois Institute at Harvard University.

Taeku Lee is a professor of political science and law and chair of the department of political science at the University of California, Berkeley. He is the author or editor of several books including *Mobilizing Public Opinion; Transforming Politics, Transforming America* (with S. Karthick Ramakrishnan and Ricardo Ramírez); *Why Americans Don't Join the Party* (with Zoltan Hajnal); and *Asian American Political Participation* (with Janelle Wong, S. Karthick Ramakrishnan, and Jane Junn), among others. Lee is co-principal investigator of the National Asian American Survey. He has been an assistant professor at Harvard's Kennedy School and the Robert Wood Johnson Scholar at Yale. He holds an AB from the University of Michigan, a master's in public policy from Harvard University, and a PhD from the University of Chicago. Born in South Korea, Lee grew up in rural Malaysia, Manhattan, and suburban Detroit, and is a proud graduate of K–12 public schools.

Glenn C. Loury is a distinguished economist and is the Merton P. Stoltz Professor of the Social Sciences and a professor of economics and public policy at Brown University. He has contributed to a variety of areas in applied microeconomic theory including welfare economics, game theory, industrial organization, natural resource economics, and the economics of income distribution. A recipient of a Guggenheim Fellowship and the John von Neuman Award, and a member of the Council on Foreign Relations, he was for many years a contributing editor at the *New Republic* and at the *American Interest*, and he currently serves on the editorial advisory board of the *Boston Review*. His books include *One by One from the Inside Out: Essays and Reviews on Race and Responsibility in America* (winner of the American Book Award); *The Anatomy of Racial Inequality*; and *Race, Incarceration, and American Values*, among others.

Kenneth W. Mack is a professor of law at Harvard University. He worked as an electrical engineer at Bell Laboratories before turning to law and history, receiving his JD from Harvard and his MA and PhD in history from Princeton. He is a former law clerk to Federal District Judge Robert L. Carter. He is also a faculty associate in the Joint Center for History and Economics at Harvard University and the University of Cambridge. He is a recipient of the Alphonse Fletcher Sr. Fellowship. Mack is the author of *Representing the Race: The Creation of the Civil Rights Lawyer* and numerous scholarly articles in leading law and history journals. He has also written opinion pieces for the national press and leading online journals of opinion. During the 2008 and 2012 presidential election cycles, he offered commentary on the candidates in a number of national media outlets, and during the last two presidential inaugurations he offered live commentary seen worldwide on the BBC.

Angela Onwuachi-Willig is the Charles M. and Marion J. Kierscht Professor of Law at the University of Iowa, where she joined the faculty in 2006 after three years at the University of California Davis School of Law. She has clerked for Judge Solomon Oliver, now Chief U.S. District Judge for the Northern District of Ohio, and Judge Karen Nelson Moore, U.S. Circuit Judge for the Sixth Circuit. A former labor and employment lawyer in Cleveland and Boston, Onwuachi-Willig was selected as a 2011 finalist for the Iowa Supreme Court and in that same year was named one of America's top young legal professionals by the *National Law Journal*. Her first book, *According to Our Hearts: Rhinelander v. Rhinelander and the Law of the Multiracial Family*, is an examination of the present and historical legal contexts for multiracial couples and families in the United States.

Orlando Patterson, a historical and cultural sociologist, is John Cowles Professor of Sociology at Harvard University. His academic interests include the culture and practice of freedom, the comparative study of slavery and ethno-racial relations, the sociology of underdevelopment with special reference to the Caribbean, and the problems of gender and familial relations in the black societies of the Americas. A prolific writer, Patterson has been published widely in journals of opinion and the national press. His books include *Slavery and Social Death, The Ordeal of Integration*, and *Freedom in the Making of Western Culture*, for which he won the National Book Award for Nonfiction in 1991. A public intellectual, Professor Patterson was, for eight years, special advisor for social policy and development to Prime Minister Michael Manley of Jamaica.

Cristina Rodríguez is the first Latina tenured law professor at Yale Law School. For two years she served as deputy assistant attorney general in the Office of Legal Counsel in the U.S. Department of Justice, and prior to that she was on the faculty at the NYU School of Law. Her fields of research include immigration law, constitutional law and theory, administrative law and process, language rights and language policy, and citizenship theory. Before beginning her academic career, Rodríguez was a Rhodes Scholar at Oxford University, where she earned a master of letters in modern history. After graduating from law school, she served as a clerk to Judge David S. Tatel of the U.S. Court of Appeals for the D.C. Circuit, and to Justice Sandra Day O'Connor of the U.S. Supreme Court.

Gerald Torres holds the Bryant Smith Chair in Law at the University of Texas at Austin. He is an expert in agricultural law, environmental law, and critical race theory. He has been a visiting professor at Harvard and Stanford law schools, and with Lani Guinier is the author of *The Miner's Canary*. He has served as the deputy assistant attorney general for the Environment and Natural Resources Division of the U.S. Department of Justice and as counsel to former U.S. attorney general Janet Reno. A past president of the Association of American Law Schools, Torres was honored with the 2004 Legal Service Award from the Mexican American Legal Defense and Educational Fund (MALDEF) for his work to advance the legal rights of Latinos. He is currently board chair of the Advancement Project, one of the nation's most prominent social and racial justice organizations.

NOTES

Preface

1. See John Hope Franklin, "The Two Worlds of Race: A Historical View," in *Race and History: Selected Essays, 1938–1988* (Baton Rouge: Louisiana State University Press, 1992).
2. For an overview of the present condition of African Americans from which these figures are drawn, see Orlando Patterson, "Black Americans," in *Understanding America: The Anatomy of an Exceptional Nation*, ed. Peter Schuck and James Wilson (New York: PublicAffairs, 2008), chap. 13.
3. John Hope Franklin, *Mirror to America: The Autobiography of John Hope Franklin* (New York: Farrar, Straus, 2005), 379.
4. Julia B. Isaacs, "Economic Mobility of Black and White Families," Pew Charitable Trust, November 13, 2007, pewtrusts.org/uploadedFiles/wwwpewtrustsorg/Reports/Economic_Mobility/EMP%20Black%20and%20White%20Families%20ES+Chapter.pdf.
5. For example, see Gary Orfield and Chungmei Lee, *Racial Transformation and the Changing Nature of Segregation* (Cambridge, MA: The Civil Rights Project at Harvard University, 2006).
6. For a discussion of the role of culture and how it has been treated, see Orlando Patterson, "Taking Culture Seriously: A Framework & Afro-American Illustration," in *Culture Matters: How Values Shape Human Progress*, ed. Lawrence Harrison and Samuel Huntington (New York: Basic Books, 2001), 202–18.

Introduction:
The New Black and the Death of the Civil Rights Idea

1. Martha Minow, *In Brown's Wake: Legacies of America's Educational Landmark* (New York: Oxford University Press, 2010), 169–89.
2. Thomas J. Sugrue, *The Origins of the Urban Crisis: Race and Inequality in Postwar Detroit* (Princeton, NJ: Princeton University Press, 2005);

Kevin M. Kruse, *White Flight: Atlanta and the Making of Modern Conservatism* (Princeton, NJ: Princeton University Press, 2005).

3. Howard Schuman, Charlotte Steeh, Lawrence Bobo, and Maria Krysan, *Racial Attitudes in America: Trends and Interpretation*, 2nd ed. (Cambridge, MA: Harvard University Press, 1997), 153–83.

4. Nancy MacLean, *Freedom Is Not Enough: The Opening of the American Workplace* (Cambridge, MA: Harvard University Press, 2006), 225–61.

5. Dalton Conley, *Being Black, Living in the Red: Race, Wealth, and Social Policy in America* (Berkeley: University of California Press, 1999).

6. According to one well-respected social scientist, between 1979 and 1999, the risk of imprisonment increased two-and-a-half times for black men who had not been to college, while it actually *decreased* for black men with some college education. Bruce Western, *Punishment and Inequality in America* (New York: Russell Sage Foundation, 2006), 27.

7. For a recent, somewhat polemical, argument for the declining relevance of civil rights law, see Richard Thompson Ford, *Rights Gone Wrong: How Law Corrupts the Struggle for Equality* (New York: Farrar, Straus and Giroux, 2011).

8. Jennifer L. Hochschild, Vesla M. Weaver, and Traci Burch, "Destabilizing the American Racial Order," *Daedalus* 140, no. 2 (Spring 2011): 151–65; Richard Alba, *Remaking the American Mainstream: Assimilation and Contemporary Immigration* (Cambridge, MA: Harvard University Press, 2003).

9. Michelle Alexander, *The New Jim Crow: Mass Incarceration in the Age of Colorblindness* (New York: The New Press, 2010).

10. Stephen Ansolabehere, Nathaniel Persily, and Charles Stewart III, "Race, Region, and Vote Choice in the 2008 Election: Implications for the Future of the Voting Rights Act," *Harvard Law Review* 123 (2010): 1385.

11. Michael Tesler and David O. Sears, *Obama's Race: The 2008 Election and the Dream of a Post-Racial America* (Chicago: University of Chicago Press, 2010); Randall Kennedy, *The Persistence of the Color Line: Racial Politics and the Obama Presidency* (New York: Pantheon Books, 2011).

12. See also William Julius Wilson, *More Than Just Race: Being Black and Poor in the Inner City* (New York: Norton, 2009).

13. Schuman et al., *Racial Attitudes in America*, 114–18.

14. Jon Hanson, ed., *Ideology, Psychology, and Law* (New York: Oxford University Press, 2010).

1. Political Race and the New Black

1. Charles LeDuff, "At a Slaughterhouse Some Things Never Die: Who Kills, Who Cuts, Who Bosses Can Depend on Race," *New York Times*, June 16, 2000, http://www.nytimes.com/2000/06/16/us/slaughterhouse -some-things-never-die-who-kills-who-cuts-who-bosses-can-depend .html?pagewanted=print&src=pm.
2. Ibid.
3. Ibid.
4. Ibid.
5. Ibid.
6. Ibid.
7. Krissah Thompson, "NAACP President Benjamin Jealous Reaches Out to a Changing Membership," *Washington Post*, November 3, 2009, http://www.washingtonpost.com/wp-dyn/content/article/2009/11/02/ AR2009110202850.html.
8. Ibid.
9. Ibid.
10. Ibid.
11. Ibid.
12. Ibid.
13. But shared hardships don't necessarily make allies. "As linked fate rises, so does competition," said Michael Jones-Correa, a professor of government at Cornell who specializes in immigration and interethnic relations. "It's like a sibling rivalry," he said. "This is not a painless relationship." Isabel Wilkerson, "In Florida: A Death Foretold," *New York Times*, April 1, 2012, http://www.ny times.com/2012/04/01/opinion/sunday/a-native-caste-society.html ?pagewanted=all.
14. See, e.g., Lani Guinier and Gerald Torres, *The Miner's Canary: Enlisting Race, Resisting Power, Transforming Democracy* (Cambridge, MA: Harvard University Press, 2003), chap. 7.
15. See Gerald Torres, "The Legacy of Conquest and Discovery," in *Borderless Borders*, ed. Frank Bonilla and Maria Elena Torres (Philadelphia: Temple University Press, 2000), 153, 167–68.
16. Wilkerson, "In Florida, a Death Foretold."
17. Lani Guinier, "From Racial Liberalism to Racial Literacy," *Journal of American History* 91 (2004): 108.

18. David Levering Lewis, "The Souls of Black Folk: A Century Hence," *New Crisis* 110 (2003): 18.
19. Guinier and Torres, *The Miner's Canary*, 75.
20. LeDuff, "At a Slaughterhouse."
21. See Neil Foley, *Quest for Equality: The Failed Promise of Black-Brown Solidarity* (Cambridge, MA: Harvard University Press, 2010).
22. Beth Roy, *Bitters in the Honey: Tales of Hope and Disappointment Across Divides of Race and Time* (Fayetteville: University of Arkansas Press, 1999), 324–25, 338–44.
23. "From Slavery to Freedom to the White House: Race in 21st Century America, a Conference in Honor of John Hope Franklin," April 8, 2010, http://law.duke.edu/webcast/?match=Center+on+Law%2C+Race%2C+and+Politics.
24. Although we have taken some liberties with the transcript, we have been honest with the substance and the tone of the conversation. In our view the conversation reveals some of the fractures within a racialized social policy that our idea of political race must confront.
25. Illegal immigrants don't have social security numbers, but they can get what's called an I-10 number to pay taxes. See, e.g., http://www.npr.org/templates/story/story.php?storyId=9615621; see also http://www.us-immigration.com/?gclid=CKTth-vJ4K8CFYhM4Aod51wQ2g.
26. See, e.g., "Black Mamba: Illegal Immigrants Are the New Black," *New York Times* Room for Debate, December 13, 2011 a black woman ("blackmamba") from Dearborn, Michigan? Kay, Dearborn, MI

    "I remember reading a treatise in college many years ago, written by Benjamin Franklin, about why white people will fall behind in population. He looked at black slaves, Native Americans and Latinos and made the case for whites losing their majority in the United States. Didn't happen due to immigration. So much for that. The problem today is loss of "The American Dream" that many of us grew up with. The jobs we once had were outsourced due to corporate greed and their willing enablers in Congress.

    As an African American whose ancestors were forced to this country, I struggle with why there is so much antipathy aimed at Hispanic immigrants. Go to any hotel, or landscaping crews or migrant workers and you will see how Hispanic workers are doing important jobs that few others want. I am sorry to say that the real issue is racism. The jobs that we once had making things have gone overseas. This has nothing to do with immigration. I am ashamed by the outright racism."

27. See, e.g., Alexander Stille, "The Paradox of the New Elite," *New York Times*, October 24, 2011, http://www.nytimes.com/2011/10/23/opin ion/sunday/social-inequality-and-the-new-elite.html?pagewanted=all.
28. See, e.g., http://1nedrop.com/susie-guillory-phipps-the-state-of-lou isiana-and-the-one-drop-rule. (Although Louisiana repealed its one-drop rule in 1983, a woman who contested her status as black lost because the 1983 law was not retroactive.) Apparently, the onus of proving that one is not black still rests on the individual.
29. This does not mean that King and others were unaware of the necessity to challenge economic injustice directly and systemically. See, e.g., Thomas Jackson, "'Bread of Freedom': Martin Luther King, Jr. and Human Rights," *OAH Magazine of History* 22 (2008): 14. Abolishing class inequality and institutional racism meant "restructuring the architecture of American society" and would require organizing "new multiracial alliances" (quoting Dr. King).
30. Andrew Young, foreword to Gary Orfield and Carole Ashkinaze, *The Closing Door: Conservative Policy and Black Opportunity* (Chicago: University of Chicago Press, 1991), viii.
31. See Michael Dawson, "The Future of Black Politics," *Boston Review*, Jan./Feb. 2012, http://www.bostonreview.net/BR37.1/ndf_michael_ dawson_black_politics.php. See also our response, "Don't Go It Alone," *Boston Review*, Jan./Feb. 2012, http://www.bostonrevie.net/BR37.1/ ndf_lani_guinier_gerald_torres_black_politics.php.
32. Guinier and Torres, *The Miner's Canary*, 107.
33. Jackson, Martin Luther King Jr.; "Statement," December 15,1966, in U.S. Senate, Subcommittee on Executive Reorganization, Committee on Government Operations, Federal Role in Urban Affairs (Washington, DC, Government Printing Office, 1966), 2981–82. King voiced these themes explicitly as early as 1964. Martin Luther King Jr., *Why We Can't Wait* (New York: Mentor, 1964), 141, 151; King, "The Stall-In in Review," *New York Amsterdam News*, May 9, 1964; Thomas F. Jackson, *From Civil Rights to Human Rights: Martin Luther King, Jr., and the Struggle for Economic Justice* (Philadelphia: University of Pennsylvania Press, 2007), 203, 244.

2. Déjà Vu All Over Again?

1. W.E.B. DuBois, *The Souls of Black Folk* (Chicago: A.C. McClurg, 1903).
2. Shelby Steele, "America's Post-Racial Promise," *Los Angeles Times*,

November 5, 2008; Touré, *Who's Afraid of Post-Blackness? What It Means to Be Black Now* (New York: Free Press, 2011); Matt Bai, "Is Obama the End of Black Politics?" *New York Times Magazine*, August 6, 2008.

3. This essay was completed too soon after the 2012 election to fully integrate its results. Preliminary assessments indicate that the voting coalition that elected Obama in 2012 was similar to that of 2008, with the most significant difference being the shift of some white voters out of Obama's column in 2012, and the shift of some Latino voters in the opposite direction. For preliminary results, see the Pew Research Center analysis at http://www.people-press.org/2012/11/07/changing-face-of-america-helps-assure-obama-victory/.

4. Office of the Press Secretary, press release, "Remarks by the President in Remembrance of Dr. Martin Luther King, Jr.," January 17, 2010, http://www.whitehouse.gov/the-press-office/remarks-president-remebrance-dr-martin-luther-king-jr.

5. Gunnar Myrdal, *An American Dilemma* (New York: Harper and Row, 1944).

6. David Hollinger "The Concept of Post-Racial: How Its Easy Dismissal Obscures Important Questions," *Daedalus* 140, no. 1 (Winter 2011): 174–82.

7. See, for example, Desmond King and Rogers Smith, *Still a House Divided: Race and Politics in Obama's America* (Princeton, NJ: Princeton University Press, 2011); Ian Haney López, "Is the 'Post' in Post-Racial the 'Blind' in Colorblind?" *Cardozo Law Review* 32, no. 3 (Jan. 2011): 807–31; Thomas Sugrue, *Not Even Past: Barack Obama and the Burden of Race* (Princeton, NJ: Princeton University Press, 2010).

8. Lawrence Bobo and Camille Z. Charles, "Race in the American Mind: From the Moynihan Report to the Obama Candidacy," *The ANNALS of the American Academy of Political and Social Science* 621 (2009): 243.

9. Bobo and Charles, "Race in the American Mind," 244.

10. For reviews of this literature, see Vincent Hutchings and Nicholas Valentino, "The Centrality of Race in American Politics," *Annual Review of Political Science* 7 (2004): 383–408; Taeku Lee and Nicole Willcoxon, "Public Opinion, the Media, Race, and Civil Rights," in *Oxford Handbook of American Public Opinion and the Media*, ed. Robert Shapiro and Lawrence Jacobs (New York: Oxford University Press, 2011).

11. David Canon, *Race, Redistricting, and Representation: The Unintended*

Consequences of Black Majority Districts (Chicago: University of Chicago Press, 1999).

12. Nadya Terkildsen, "When White Voters Evaluate Black Candidates: The Processing Implications of Candidate Skin Color, Prejudice, and Self-Monitoring," *American Journal of Political Science* 37, no. 4 (1993): 1032–53.

13. See, e.g., Lawrence D. Bobo, "Racial Attitudes and Relations at the Close of the Twentieth Century," in *America Becoming: Racial Trends and Their Consequences*, volume 1, ed. Neil Smelser, William Julius Wilson, and Faith Mitchell (Washington, DC: National Academies Press, 2001); Donald Kinder and Lynn Sanders, *Divided by Color: Racial Politics and Democratic Ideals* (Chicago: University of Chicago Press, 1996).

14. For a good synthesis, see Shankar Vedantam, "See No Bias," *Washington Post Magazine* (January 23, 2005), 12–17, 38–42.

15. For one engagement with this question, see Kristin Lane and John Tost, "Black Man in the White House: Ideology and Implicit Racial Bias in the Age of Obama," in *The Obamas and a (Post) Racial America?* ed. Gregory S. Parks and Matthew W. Hughey (New York: Oxford University Press, 2011).

16. See, e.g., Tukufu Zuberi, *Thicker Than Blood: How Racial Statistics Lie* (Minneapolis: University of Minnesota Press, 2001); Taeku Lee, "Race, Immigration, and the Identity-to-Politics Link," *Annual Review of Political Science* 11 (2008): 457–78.

17. See, e.g., Stephen Ansolabehere, Nathaniel Persily, and Charles Stewart III, "Race, Region, and Vote Choice in the 2008 Election: Implications for the Future of the Voting Rights Act," *Harvard Law Review* 123, 2010: 1385–1436.

18. See, for example, A. G. Greenwald et al., "Race Attitude Measured Predicted Vote in the 2008 U.S. Presidential Elections," *Analyses of Social Issues and Public Policy* 9 (2009): 241–53; B. K. Payne et al., "Implicit and Explicit Prejudice in the 2008 American Presidential Election," *Journal of Experimental Social Psychology* 46 (2010): 367–74; Donald Kinder and Allison Dale-Riddle, *The End of Race? Obama, 2008, and Racial Politics in America* (New Haven, CT: Yale University Press, 2012); Michael Tesler and David O. Sears, *Obama's Race: The 2008 Election and the Dream of a Post-Racial America* (Chicago: University of Chicago Press, 2010); Lane and Tost, "Black Man in the White House."

19. See Payne, "Implicit and Explicit Prejudice"; Michael Lewis-Beck, Charles Tien, and Richard Nadeau, "Obama's Missed Landslide: A Racial Cost?" *PS: Political Science and Politics* 43, no. 1 (2010): 69–76; Simon Jackman and Lynn Vavreck, "How Does Obama Match-Up? Counterfactuals and the Role of Obama's Race in 2008," unpublished manuscript, 2011; Seth Stephens-Davidowitz, "The Effects of Racial Animus on Voting: Evidence Using Google Search Data," unpublished manuscript, 2011.

20. Taeku Lee, "Somewhere Over the Rainbow? Post-Racial and Pan-Racial Politics in the Age of Obama," *Daedalus* 140, no. 2 (Spring 2011): 136–50.

21. See, e.g., Toni Morrison, *Playing in the Dark* (Cambridge, MA: Harvard University Press, 1990); Ian Haney López, *White by Law* (New York: New York University Press, 1996).

22. In this section, I rely heavily on Zoltan Hajnal and Taeku Lee, *Why Americans Don't Join the Party: Race, Immigration, and the Failure (of Political Parties) to Engage the Electorate* (Princeton, NJ: Princeton University Press, 2011).

23. Ibid.

24. U.S. Citizenship and Immigration Services, *Yearbook of Immigration Statistics: 2008* (Washington, DC: U.S. Department of Homeland Security, Office of Immigration Statistics, 2009).

25. Ansolabahere et al. further report that "the increase in the Democratic share of the electorate was due almost completely to increased turnout among minorities, and the decrease in the Republican share of the electorate is due to the drop off of whites," 1411.

26. For a notable exception, see Lani Guinier, "Beyond Electocracy: Rethinking the Political Representative as Powerful Stranger," *Modern Law Review* 71, no. 1 (2008): 1–35.

27. See, e.g., Richard D. Shingles, "Black Consciousness and Political Participation: The Missing Link," *American Political Science Review* 75, no. 1 (1981): 76–91; Lawrence D. Bobo and Franklin D. Gilliam Jr., "Race, Sociopolitical Participation, and Black Empowerment," *American Political Science Review*, 84, no. 2 (1990): 377–93; Michael C. Dawson, *Behind the Mule: Race and Class in African-American Politics* (Princeton, NJ: Princeton University Press, 1994); Katherine Tate, *From Protest to Politics: The New Black Voters in American Elections* (Cambridge, MA: Harvard University Press, 1993).

28. See, e.g., Tommie Shelby, *We Who Are Dark: The Philosophical*

Foundations of Black Solidarity (Cambridge, MA: Belknap Press of Harvard University Press, 2005); Wendy Brown, *States of Injury* (Princeton, NJ: Princeton University Press, 1995); Iris Marion Young, *Inclusion and Democracy* (New York: Oxford University Press, 2000).

29. The concept of a linked-fate heuristic is developed in Dawson, *Behind the Mule* and Tate, *From Protest to Politics*. See also Paula McClain et al., "Group Membership, Group Identity, and Group Consciousness: Measures of Racial Identity in American Politics?" *Annual Review of Political Science* 12 (2009): 471–85; Jane Junn, "Mobilizing Group Consciousness: When Does Ethnicity Have Political Consequences?" in *Transforming Politics, Transforming America: The Political and Civic Incorporation of Immigrants in the United States*, ed. Taeku Lee, S. Karthick Ramakrishnan, and Ricardo Ramírez (Charlottesville: University of Virginia Press, 2006); Dennis Chong and Reuel Rogers, "Reviving Group Consciousness," in *The Politics of Democratic Inclusion*, ed. Christina Wolbrecht and Rodney E. Hero (Philadelphia: Temple University Press, 2005).

30. Cathy Cohen, *Boundaries of Blackness: AIDS and the Breakdown of Black Politics* (Chicago: University of Chicago Press, 1999). See also Michael C. Dawson, *Black Visions: The Roots of Contemporary African-American Political Ideologies* (Chicago: University of Chicago Press, 2001); Melissa V. Harris-Perry, *Sister Citizen: Shame, Stereotypes, and Black Women in America* (New Haven, CT: Yale University Press, 2011).

3. Immigration and the Civil Rights Agenda

1. A 2006 survey by the Pew Hispanic Center found that 62 percent of native-born Latinos and 64 percent of foreign-born Latinos believed the immigrants' rights marches of May 2006 signaled the start of a new civil rights movement that will go on for a long time. See Roberto Suro and Gabriel Escobar, "National Survey of Latinos: The Immigration Debate," Pew Hispanic Center, July 13, 2006, http://www.pewhispanic.org/files/reports/68.pdf.

2. I have elaborated on this observation elsewhere. Cristina M. Rodríguez, "Latinos and Immigrants," *Harvard Latino Law Review* 11 (2008): 247.

3. Harry S. Truman, "Veto of Bill to Revise the Laws Relating to Immigration, Naturalization, and Nationality," June 25, 1952, the American

Presidency Project, http://www.presidency.ucsb.edu/ws/index.php ?pid=14175. In the letter, President Truman referenced his 1948 message to Congress: "I have long urged that racial or national barriers to naturalization be abolished. This was one of the recommendations in my civil rights message to the Congress on February 2, 1948."

4. Ibid. President Truman stated, "The idea behind this discriminatory policy was, to put it baldly, that Americans with English or Irish names were better people and better citizens than Americans with Italian or Greek or Polish names. It was thought that people of West European origin made better citizens than Rumanians or Yugoslavs or Ukrainians or Hungarians or Baits or Austrians. Such a concept is utterly unworthy of our traditions and our ideals. It violates the great political doctrine of the Declaration of Independence that 'all men are created equal.' It denies the humanitarian creed inscribed beneath the Statue of Liberty proclaiming to all nations, 'Give me your tired, your poor, your huddled masses yearning to breathe free.' "

5. A long list of these connections could be written. When Congress in 1964 finally put an end to the Mexican guest worker regime known as the Bracero program, begun at the close of World War II to address wartime labor shortages in the Southwest, it was in part due to the political pressure exerted by unions and other civil rights activists, who drew attention to the gross exploitation of the Bracero workers, as well as to the program's negative effects on the working conditions and wages of U.S. citizens—realities brought to the general public's attention through Edward R. Murrow's documentary *Harvest of Shame*, CBS, November 25, 1960. For a discussion of the Bracero program's history, see Adam B. Cox and Cristina M. Rodríguez, "The President and Immigration Law," *Yale Law Journal* 119 (2009): 458, 485–91.

6. See, for example, *Sugarman v. Dougall*, 413 U.S. 634, 646–47 (1973); *Graham v. Richardson*, 403 U.S. 365, 372, 376 (1971); cf. *Mathews v. Diaz*, 426 U.S. 67, 80–81 (1976).

7. 457 U.S. 202 (1982).

8. For an extended argument that the passage of time, which transforms illegal immigrants into members of the polity, gives rise to a moral argument for legalization, see Joseph Carens, "The Case for Amnesty: Time Erodes the State's Right to Deport," *Boston Review*, May/June 2009, http://bostonreview.net/BR34.3/carens.php.

9. The Supreme Court says as much in *Plyler v. Doe*, rejecting calls to

apply strict scrutiny to unauthorized immigrants on the ground that the status is not morally irrelevant. 457 U.S. 202, 220 (1982).

10. In this context, it is worth pointing out that the major civil rights statutes were enacted against a backdrop of social movement protest, but major immigration reforms have more closely fit the model of interest group–driven legislation. Even the Hart-Celler Act of 1965, which made its way through Congress the same year as the Voting Rights Act and was animated by civil rights principles of equal treatment, did not result from widespread popular mobilization, but rather from lobbying by discrete ethnic groups and the State Department. 1965 Immigration and Nationality Act, H.R. 2580, 89th Cong. (1965) (enacted).

11. See Dowell Myers, *Immigrants and Boomers: Forging a New Social Contract for the Future of America* (New York: Russell Sage Foundation, 2007), 36–40.

12. T. Alexander Aleinikoff has articulated the pragmatic case for legalization using cost-benefit language, which is congenial to a mutual benefit narrative. See Alexander Aleinikoff, "Legalization Has Its Costs, but They Are Outweighed by the Benefits; Pragmatic Arguments May, in the End, Be Most Persuasive," *Boston Review*, May/June 2009, http:// bostonreview.net/BR34.3/aleinikoff.php.

13. For an astute discussion of the politics of immigration reform, noting that the obstacles to immigration reform, which in and of itself is treacherous for presidents and congressional leaders, are heightened when focused on illegal immigration, see Daniel J. Tichenor, "Navigating an American Minefield: The Politics of Illegal Immigration," *The Forum* 7, no. 3 (2009): 1.

14. N. C. Aizenman, "Latinos Skeptical of Obama Immigration Efforts," *Washington Post*, March 20, 2010, A3. In this article, Aizenman notes that, in fiscal year 2009, the rate of removal increased 5 percent to 387,790 removals, and that the removal of immigrants who have committed crimes increased by 19 percent.

15. For a discussion of the evolution of the 287(g) program and other programs involving federal-state collaboration in enforcement that contain similar priorities, see Cristina M. Rodríguez, Muzaffar Chishti, Randy Capps, and Laura St. John, *A Program in Flux: New Priorities and Implementation Challenges for 287(g)* (Washington, DC: Migration Policy Institute, 2010).

16. Another important procedural shift initiated by executive officials

in 2009 was attorney general Holder's decision to vacate the opinion issued by former attorney general Mukasey denying that ineffective assistance of counsel could be a basis for a motion to reopen, overturning twenty years of precedent and essentially establishing that, because immigrants do not have a constitutional right to counsel, they cannot claim relief based on their lawyers' mistakes. Holder ordered the Bureau of Immigration Appeals to continue applying past precedent on ineffective assistance of counsel pending a rulemaking on the subject. Compean, 25 I&N Dec. 1 (A.G. 2009). Interim Decision #3643. This move simultaneously acknowledges the importance of counsel to the immigrant's ability to defend his interests in removal proceedings and the value of procedural protections, such as the right to counsel, to the integrity of the regime of immigration adjudication, because of the role that counsel plays both in checking the government's power and helping to approximate the correct outcome in adjudications.

17. U.S. Immigration and Customs Enforcement, "ICE Announces Major Reforms to Immigration Detention System," news release, Aug. 6, 2009, http://www.ice.gov/pi/nr/0908/090806washington.htm.

18. See Dora Schriro, "Immigration Detention Overview and Recommendations," U.S. Immigration and Customs Enforcement, Department of Homeland Security, October 6, 2009, http://www.ice.gov/doclib/about/offices/odpp/pdf/ice-detention-rpt.pdf.

4. The President and the Justice

1. *People v. Hall*, 4 Cal. 399 (1854).

2. Noel Ignatiev, *How the Irish Became White* (New York: Routledge, 1995), 2.

3. David Roedriger, *Working Toward Whiteness: How America's Immigrants Became White* (New York: Basic Books, 2005), 27.

4. Touré, *Who's Afraid of Post-Blackness: What It Means to Be Black Now* (New York: Free Press, 2011), 32.

5. Ibid.

6. Ibid., 25.

7. See James Baldwin, "A Talk to Teachers," *Saturday Review*, December 21, 1963.

8. Zora Neale Hurston, "How It Feels to Be Colored Me," *World Tomorrow*, May, 11 1928.

9. Ibid.
10. Ibid.
11. For a provocative essay on what it means to be white or nonwhite, see Eric Liu, "Notes of a Native Speaker," *Washington Post*, May 17, 1998.
12. Andrew Malcolm, "Chris Matthews Approvingly Says 'I Forgot He Was Black' of Obama's Speech," *Los Angeles Times*, January 27, 2010.
13. Jeffrey Toobin, "Annals of Law: Partners," *New Yorker*, August 29, 2011.
14. Barack Obama, *The Audacity of Hope: Thoughts on Reclaiming the American Dream* (New York: Crown, 2006), 231.
15. Michael Fletcher, "Justice Thomas Faces Down Critics," *Washington Post*, July 30, 1998.
16. W.E.B. DuBois, *The Souls of Black Folk* (Chicago: A.C. McClurg, 1903).
17. Jane Mayer and Jill Abramson, *Strange Justice: The Selling of Clarence Thomas* (Boston: Houghton Mifflin, 1994), 52.
18. Barack Obama, "The America We Love" (address, Independence, MO., June 30, 2008).
19. Fletcher, "Justice Thomas Faces Down Critics."
20. Barack Obama, "A More Perfect Union" (address, National Constitution Center, Philadelphia, PA, March 18, 2008).
21. Helene Cooper, "Attorney General Chided for Language on Race," *New York Times*, March 7, 2009. Obama agreed with Holder that "we're oftentimes uncomfortable talking about race until there's some sort of racial flare up or conflict," but said, "I think it's fair to say that if I had been advising my attorney general, we would have used different language."
22. See Stephen F. Smith, "Clarence X? The Black Nationalist Behind Justice Thomas's Constitutionalism," *New York University Journal of Law and Liberty* 4 (2009): 583; Angela Onwuachi-Willig, "Just Another Brother on the SCT?: What Justice Clarence Thomas Teaches Us About the Influence of Racial Identity," *Iowa Law Review* 90 (2005): 931.
23. Smith, "Clarence X?," Onwuachi-Willig, "Just Another Brother?"
24. 538 U.S. 343 (2003) (Thomas, J., dissenting).
25. Linda Greenhouse, "An Intense Attack by Justice Thomas on Cross Burning," *New York Times*, December 12, 2002.
26. Ibid.
27. Jeffrey Rosen, "Annals of Law: Moving On," *New Yorker*, April 29, 1996.
28. 558 U.S. 310 (2010).
29. Toobin, "Annals of Law."
30. 561 U.S. 3025 (2010) (Thomas, J., concurring).

31. Derrick Bell, "Who's Afraid of Critical Race Theory?" *University of Illinois Law Review,* 1995, no. 4: 908.
32. Obama, *The Audacity of Hope,* 239.
33. David Jackson, "Obama Rejects Congressional Black Caucus Criticism," *USA Today,* December 3, 2009.
34. Juan Williams, "A Question of Fairness," *Atlantic,* February 1987, 56.
35. Rosen, "Annals of Law."
36. Derrick Bell, "Racial Realism," *Connecticut Law Review* 24 (1992): 363–79.
37. "Clarence Thomas: The Justice Nobody Knows," *60 Minutes,* February 11, 2009.
38. Obama, "A More Perfect Union."
39. Terry McDermott and Mark Z. Baraban, "Crowds Adore Obama," *Los Angeles Times,* December 11, 2006.
40. 515 U.S. 200, 240 (1995) (Thomas, J., concurring).
41. 551 U.S. 701, 780–81 (2007) (Thomas, J., concurring).
42. Clarence Thomas, *My Grandfather's Son: A Memoir* (New York: Harper, 2007), 87, 99.
43. Cooper, "Attorney General Chided."
44. David Paul Kuhn, "Obama Shifts Affirmative Action Rhetoric," Politico, August 10, 2008.
45. Obama, *The Audacity of Hope,* 245–46.
46. Ibid., 247.
47. Maureen Dowd, "McCain's Green-Eyed Monster," *New York Times,* August 5, 2008.
48. Kuhn, "Obama Shifts."
49. Ibid.
50. Obama, "A More Perfect Union."
51. Juan Williams, "EEOC Chairman Blasts Black Leaders," *Washington Post,* October 25, 1984.
52. Barack Obama, address to the Congressional Black Caucus (CBC) Foundation Gala, September 24, 2011, Washington, DC.
53. Barack Obama, address to the National Association for the Advancement of Colored People (NAACP) Centennial Convention, July 16, 2009, New York, NY.
54. Ibid.
55. Barack Obama, address to the Apostolic Church of God, June 15, 2008, Chicago, IL, http://www.huffingtonpost.com/2008/06/15/obamas-fathers-day-speech_n_107220.html.

56. "Obama's Racial Identity Still an Issue," CBSNews.com, February 11, 2009.
57. U.S. Congress. Senate. Committee on the Judiciary. *Nomination of Judge Clarence Thomas to Be Associate Justice of the Supreme Court of the United States.* 102nd Cong., October 11, 1991.
58. "The President's Agenda and the African American Community," November 2011, http://www.whitehouse.gov/sites/default/files/af_am_report_final.pdf.
59. Suzanne Gamboa, "Obama Seeks Ideas on Reducing Black Joblessness," Associated Press, November 10, 2011, http://www.businessweek.com/ap/financialnews/D9QTU5RO0.htm.
60. Ibid.
61. Rakesh Kochnar et al., *Wealth Gaps Rise to Record Highs Between Whites, Blacks, Hispanics* (Pew Research Center, July 2011), http://pewresearc.org/pubs/2069/housing-bubble-subprime-mortgages-hispanics-blacks-household-wealth-disparity.
62. Ibid.
63. Ibid.
64. Marc Mauer and Ryan S. King, *Uneven Justice: State Rates of Incarceration by Race and Ethnicity* (Washington, DC: The Sentencing Project, July 2007), http://sentencingproject.org/doc/publications/rd_stateratesofincbyraceandethnicity.pdf.
65. Lauren Glaze and Laura Maruschak, *Parents in Prison and Their Minor Children* (Washington, DC: BJS Special Report, March 2010), http://bjs.ojp.usdoj.gov/content/pub/pdf/pptmc.pdf.
66. William Sabol and Heather Couture, *Prison Inmates at Midyear 2007* (Washington, DC: BJS Bulletin, June 2008), http://bjs.ojp.usdoj.gov/content/pub/pdf/pim07.pdf.
67. 539 U.S. 306, 349–50 (2003) (Thomas, J., separate opinion).
68. Randall Kennedy, *The Persistence of the Color Line* (New York: Pantheon Books, 2011), 224.
69. Obama, address to the National Association for the Advancement of Colored People (NAACP) Centennial Convention.
70. Barack Obama, remarks in a town hall meeting, August 15, 2011, Decorah, Iowa, http://www.whitehouse.gov/the-press-office/2011/08/15/remarks-president-town-hall-meeting-decorah-iowa.
71. *Regents of Univ. of California v. Bakke*, 438 U.S. 265, 407 (1978) (Blackmun, J., separate opinion).
72. "Obama's Hip-Hop BBQ Didn't Create Jobs," Fox Nation, August 5,

2011, http://nation.foxnews.com/president-obama/2011/08/05/obama
-parties-chris-rock-jay-z-and-whoopi-while-rome-burns.

5. The Racial Metamorphosis of Justice Kennedy and the Future of Civil Rights Law

1. Noah Feldman, "The United States of Justice Kennedy," Bloomberg, May 30, 2011, http://www.bloomberg.com/news/2011-05-30/how-it -became-the-united-states-of-justice-kennedy-noah-feldman.html.
2. 129 S. Ct. 2658 (2009).
3. Ibid., (Scalia, J., concurring).
4. 539 U.S. 461 (2003).
5. Ibid., 491 (Kennedy, J., concurring).
6. The term "Second Reconstruction" was popularized by the historian C. Vann Woodward, referring to the modern civil rights movement during which African Americans regained many of the rights that were lost at the close of the post–Civil War Reconstruction. In this essay, the term refers to the major civil rights acts of the 1960s, which enshrined these rights: the Civil Rights Act of 1964, and the Voting Rights Act of 1965.
7. See *Grutter v. Bollinger*, 539 U.S. 306 (2003); see also *Chisom v. Roemer*, 501 U.S. 380 (1991) (Kennedy, J., dissenting); *Johnson v. DeGrandy*, 512 U.S. 997, 1026 (1994) (Kennedy, J., concurring).
8. 548 U.S. 399 (2006).
9. 551 U.S. 701, 797 (2007).
10. 129 S. Ct. 1231 (2009).
11. 129 S. Ct. 2658 (2009).
12. See Adam Liptak, "A Significant Term, with Bigger Cases Ahead," *New York Times*, June 28, 2011 (citing Professors Lee Epstein and Andrew Martin for the conclusion that the odds that "nine truly independent judges finding themselves in just two configurations a dozen times out of 14" is 1 in 44.2 quintillion).
13. See Luis Fuentes-Rohwer, "The End of the Second Reconstruction" (draft on file).
14. See Lee Epstein and Tonja Jacobi, "Super Medians," *Stanford Law Review* 61 (2008): 37.
15. Ibid., 51.
16. See ibid., 54 (fig. 3).
17. 488 U.S. 469 (1989).

18. 497 U.S. 547 (1990).
19. 488 U.S. 519.
20. *Metro Broadcasting*, 497 U.S. 632, 633 n.1, and 635.
21. See, e.g., *Miller v. Johnson*, 515 U.S. 900 (1995); *Rice v. Cayetano*, 528 U.S. 495 (2000).
22. *Presley v. Etowah County Commission*, 502 U.S. 491 (1992); *Holder v. Hall*, 512 U.S. 874 (1994).
23. 512 U.S. 997 (1994).
24. Ibid., 1026.
25. Ibid.
26. 42 U.S.C. sec. 1973 (cited ibid., 1026–27).
27. *DeGrandy*, 512 U.S. 1027.
28. Ibid. (citing *Voinovich v. Quilter*, 507 U.S. 146, 151–52 (1993); Abigail Thernstrom, *Whose Votes Count? Affirmative Action and Minority Voting Rights*, 210–16 (Cambridge, MA: Harvard University Press, 1987); Carol Swain, *Black Faces, Black Interests*, ch. 6 (Cambridge, MA: Harvard University Press, 1993)).
29. *DeGrandy*, 512 U.S. 1027 (citing *Metro Broadcasting, Inc. v. FCC*, 497 U.S. 547, 636 (1990) (Kennedy, J., dissenting)).
30. Ibid., 1029 (citing *Metro Broadcasting, Inc. v. FCC* 497 U.S. 636–37 (Kennedy, J., dissenting)).
31. Ibid., 1030 (citing *Shaw v. Reno*, 509 U.S. 630, 657 (1993)).
32. Ibid., 1029 (citing *City of Richmond v. Croson*, 488 U.S. 469 (1989) (Kennedy, J., concurring)).
33. Heather K. Gerken, "Justice Kennedy and the Domains of Equal Protection," *Harvard Law Review* 121 (2007): 104.
34. 551 U.S. 701 (2007).
35. Ibid., 787–88.
36. *Parents Involved*, 551 U.S. 788.
37. 548 U.S. 399 (2006).
38. See *Georgia v. Ashcroft*, 539 U.S. 461, 491 (2003) (Kennedy, J., concurring).
39. On this point, see *LULAC*, 548 U.S. 399, 497 (2006) (Roberts, J., dissenting).
40. See ibid., 498–500.
41. 515 U.S. 900 (1995).
42. Ibid., 927–28.
43. Ibid., 440.
44. *Miller v. Johnson*, 515 U.S. 900, 911–12 (1995) (quoting *Shaw v. Reno*,

509 U.S. 630, 647 (1993)); see *Metro Broadcasting v. FCC*, 497 U.S. 547, 636 (1990) (Kennedy, J., dissenting): "The perceptions of the excluded class must also be weighed, with attention to the cardinal rule that our Constitution protects each citizen as an individual, not as a member of a group.").

45. Epstein and Jacobi, "Super Medians," 51.
46. 515 U.S. 900 (1995).
47. 532 U.S. 234 (2001).
48. See Pamela S. Karlan, "The Law of Small Numbers: *Gonzalez v. Carhart, Parents Involved in Community Schools*, and Some Themes from the First Full Term of the Roberts Court," *North Carolina Law Review* 86 (2008): 1369.
49. Ibid., 1377.
50. Ibid.
51. Gerken, "Justice Kennedy," 118; Reva B. Siegel, "From Colorblindness to Antibalkanization: An Emerging Ground of Decision in Race Equality Cases," *Yale Law Journal* 120 (2011): 1278.
52. Ibid., 1299.
53. See *Ricci v. DeStefano*, 129 S. Ct. 2658, 2676–77 (2009).
54. See Michelle Adams, "Is Integration a Discriminatory Purpose?" *Iowa Law Review* 96 (2011): 837; Cheryl I. Harris and Kimberly West-Faulcon, "Reading *Ricci*: Whitening Discrimination, Racing Test Fairness, *UCLA Law Review* 58 (2010): 73.
55. Siegel, "From Colorblindness," 1337.
56. See ibid., 1345.
57. See Jeffrey A. Segal and Harold J. Spaeth, *The Supreme Court and the Attitudinal Model Revisited* (Cambridge, UK: Cambridge University Press, 2002).
58. Feldman, "United States."
59. See *Alden v. Maine*, 527 U.S. 706, 715 (1999): "The States thus retain 'a residuary and inviolable sovereignty.' They are not relegated to the role of mere provinces or political corporations, but retain the dignity, though not the full authority, of sovereignty" (quoting *The Federalist* 39, 245 (C. Rossiter ed. 1961) (J. Madison)).
60. See *Georgia v. Ashcroft*, 539 U.S. 461, 491 (2003) (Kennedy, J., concurring).
61. See *Ricci v. DeStefano*, 129 S. Ct. 2658 (2009).
62. 521 U.S. 507 (1997).
63. Ibid., 519.
64. Ibid., 520.

65. Ibid., 529 (citing *Marbury v. Madison*).
66. See Douglas Laycock, "Conceptual Gulfs in *City of Boerne v. Flores*," *William and Mary Law Review* 39 (1998): 743.
67. *City of Rome v. United States*, 446 U.S. 156, 210–11 (1980) (Rehnquist, J., dissenting).
68. See *Katzenbach v. Morgan*, 384 U.S. 641, 688 (1966) (Harlan, J., dissenting).
69. *NAMUDNO v. Holder*, oral argument, 36.
70. Ibid., 35–36.
71. *NAMUDNO v. Holder*, 129 S. Ct. 2504, 2512 (2009).
72. See Voting Rights Act: Hearings on S. 1564 Before the Senate Comm. on the Judiciary, 89th Cong. 564 (1965) (testimony of Leander Perez). This charge was later echoed by Justice Black in his partial dissent in *South Carolina v. Katzenbach*, 383 U.S. 301, 358–60 (1966) (Black, J., dissenting in part).
73. See *NAMUDNO v. Holder*, 129 S. Ct. 2504, 2511 (2009).
74. See *NAMUDNO v. Holder*, oral argument, 27.
75. 129 S. Ct. 2504 (2009).
76. For example, in *Vieth v. Jubelirer*, 541 U.S. 267 (2004), four justices were ready to brand political gerrymandering cases as political questions, while four justices were prepared to provide judicially manageable standards. Unable to agree with either side, yet unsure that either side had the better argument, Justice Kennedy set the question aside for the future. An answer still awaits.
77. Randall Kennedy, *The Persistence of the Color Line: Racial Politics and the Obama Presidency* (New York: Pantheon Books, 2011), 255.
78. See Alexander M. Bickel, *The Least Dangerous Branch: The Supreme Court at the Bar of Politics*, 2nd ed. (Binghamton, NY: Vail-Ballou Press, 1986).
79. See Derrick A. Bell, "Brown v. Board of Education and the Interest-Convergence Dilemma," *Harvard Law Review* 93 (1980): 518.

6. The Right Kind of Family

1. Author to Chris Johnson, electronic mail, 25 Jan. 2010.
2. Chris Johnson to author, electronic mail, 25 Jan. 2010.
3. Brian Holloway to author, electronic mail, 27 Jan. 2010.
4. Ibid.
5. Brian Holloway to author, electronic mail, 28 Jan. 2010.

6. Karen Holloway to author, electronic mail, 28 Jan. 2010.
7. Wendell Holloway to author, electronic mail, 27 Jan. 2010.
8. Wendell Holloway, telephone interview with author, Jan. 2010. Later on, in a follow-up conversation, my father was more pointed, saying he had to get out of the Air Force because he was "tired of killing people." My father also feels to this day that the death of his first child, David—an older brother I never met—was caused by radiation exposure at one of the Air Force bases where the family was stationed. All of the pilots had to walk around with dosimeters on their chests to gauge radiation exposure, but there was nothing available for the families. That the Air Force "took enough of" him reads on multiple levels, all shot through with trauma.

7. John Hope Franklin

1. Peter Applebome, "John Hope Franklin, Scholar and Witness," Week in Review, *New York Times*, March 28, 2009.
2. John Hope Franklin, *Mirror to America: The Autobiography of John Hope Franklin* (New York: Farrar, Straus and Giroux, 2005), 3.
3. Ibid., 62.
4. Applebome, "John Hope Franklin."
5. Franklin, *Mirror to America*, 376.
6. John Hope Franklin, "The Historian and the Public Policy," in his *Race and History* (Baton Rouge: Louisiana State University Press, 1990; rep. 1992).
7. *The Free Negro in North Carolina, 1790–1860* (Chapel Hill: University of North Carolina Press, 1943; 1995).
8. *Reconstruction After the Civil War* (University of Chicago Press, 1961; pbk. ed., 1963, 1995).
9. *The Militant South, 1800–1861* (Belknap Press of Harvard University, 1956; rep., University of Illinois Press, 2002).
10. [With Loren Schweninger] *Runaway Slaves: Rebels on the Plantation*, (Oxford University Press, 2005).
11. *George Washington Williams: A Biography* (University of Chicago Press, 1985; repr., Duke University Press, 1998).
12. *The Color Line: Legacy for the Twenty-first Century* (University of Missouri Press, 1993); *Racial Equality in America* (University of Chicago Press, 1976; rep., University of Missouri Press, 1993).

13. "Edward Bellamy and the Nationalist Movement," *New England Quarterly* 11 (December 1938): 739–72.

14. *A Southern Odyssey: Travelers in the Antebellum North* (Louisiana State University Press, 1976).

15. *From Slavery to Freedom: A History of African Americans* (Alfred A. Knopf, 1947; revised and enlarged, 1957, 1967; with Alfred Moss, 1974, 1980, 1987, 1994, and 2000; Vintage pbk. ed., Random House, 1969; Indian edition, 1973; Japanese translation, 1974; German translation, 1978; French translation, 1984; Portuguese translation, 1989; Chinese translation, 1990; revised with Evelyn Brooks Higginbotham: McGraw-Hill, 2010).

16. Franklin, *Mirror to America*, 127–28.

17. Kenneth M. Stampp, *The Peculiar Institution: Slavery in the Ante-Bellum South* (New York: Vintage Books, 1956; 1989).

18. Ulrich B. Phillips, *American Negro Slavery* (New York: Appleton, 1918; BiblioLife, 2008).

19. Malcolm X, *The Autobiography of Malcolm X* (New York: Ballantine Books, 1999), 205.

20. For an appraisal of this historiography, see Orlando Patterson, "Rethinking Black History," *Harvard Educational Review* 41, no. 3 (1971): 297–315; see also, Orlando Patterson, *The Ordeal of Integration* (New York: Civitas, 1997), 77–81.

21. John Hope Franklin, "The Two Worlds of Race: A Historical View," in *Race and History: Selected Essays, 1938–1998* (Baton Rouge: Louisiana State University Press, 1992), 41; Franklin, *Mirror to America*, 381.

22. Franklin, "Slavery and the Martial South," *Journal of Southern History* 37 (1952); reprinted in *Race and History*, 102–103.

23. The influence of W. J. Cash's great work *The Mind of the South*, first published in 1941, must be acknowledged. Franklin, however, was one of the earliest to explore this thesis in a major academic work.

24. Franklin, "The Practices of History," in *Race and History*, 71.

25. Peter Applebome, "John Hope Franklin."

26. Franklin, *Mirror to America*, 37.

27. Ibid., 379.

28. For a discussion of the role of culture and how it has been treated, see Orlando Patterson, "Taking Culture Seriously: A Framework and Afro-American Illustration," in Lawrence Harrison and Samuel Huntington, ed., *Culture Matters: How Values Shape Human Progress* (New

York: Basic Books, 2001), 202–18. On culture and black youth, see the forthcoming collaborative work edited by Orlando Patterson and Ethan Fosse, to be published by Harvard University Press, 2013.
29. Franklin, *Mirror to America*, 380.
30. Ibid., 382.
31. Ibid., 381.

8. The Puzzles of Racial Extremism in a "Postracial" World

1. See, for example, Robert H. Frank, "When It Really Counts Qualifications Trump Race," *New York Times*, November 16, 2008; Michael Eric Dyson, "Barack Obama's Victory Represents a Quantum Leap in the Racial Progress of White America," *Los Angeles Times*, November 5, 2008; Abigail Thernstrom and Stephan Thernstrom, "Racial Gerrymandering Is Unnecessary," *Wall Street Journal*, November 11, 2008.
2. Bob Herbert, "Take a Bow America," *New York Times*, November 8, 2008.
3. See, for example, Michael Crowley, "Post-Racial, Even White Supremacists Don't Hate Obama," *New Republic*, March 12, 2008, 7; Shelby Steele, "Obama's Post-Racial Promise," *Los Angeles. Times*, November 5, 2008; Tim Rutten, "The Good Generation Gap," *Los Angeles Times*, February 6, 2008.
4. See, for example, Michael Fauntroy, "Enough of This 'Post Racial' America Stuff," Huffington Post, December 28, 2008, http://www.huffington post.com/michael-fauntroy-phd/enough-of-this-post-racia_b_15449.html; "A New 'Post-Racial' Political Era in America," narrated by Daniel Schorr, NPR, January 28, 2008, http://www.np.org/templates/story/story.php?story Id=18489466; see also Leonard Pitts Jr., "Commentary: 'Post-Racial' America Isn't Here Yet," CNN, March 28, 2009, http://www.cnn.com/2009/POLITICS/03/28/pitts.black.america/index.html.
5. Thernstrom and Thernstrom, "Racial Gerrymandering."
6. See, for example, Mark K. Warren, *Fire in the Heart: How White Activists Embrace Racial Justice* (New York: Oxford University Press, 2010), 2; Reginald T. Shuford, "Why Affirmative Action Remains Essential in the Age of Obama," *Campbell Law Review* 31 (May 2009): 503; Matthew T. Hughey, "Measuring Racial Progress in America: The Tangled Path," in *The Obamas and a (Post) Racial America?*, ed. Gregory S. Parks and Matthew W. Hughey (New York: Oxford University Press, 2011), 13–20; Pitts, " 'Post-Racial' America Isn't Here Yet."

7. Frank Newport, "Americans See Obama Election as Race Relations Milestone," November 5, 2008, http://www.gallup.com/poll/111817/ americans-see-obama-election-race-relations-milestone.aspx.
8. Ibid.
9. Fauntroy, "Enough of This 'Post Racial' America Stuff"; "A New 'Post-Racial' Political Era in America"; see also Pitts, " 'Post-Racial' America Isn't Here Yet."
10. Howard Schuman, Charlotte Steeh, Lawrence Bobo, and Maria Krysan, *Racial Attitudes in America: Trends and Interpretations*, 2nd ed. (Cambridge, MA: Harvard University Press, 1997), 104.
11. Ibid.
12. Lawrence T. Bobo and Camilla Z. Charles, "Race in the American Mind: From the Moynihan Report to the Obama Candidacy," in *The Moynihan Report Revisited: Lessons and Reflections After Four Decades*, ed. Douglass S. Massey and Robert J. Sampson (Thousand Oaks, CA: SAGE, 2009), 245.
13. Jeffrey M. Jones, "Record-High 86% Approve of Black-White Marriages," Gallup, September 12, 2011, http://www.gallup.com/poll/149390/ Record-High-Approve-Black-White-Marriages.aspx?ref=more. When this question was first asked by Gallup in the 1950s, just 4 percent approved.
14. Husna Haq, "Interracial Marriage: More Than Double the Rate in the 1980s," *Christian Science Monitor*, June 4, 2010, http://www.csmonitor .com/USA/Society/2012/0216/Interracial-marriage-rate-doubles-in-30 -years-how-US-attitudes-have-changed.
15. Shuford, "Why Affirmative Action Remains Essential," 507.
16. Ibid.
17. Notable events include the vitriolic attacks directed at President Obama at town hall meetings to promote his health care plan.
18. One such event includes the "You lie" outburst by GOP representative Joe Wilson during the president's 2009 State of the Union.
19. Darrel Enck-Wanzer, "Barack Obama, the Tea Party, and the Threat of Race: On Racial Neoliberalism and Born Again Racism," *Communication, Culture and Critique* 4, no. 1 (2011): 26.
20. Ibid.
21. Ibid.
22. Southern Poverty Law Center, "Hard-Line 'Birthers' Soldier on After Certificates Release," *Intelligence Report* 143 (Fall 2011).
23. Ibid.

24. Ibid.
25. "Hate Crime Statistics," Criminal Justice Information Services Division, accessed September 8, 2011, http://www2.fbi.gov/ucr/hc2009/incidents.html.
26. For a detailed description of incidents, see Jeannine Bell, *Hate Thy Neighbor: Racial Violence and the Persistence of Segregation in American Housing* (forthcoming, NYU Press).
27. The Fair Housing Act and hate crimes legislation may be used to prosecute acts of anti-integrationist violence. Jeannine Bell, "The Fair Housing Act and Extralegal Terror" *Indiana Law Review* 41 (2008): 543–48.
28. See, for example, *United States v. Stewart*, 65 F.3d 918 (11th Cir. 1995) (cross burned on lawn of black family because perpetrators wanted to communicate that they "were not wanted" in the all-white neighborhood); *United States v. J.H.H.*, 22 F.3d 821 (8th Cir. 1994) (cross burned because burner was disgusted at having an African American family living in the neighborhood); *United States v. Montgomery*, 23 F.3d 1130 (7th Cir. 1994) (cross burned to drive out shelter for homeless black veterans); *United States v. Lee*, 6 F.3d 1297 (8th Cir. 1993) (cross burned to "scare off" African Americans); *United States v. Long*, 935 F.2d 1207 (11th Cir. 1991) (cross burned on lawn of black family in formerly all-white neighborhood to intimidate them because of their race); *United States v. Anzalone*, 555 F.2d 317 (2d Cir. 1997) (vandalism and arson directed against a black family that intended to move into a house); *United States v. Redwine*, 715 F.2d 315 (7th Cir. 1983) (after black couple moved into the all-white neighborhood approximately a block and a half away from defendants' homes, the latter engaged in conduct intended to get the black couple to move out).
29. Jack Levin and Jack McDevitt, *Hate Crimes Revisited: America's War Against Those Who Are Different* (Boulder, CO: Westview Press, 2002), 11.
30. See, for example, Lisette Livingston, "Louisiana Man Sentenced for Civil Rights Violation in Connection with Cross-Burning," *Chicago Citizen*, July 2, 2010, 13 (cross burning directed at home of interracial couple in Athens, LA); Ginny Laroe, "Burnt Cross Lands 2 More in Prison," *Arkansas Democrat-Gazette*, December 8, 2009 (cross burning directed at white woman and biracial children); Leonard Sparks, "Residents Confront Racism in Maryland," *Afro-American* (Baltimore, MD), May 20–26, 2006 (racist fliers targeted at white woman dating

black man); *United States v. Hartbartger*, 148 F.3d 777 (7th Cir. 1998) (cross burned to force biracial couple to move from trailer park); *United States v. Smith*, 161 F.3d 5 (4th Cir. 1998) (cross burned to frighten biracial couple so they would move from the area); *United States v. May*, 359 F.3d 683 (4th Cir. 2004) (cross burned on lawn of white woman who lived with a black man); *United States v. Gilbert*, 884 F.2d 454 (9th Cir. 1989) (defendant convicted under section 3631 for sending letter aimed at discouraging the white head of an adoption agency from promoting the placement of black and Asian adopted children with white families); *United States v. Hayward*, 6 F.3d 1241 (7th Cir. 1993) (defendant convicted under section 3631 for burning two crosses on the property of a white family who had entertained black friends); *United States v. Sheldon*, 107 F.3d 868 (4th Cir. 1997) (unpublished) (defendant convicted for burning a cross on the front lawn of an interracial couple's house); *United States v. Ramey*, 24 F.3d 602 (4th Cir. 1994) (Molotov cocktail burned down trailer of biracial couple).

31. The highest number of incidents were identified in California (48), Florida (40), Illinois (32), New York (26), Pennsylvania (24), Massachusetts (24), Missouri (24), and Ohio (23). See, Bell, *Hate Thy Neighbor*.

32. See, for example, Daryl Glover, "The Hateful Truth: Racists Are Targeting Black Family," *Seattle Post-Intelligencer*, July 16, 1991; "Cross Burning; Family Calls for National Investigation" *Westside Gazette*, August 19–25, 2004. A similar incident involved a large cross burned into the lawn of a Jewish family in an upscale development in Lake Oswego, Oregon. Nia Carlson, "Cross Seared into Family's Lawn," *The Oregonian*, June 23, 2004.

33. "Hate Crime May Be Culprit of $10 Million Maryland Arson," *Westside Gazette*, January 20–26, 2005.

34. Ibid.

35. See, for example, *Johnson v. Smith*, 810 F.Supp. 235, 238–39 (N.D.Ill. 1992); *Egan v. Schmock*, 93 F.Supp. 1090, 1092–93 (N.D. Cal. 2000) (holding a section 3617 claim may be based on discriminatory conduct designed to drive an individual out of his or her home); *Ohana v. 180 Prospect Place Realty Corp.*, 996 F.Supp. 238, 239–243 (E.D.N.Y. 1998) (holding FHA protects individuals from interference by neighbors for discriminatory reasons in the peaceful enjoyment of their homes); *Johnson v. Smith*, 810 F.Supp. 235, 238–39 (N.D. Ill. 1992)

(allegations that defendants participated in cross burning on plaintiff's lawn stated claim under section 3617); *Stirgus v. Benoit,* 720 F.Supp. 119, 123 (N.D. Ill. 1989) (holding allegation that plaintiff's home had been firebombed in order to intimidate and coerce her to move out of the neighborhood was sufficient to state a claim under section 3617); *Stackhouse v. DeSitter,* 620 F.Supp. 208 (N.D. Ill. 1985) (firebombing of family's car in effort to drive them from the neighborhood sufficient to state claim under section 3617).

36. *United States v. Nichols,* 149 Fed.Appx. 149, C.A .4 (N.C.) 2005 (unpublished).
37. Ibid., 1.
38. Ibid.
39. Ibid.
40. Ibid.
41. Another prominent example of a similar situation was the beating to death of Vincent Chin, a Chinese American. Chin was killed in 1982 by two out-of-work Detroit auto workers who blamed Asian Americans for their employment difficulties.
42. Russell Walker, "Bigotry Kindling for Tremont Arson Fires?" *Call & Post* (Cleveland, OH), Aug. 22–28, 2007.
43. Brian Schwartzman, " 'Once I Leave, I Don't Think I'll Ever Come Back': Two Towns, and Their Inhabitants, Grapple with a Number of Disturbing Racist Incidents," *Jewish Exponent,* February 17, 2005.
44. Ibid.
45. Ibid.
46. Walker, "Bigotry Kindling."
47. For discussion of this, see Leonard S. Rubinowitz and Imani Perry, "Crimes Without Punishment: White Neighbors Resistance to Black Entry," *Journal of Criminal Law and Criminology* 92, no. 2 (2001).
48. Leslie Ashburn-Nardo, Robert W. Livingston, and Joshua Waytz, "Implicit Bias: A Better Metric for Racial Progress," in Parks and Hughey, *The Obamas,* 33.
49. Ibid.
50. Ibid.
51. Kathleen Schmidt and Brian Nosek, "Implicit (and Explicit) Racial Attitudes Barely Changed During Barack Obama's Presidential Campaign and Early Presidency," *Journal of Experimental Social Psychology* 46 (2010): 310.
52. Vincent L. Hutchings, "Change or More of the Same? Evaluating

Racial Attitudes in the Obama Era," *Public Opinion Quarterly* 73 (2009): 919.

53. Ibid., 923.
54. Ibid., 928.
55. See, generally, Jeannine Bell, "The Hangman's Noose and the Lynch Mob: Hate Speech and the Jena 6," *Harvard Civil Rights and Civil Liberties Law Review* 44 (2009): 329, which discusses cases with noose hangers who insist that they are not racist, and Jeannine Bell, "O Say, Can You See: Free Expression by the Light of Fiery Crosses," *Harvard Civil Rights and Civil Liberties Law Review* 39 (2004): 335, discussing cross burners who claim not to be racist.
56. John Williams, "Hateful Speech," *Arkansas Times*, July 19, 2007.
57. Ibid.
58. Ibid.
59. Ibid. As part of her worries, she cited a rape case involving an African American suspect the previous year at the local middle school.
60. Ibid.
61. Tony Ortega, "The Hood: A Black Couple in Independence Wonders About the Price of Peace and Quiet," *PitchWeekly* (Kansas City, MO), July 21, 2005.
62. See, generally, Bell, *Hate Thy Neighbor*.
63. David Gamacorta, Damon C. Williams, and Regina Medina, "Advice About Racism Proved to Be Prophetic," *Philadelphia Daily News*, December 14, 2007.
64. Ibid.
65. Ibid.
66. Eduardo Bonilla-Silva and David G. Embrick, " 'Every Place Has a Ghetto . . . ': The Significance of Whites' Social and Residential Segregation," *Symbolic Interaction* 30, no. 3, 323–345, 327.
67. Ibid.
68. Ibid.
69. Ibid., 340.
70. Bill Brioux, "Welcome Already Worn Out: Edgy Reality Series Yanked from ABC Lineup at Last Minute," *Toronto Sun*, July 22, 2005.
71. Felix Gillette, "In This Neighborhood, Reality TV Falls Short," *New York Times*, July 14, 2005.
72. Ibid.
73. Ibid.

9. An Officer and a Gentleman

1. Tracy Jan, "Harvard Professor Gates Arrested at Cambridge Home," *Boston Globe*, July 20, 2009, http://www.boston.com/news/local/break ing_news/2009/07/harvard.html.
2. Tracy Jan, "Racial Talk Swirls with Gates Arrest," *Boston Globe*, July 21, 2009; Michael Eric Dyson, "Professor Arrested for 'Housing While Black,'" CNN.com, July 22, 2009, http://www.cnn.com/2009/LIVING/ 07/22/dyson.police/index.html?iref=mpstoryview.
3. Cambridge Police Department, Cambridge, MA., Incident Report #9005127, July 16, 2009, at 13:21:34.
4. "Lawyer's Statement on the Arrest of Henry Louis Gates Jr.," The Root, July 20, 2009, http://www.theroot.com/views/lawyers-statement -arrest-henry-louis-gates-jr.
5. Jan, "Harvard Professor."
6. See Ronald Weitzer and Steven Tuch, "Race and Policing in America," *Conflict and Reform* 1–4 (2006); see also Richard Delgado, "Law Enforcement in Subordinated Communities: Innovation and Response," *Michigan Law Review* 106 (2008): 1193, 1199.
7. Martha St. Jean, "Race in America: Comments on the Arrest of Henry Louis Gates Jr.," Huffington Post, July 21, 2009, http://www.huffington post.com/martha-st-jean/race-in-america-comments_b_242093.html.
8. Ibid.
9. "Sergeant Gets Backup, Cambridge Chief Defends Arrest but Promises a Review," *Boston Globe*, July 24, 2009, http://www.boston.com/ news/local/massachusetts/articles/2009/07/24/cambridge_police_chief _backs_sergeant_but_promises_review_of_gates_arrest/.
10. "Friends and Police Rally Behind Sgt. James Crowley, Who Arrested Harvard Professor," *MetroWest Daily News*, July 24, 2009, http://www .metrowestdailynews.com/homepage/x905592581/Friends-and-police -rally-behind-Sgt-James-Crowley-who-arrested-Harvard-professor.
11. Andrew Ryan, "Cambridge Sergeant Declines to Criticize Obama," *Boston Globe*, July 23, 2009, http://www.boston.com/news/local/break ing_news/2009/07/cambridge_sgt_d.html (emphasis added); Joseph Williams, "Obama Scolds Cambridge Police," *Boston Globe*, July 23, 2009, http://www.boston.com/news/nation/washington/articles/2009 /07/23/obama_scolds_cambridge_police/.
12. "Obama's Ratings Slide Across the Board, Pew Research Center for

the People and the Press, July 30, 2009, http://people-press.org/report/ ?pageid=1560.

13. See, generally, Kevin R. Johnson, "How Racial Profiling in America Became the Law of the Land: *United States v. Brignoni-Ponce* and *Whren v. United States* and the Need for Truly Rebellious Lawyering," *Georgetown Law Review* 98 (2010): 1005.

14. Karlyn Bowman, "Obama, Gates, and Crowley," Forbes.com, August 3, 2009, http://www.forbes.com/2009/08/02/obama-gates-crowley-opin ions-columnists-polls.html.

15. Johnson, "How Racial Profiling," 1047.

16. Ian Ayres and Jonathan Borowsky, "A Study of Racially Disparate Outcomes in the Los Angeles Police Department" 8 (2008), available at http://www.aclu-sc.org/documents/view/47; see, generally, L. Song Richardson, "Arrest Efficiency and the Fourth Amendment," *Minnesota Law Review* 95 (2011): 2035.

17. Georgiana Melendez and Robert L. Turner, The Unfinished Work of Equality," *Boston Globe*, July 22, 2009, http://www.boston.com/bos tonglobe/editorial_opinion/oped/articles/2009/07/22/the_unfinished _work_of_equality/.

18. Lydia Lum, "The Obama Era: A Post-Racial Society?" Diverse Online, February 5, 2009, http://diverseeducation.com/article/12238/.

19. Richardson, "Arrest Efficiency," 2039.

20. "Sergeant Gets Backup."

21. Richardson, "Arrest Efficiency," 2039, 2053–54.

22. Michael Eric Dyson, "Commentary: Professor arrested for 'housing while black,'" CNN.com, July 22, 2009, http://www.cnn.com/2009/ LIVING/07/22/dyson.police/.

23. Richardson, "Arrest Efficiency," 2047.

24. Ryan, "Cambridge Sergeant."

25. Frank Rudy Cooper, "'Who's the Man?': Masculinities Studies, Terry Stops, and Police Training," *Columbia Journal of Gender and Law* 18 (2009): 671, 674–75, 698–702.

26. Frank Rudy Cooper, "Masculinities, Post-Racialism and the Gates Controversy: The False Equivalence Between Officer and Civilian," *Nevada Law Journal* 11 (2010): 1, 5.

27. Cooper, "Masculinities," 37.

28. Bob Herbert, "Anger Has Its Place," *New York Times*, August 1, 2009, http://www.nytimes.com/2009/08/01/opinion/01herbert.html.

29. Richardson, "Arrest Efficiency," 2053.

30. See, e.g., "Friends and Police Rally."
31. Ibid. Also noteworthy is Crowley's statement about his actions in trying to save Lewis. Crowley said, "Looking back on it, . . . [Reggie Lewis] was probably already gone. But I did to him what I would do to *anything* else in that situation." (emphasis added)
32. Cambridge Police Department, Incident Report #9005127.
33. See Angela Onwuachi-Willig, "Volunteer Discrimination," *UC Davis Law Review* 40 (2007): 1895.
34. Richardson, "Arrest Efficiency," 2064.
35. Paul Butler, "More Ways of Looking at a Black Man," in "The Gates Case and Racial Profiling," *New York Times* "Room for Debate," July 22, 2009.
36. Herbert, "Anger Has Its Place."
37. "Local, National Figures Weigh in on Gates' Case," boston.com, July 21, 2009, http://www.boston.com/news/local/breaking_news/2009/07/local_national.html.

10. Obama Is No King

1. See www.youtube.com/watch?v=8atfjvN488s.
2. See www.nobelprize.org/Nobel_prizes/peace/Laureates/2009/Obama-Lecture-en.html.
3. http://mlk-kpp01.stanford.edu/kingweb/publications/speeches/Beyond_Vietnam.pdf.
4. For an attempt to hold Obama accountable to the historical tradition of King and others, see Frederick C. Harris, "The Price of a Black President," *New York Times*, October 28, 2012, SR1.
5. Martin Luther King Jr., *A Testament of Hope: The Essential Writings of Martin Luther King, Jr.*, ed. James Washington (San Francisco: Harper & Row, 1986), 191, 207, 230, 277, 438; Sheryl Gay Stolberg, "A New Look for the Oval Office," *New York Times*, The caucus, August 31, 2010. The phrase originates with the nineteenth-century abolitionist minister, Theodore Parker. Taylor Branch, *Parting the Waters: America in the King Years, 1954–63* (New York: Simon and Schuster, 1988), 197n.
6. Rahaf Harfoush, *Yes We Did: An Inside Look at How Social Media Built the Obama Brand* (Berkeley, CA: New Riders, 2009), 36.
7. James T. Patterson, *Freedom is Not Enough: The Moynihan Report and*

America's Struggle Over Black Family Life—from LBJ to Obama (New York: Basic Books, 2010), ix–x.

8. For a reading of Obamas' views of history and other matters, see James T. Kloppenberg, *Reading Obama: Dreams, Hope, and the American Political Tradition* (Princeton: Prenceton Universtiy Press, 2011).

9. See www.nytimes.com/2008/03/18/us/politics/18text-obama.html ?pagewanted-all.

11. Free Black Men

1. "Primary Choices: Hillary Clinton," *New York Times*, January 25, 2008, http://www.nytimes.com/2008/01/25/opinion/25fri1.html?page wanted=all.

2. During the 2012 campaign season, Obama again shed tears in public on at least two occasions—during his final speech in Iowa, and in his postelection speech to campaign workers. *New York Times*, November 9, 2012, and November 5, 2012.

3. *The Concise History of Woman Suffrage: Selections from the Classic Work of Stanton, Anthony, Gage and Harper*, Mary Jo and Paul Buhle, eds. (Urbana: University of Illinois Press, 1978), 219, 259; "Catt, Carrie Chapman," in *American Dissidents: An Encyclopedia of Actitvists, Subversives, and Prisoners of Conscience*, Kathlyn Gay, ed. (Santa Barbara: ABC-CLIO, 2012), 115. Katharine Q. Seelye and Julie Bosman, "Ferraro's Obama Remarks Become Talk of Campaign," *New York Times*, March 12, 2008, http://www.nytimes.com/2008/03/12/politics/12campaign.html.

4. Marc Santora, "Pointed Question Puts McCain in a Tight Spot," *New York Times*, November 14, 2007, http://www.nytimes.com/2007/11/14/us/politics/14mccain.html.

5. Elsa Barkeley-Brown, "Negotiating and Transforming the Public Sphere: African American Political Life in the Transition from Slavery to Freedom," *Public Culture* 7, no. 1 (Fall 1994): 107–46.

6. "The Personal Transition," *60 Minutes*, November 16, 2008, http://www.cbsnews.com/video/watch/?id=4608194n.

7. Peter Slevin, "Her Heart's in the Race," *Washington Post*, November 28, 2007, http://www.washingtonpost.com/wp-dyn/content/article/2007/11/27/AR2007112702670.html.

8. Maureen Dowd, "She's Not Buttering Him Up," *New York Times*,

April 25, 2007, http://select.nytimes.com/2007/04/25/opinion/25dowd.html.

9. Andrew Ironside, "O'Reilly: 'I Don't Want to Go on a Lynching Party Against Michelle Obama Unless There's Evidence, Hard Facts, That Say This Is How the Woman Really Feels," Media Matters, February 20, 2008, http://mediamatters.org/research/2008/02/20/oreilly-i-dont-want-to-go-on-a-lynching-party-a/142610.

10. See http://wasiwasi.blogspot.com/2007_07_01_archive.html.

11. John Hope Franklin and Evelyn Brooks Higginbotham, *From Slavery to Freedom* (New York: McGraw-Hill, 2010).

PUBLISHING IN THE PUBLIC INTEREST

Thank you for reading this book published by The New Press. The New Press is a nonprofit, public interest publisher. New Press books and authors play a crucial role in sparking conversations about the key political and social issues of our day.

We hope you enjoyed this book and that you will stay in touch with The New Press. Here are a few ways to stay up to date with our books, events, and the issues we cover:

- Sign up at www.thenewpress.com/subscribe to receive updates on New Press authors and issues and to be notified about local events
- Like us on Facebook: www.facebook.com/newpressbooks
- Follow us on Twitter: www.twitter.com/thenewpress

Please consider buying New Press books for yourself; for friends and family; or to donate to schools, libraries, community centers, prison libraries, and other organizations involved with the issues our authors write about.

The New Press is a 501(c)(3) nonprofit organization. You can also support our work with a tax-deductible gift by visiting www.thenewpress.com/donate.